to

David,

with many thanks for
the years of your modelling
to me theological thinking
and being, particularly across
faiths.

QUIET GARDENS

Quiet Gardens
The Roots of Faith?

SUSAN BOWDEN-PICKSTOCK

LONDON • NEW YORK

Published by the Continuum International Publishing Group

The Tower Building   80 Maiden Lane
11 York Road   Suite 704
London   New York
SE1 7NX   NY 10038

www.continuumbooks.com

First published 2009

British Library Cataloguing-in-Publication Data
A catalogue record for this book is available from the British Library.

ISBN 9781847063410

All photographs reproduced in this book were taken by the author.
Copyright © Susan Bowden-Pickstock

Typeset in Adobe Minion by Tony Lansbury, Tonbridge, Kent
Printed and bound in Great Britain by MPG Books Ltd, Bodmin, Cornwall

In Memoriam: Chris Bard (1952–2007)

A man who loved everybody and everything, and
whose delight in them all was thoroughly contagious

Contents

Contents

PART 1
Food for Thought

CHAPTER 1

Journey's beginning

I grew up in a village in rural East Anglia so small there was no tarmac road in or out of it. For what was a blissful eternity to me, in my pre-school state, I wandered the fields, hedgerows, lanes and wood of our boundless (though in fact tiny) Elysium in search of buttercups and daisies, plantain heads, feathers, empty acorn cups and pine cones. My mother took us on daily walks to discover the hollow tree, the stream and fallen log, the frogs in the castle moat, the fox carcass, primroses and bluebells. We ate our lunch in the cottage overlooking the lawn, watching in case the hedgehog should waddle busily across the dewy grass. Birdsong was the background music of that time, overlaid with all sorts of percussion, such as the sudden clacking of pheasants' wings, distant gunshots echoing from a wood where the Major was shooting rabbits, woodpeckers drilling in the taller trees, or the resonant bass of the frogs and thrill of the crickets. I remember the white, white moon filling my bedroom window on a clear night, and once the startling ghostly shadow of the barn owl flying beneath the eaves. It was in fact an entirely friendly world (our only enemies were patches of nettles) enshrined in the pastoral books of my early childhood – *The Adventures of Blackberry Farm* and Alison Uttley's *Little Grey Rabbit* stories.

Time imposed a barrier between that momentary and yet momentous time and what must come; but even during our periods in town or in a larger village elsewhere, family weekends and holidays were punctuated with picnics in the resinous-smelling pine forest; or hard on Suffolk's stony beaches by grey seas with the smell of salt, shells and drying seaweed; or on the sandy heaths exploring tunnels in the gorse bushes, picking blackberries, breathing the scent of hot bracken and watching the sparrows and finches squabbling about their business. We knew one neighbouring heath and golf course like the back of our hand, riding ponies across it, watching the heath fires lay waste the rabbits' cover, or inhabiting endless games and stories of subterfuge and stealth – just about remembering to come back for meals. We visited our only set of grandparents every week. They lived on the edge of another village, across from the water meadows of the River Gipping where the cows grazed in clumpy grass and left aromatic deposits scattered like mines for innocent bare feet. Here we took more walks, accompanied or alone; and we went summer swimming in the silky cool river, on and off the sandy muddy banks, looking for tadpoles and small shoals of fish, turning over slippery stones and avoiding the denser water weed with a shiver.

My grandparents had lived through World War II with a big family and were self-sufficient with three allotments and a large garden. They had chickens and rabbits and apple trees. The chickens and rabbits were not a memory I knew, but every time we were there my grandfather would spend some of the time digging, or weeding, or picking out young carrots and beetroot. He would let us pull fat, fleshy, dark green broad bean pods with their silky lining, like a best bed, in order to remove the large, pale beans within. We shelled peas with my grandmother out in the sun, picked apples into our held-out jumpers, or scrubbed the thin skin of new potatoes. We caught soft green caterpillars in legions from the rows of cabbages, or snails from the wet paths, and pushed them around in an old dolls' pram until they all escaped over lunch. We walked miles through fields of sighing knee-high grass or rough rustling wheat stalks with poppies. Constable clouds moved in a stately fashion overhead and under the blue sky we scrambled through the meadows and along old earthy footpaths, sunk into dimness by ancient hedgerows that were more redolent of horse and cart than the bicycles and cars we knew. They yielded leaf mould and toadstools and the brilliant red arum lily berries we knew never to touch.

Some of the pleasure of these days was captured and added to at school with the nature table, and later through the scientific study of plants and animals – counting seaweed species on the Dale peninsula on a geography field trip in Wales, drawing perfect anatomical drawings of buttercup and grasses in biology, and understanding photosynthesis and how the world holds together its living, breathing biosphere. Since then, with longer stretches living in the city or the suburbs, but with frequent forays to the wild and remote on holidays and weekend escapes, I have kept in regular touch with nature through my gardens, a period of study at evening classes, and now an allotment of my own.

However, like a small stone dropping into a pond, during the research for this book I have found that apparently we are all, through our evolutionary pre-history, subject to 'biophilia'.[1] There is a vestige, it is said, even in the most city-grown, street-wise, concrete-loving individual, of some remote and deep memory of a connection with all things green and leafy. Having looked after children from the rougher streets of Newark, New Jersey, on an American summer camp scheme one summer, I would have questioned that at first. Those children, who had barely seen a tree, and never more than one at a time, were terrified by the prospect of a walk in the woods! But it didn't last, and sometimes even a week of living in the fields, woods and lakes of the campsite was enough to gain their interest, even their fascination.

Back in a more urbanized Britain than that of my own childhood, we are now living a technological, faster, more metal/plastic/tarmac-orientated and indoor lifestyle than I ever did. I can now spend a whole day in front of a computer screen, a wind-screen and a television screen. Yet if I take a trip to the garden centre on a bank

---

1. Wilson, E. O. (1984), *Biophilia: The Human Bond with Other Species* (Cambridge, MA: Harvard University Press). See also chapter 5, 'Gardens as therapy'.

holiday weekend, I may find it difficult to get into the car park. It would be a brave developer who took no account of any outdoor space and even converted factory buildings, mills or power stations are designed with balconies or roof terraces for some pots of plants. Our computers, more likely than not, will have a natural image as a screensaver; our walls may be decorated with pictures of mountains, forests, sea or flowers; and our most re-watched television programmes may well be about natural history or gardens round the world.

We want to maintain some connection with our natural surroundings and may use holidays to volunteer in conservation, or to walk an ancient track or coastal path. We may explore the hills of Umbria or beaches of Yugoslavia, trek in Nepal, camp in the Lake District, safari in Africa or take a narrow boat along some of Britain's or Ireland's waterways. There is a realization that natural beauty, whether it is in the form of a local country park, a garden or an area of wilderness, gives us something that we don't get from the indoor or urban environment. It seems to do us good, although we may not have analysed how or why.

I enjoyed three years living in south London and working in the city. I have visited, on my own and with the family, many capital cities in Europe and elsewhere and been captivated by the buildings, the streets, the transport, art, theatre, history and culture alive in those places. I have breathed in the smell of traffic, hot roads and fast food, and listened to the sounds of car horns, sirens, construction machinery and lift music and enjoyed their place in the whole city-experience. These times have not been 'less' than the times I have spent alone on the hills, the beach, or pottering around in the garden, but they have been quite different. I would say that they have not done my soul good.

The period we are living through in the West tends to be described as a secular age: postmodernist and post-Christian. It is a time of relativity where absolute values are taboo, political correctness reigns supreme and spirituality is a sideline, sitting somewhat uncomfortably alongside our generally commercial outlook. However, although our lives still orbit Planet Consumer, what we want alongside our things are experiences. It is a time to see, taste, touch and preferably roll in it: a time to 'do before we die' and 'seize the day', to live the moment and have that gap year.

Internationally, within our global village tensions are ever present. Environmental disasters and therefore climate issues feature on all our television screens and our agendas, local, national and international. Terrorism is not a new threat, but its now broader shadow delineates new ideological differences. However, the universality of that shadow draws together those living underneath it as never before. Interfaith and ecological conversations have become necessities rather than luxury items.

I would suggest that it is in this climate – with its need to experience and its dawning understanding of collective responsibility – that the spiritual dimension can flourish. I think there is also a desire to pursue it and to come to terms with our 'soul', not necessarily in institutionalized religion and tradition, but in new ways.

This book describes a journey that seeks to reinvestigate the relationship of humanity with nature and through this an understanding of our soul and what is spiritual. Within the Judaeo-Christian tradition, the Bible begins with the story of creation and of God walking in the garden he had made, with the man and the woman, in the cool of the day. This is a powerful image and anyone who has walked in the very particular atmosphere of a garden at dusk will relate to it. For many, enjoying and perhaps making a garden is a connection with the wider environment in which we are placed. It provides a link to that which is outside us, both the plants and the trees, and perhaps also the life force behind them. This is my experience, and this book retraces the path I have taken to some of Britain's lesser-known gardens and the people behind them, who recognize that horticulture is a medium to meaning and also to spirituality.

This journey has become for me a pilgrimage, a path of discovery through therapeutic horticulture, biblical gardens and theology, the gardens of the Quiet Garden Movement, Islamic gardens, a Buddhist and a Baha'i garden. It includes conversations with three leading garden thinkers and creators, Charles Jencks, Beth Chatto and Sir Roy Strong, and the making of an interfaith garden at the Chelsea Flower Show in 2007.

The journey has also been much like the path one walks through a labyrinth. I encountered labyrinths for the first time through the gardens of the Quiet Garden Movement and I am hooked. A labyrinthine path does not take its participant on a straightforward journey and it is not, like a maze, just a bit of fun. A labyrinth is a circuitous but after a while strangely satisfying path that winds rhythmically but unexpectedly around and around and about again and again, and seems to take its traveller sometimes further from the goal of the centre rather than nearer to it.

I started the journey of a relationship with nature when I was chronologically very young, although older in the understanding of some things than I am now. The point at which I wanted to write about how we relate to nature came just a few years ago when a colleague and I, both working within the BBC in local radio, discovered that as well as our faith broadcasting in common, we also had a passion for gardens and even for hills and sea; and that we might not be alone in discovering benefits from gardens and nature that have not been much verbalized. I had worked as a colleague of the Reverend Canon Chris Bard for almost ten years before we decided it was time to explore formally the relationship of gardens and spirituality. The whole BBC approach to gardening had, we felt, for too long been quite a superficial one: concerned with the outward forms and tools and practices. Gardening, as it was most usually portrayed, was about arranging a space, preparing ground, planting and moving on to the next plot that had perhaps got a bit scruffy in the meantime. It was about makeovers, changing the surface and transforming a patch of ground from one thing into another. Chris and I felt there was more to gardening than that and we began a project called 'mYth – meaning through horticulture'. These were our premises.

– We wanted to challenge the concept of gardens simply as objects of display, and to suggest that they can in addition be expressions of meaning and identity.

 – For many, making a garden is a link to that which is outside us. It is a connection with the wider environment in which we are placed and can even provide an entry point to the spiritual. 'Why do people garden?' and 'What do they get out of it?' are questions that are often answered in terms other than the material.

   The garden is a bridge for diversity. The making of gardens is a universal activity, throughout history and across cultures. Yet in the UK, the land-based industries fail to attract the same diversity as is found in the general population. Perhaps part of this problem is the way gardening is portrayed in the media. Have we failed to allow ethnic groups to 'own' their contribution to the rich synthesis that is British horticulture?

   Our experience of 'the other' is informed in gardens. All religions have something to say about gardens and the notion of paradise, linked to a garden, is found in almost all of them. Of the activities that can unite people of faith, gardening is common ground. It can be explored without touching on difficult areas of doctrine or belief.

 – Through the garden we can also explore those physical, cognitive and spiritual aspects which draw together nature and human creativity.

For two years Chris and I journeyed the length and breadth of Britain, making a radio documentary, visiting gardens of all faiths and none, speaking to some of Britain's best-known and loved garden makers and writers, and finally creating with Capel Manor Horticultural College an interfaith garden at the Chelsea Flower Show in 2007.

However, in September 2007, one of those unforeseen twists in this labyrinthine journey occurred. Chris and I flew out to Dublin to visit gardens in both Northern and Southern Ireland. Tragically, suddenly and completely unexpectedly, Chris died at Dublin airport. The only consolation for his much-loved family, his many friends and work colleagues in so many areas of life, and myself, was that he died a happy man – involved in a work project he felt passionately about, bringing together two aspects of life he really loved: faith and gardens. I am grateful for the opportunity to articulate and share our work with a wider audience through writing this book, and in so doing to move further on in my own journey, exploring the nature of the relationship between ourselves and the natural world as particularly exemplified in gardens. I know Chris would agree.

The purpose of this book is therefore to pose a number of questions and to tell a number of stories. You have had a glimpse of some of my own story, and one of the things that inspired Chris and me as we met people who make gardens was the realization that creating a garden necessarily involves telling one's story. Furthermore, each story contributes to an understanding of the bigger questions and some possible answers. This book therefore collects together a number of leading garden makers, thinkers, writers, therapeutic horticultural practitioners, theologians and ordinary people who have provided insight into answering a number of questions, including: What is a garden for? How do some of the leading world faiths approach the concept and practice of gardens and gardening? Does Christianity currently own a relationship with nature? And do gardens provide a medium through which we can explore our own spiritual side, whether we are 'religious' or not?

This may be the time to bring in some definitions. According to the *Concise Oxford Dictionary* 'spiritual' is 'of the soul'; the *Times English Dictionary* defines it as 'relating to the spirit or soul and not to physical nature or matter; intangible'. *Chambers* suggests that the 'soul' is 'that which thinks, feels, desires; moral and emotional nature'; *Oxford* agrees: it is the 'moral and emotional part of man', the 'emotional or intellectual energy'; and the *Times English* clarifies this further as 'the seat of human personality, intellect, will and emotions'.

It became clear to me quite early on in this project that if I asked someone about their garden, what they enjoy about it or perhaps why they do it, the answers were very rarely about the physical exercise gained from it, or the economics of building it. Rather, people talked about the *satisfaction* of creating a garden, the *peace* or *tranquillity* they enjoyed while sitting in it (and many of the Quiet Gardens visited are urban or near major roads or airports), the *fascination* of watching plants grow and develop, and the *fulfilment* of co-creating with nature. It is clear from the dictionary definitions that these are all spiritual qualities that relate to what might be our long-lost soul.

I have an impression that in our current culture we have lost touch with our souls and therefore with our rooted identity. I am hoping this book will bring the reassurance, first, that whether we are Muslim, Hindu or Christian, humanist or unsure, we all have a soul and a spiritual side; second, that this is a good thing; and third, that horticulture may be a very pleasant gateway through which to become reacquainted.

CHAPTER 2

Journey into meaning
– Charles Jencks

A pilgrimage is defined by the *Times English Dictionary* as 'a journey or long search'. I want to start off on this journey of exploration into the nature of gardens by, as it were, sitting aside in the gatehouse at the start of the path for a time of preparation for the way ahead. The Quiet Garden at Arley has a castellated room overlooking the park which is called The Barbican and is a remnant of the castle-house that used to stand on the site. It is also used on Quiet Days, particularly if the weather is adverse, and is a fantastic place to sit alone. I imagine being able to sit in that quiet room, laying out appropriate books and essays on the table in front of me, and then inviting in a series of visitors who have given some thought to the purpose and meaning of gardens and gardening today.

One of the first books I came across that raised the sort of questions I really wanted to explore was *Vista: The Culture and Politics of Gardens*, edited by Noel Kingsbury. It is a collection of essays about all sorts of aspects of gardens and gardening other than the practical business of digging, planting and maintaining a plot of land. In the chapter called 'The Spirit of the Geometrician' Fernando Caruncho says:

> Today more than ever, we need to study, once again, the essential elements of the universe. This is not so much the physical-chemical composition, more the mythical-spiritual relation of man and the universe, and the potential for transforming man's spirit.[1]

Caruncho is in no doubt that there is a relationship to be had with the natural world. Further on in the *Vista* book, Lorna McNeur gives a fascinating insight into the history of Manhattan Island.[2] We know this place as 'New York', the ultimate in 'city', the home of skyscraper and breakdancing (whether or not this is actually the case!), the epitome of everything urban and urbane. However, Manhattan Island was once an Indian settlement. The disaster of 9/11 exposed some of the geological layers that had been hidden when so many of the natural contours were levelled out

---

1. Kingsbury, N. (2005), *Vista: The Culture and Politics of Gardens* (London: Frances Lincoln), p. 111.
2. Lorna McNeur, 'NYCWTC 9/11: The Healing Gardens of Paradise Lost', in *ibid.*, p. 161.

to put the 'block' street system in place. McNeur's argument is that these newly revealed geological layers bring meaning back to the island again and Central Park is the only authentic and significant part of the area because it restores some of this lost landscape back to its current inhabitants.

Another author from *Vista* who is concerned about a 'sense of place' is Tim Richardson. In his essay 'Psychotopia',[3] he explains the term he has coined as the process that happens when someone encounters a landscape. This is not a chapter to be read before breakfast, but it is worth persevering through its various ideas and challenges. Back in the eighteenth century the poet Alexander Pope invented the phrase 'genius loci' to refer to the 'spirit' of an outside space, such as a garden. Richardson wants to bring this concept into the twenty-first century:

> Psychotopia is place understood not just in terms of location, but also in terms of meaning – its history, use, ecology, appearance, status, reputation, and the people who interact with the place, its potential future. It refers to the actual life of the place as it is experienced by those who visit it … A psychotopia is a place where human psyche connects and combines with place psyche.[4]

He is concerned that gardens are understood as complex rather than simple places, because any landscape that people inhabit or visit is subsequently imbued with a presence made up of the emotions, impressions and imaginations of these people. There is no such thing, he argues, as neutral territory; every place we visit or live in we also 'co-create' or contribute something intangible to. My first and most powerful experience of a place having had the spirit of its owners instilled into it was at Haworth Rectory on the edge of Keighley Moor in Yorkshire, home of the Brontë family, where the brooding clouds over the windswept moors outside the garden walls, and the copse of tall-trunked trees in the front garden to me breathed the wild spirit of the author of *Wuthering Heights*. By contrast, Jane Austen's home at Chawton on the edge of the South Downs in Hampshire exudes, appropriately, a calm patience. Richardson suggests that both individuals and communities can have an effect on a landscape, and that our relationship with our own gardens is crucial because it is a part of our identity. Likewise, if we relate to the landscapes through which we travel each day on the way to work, school or the shops rather than being oblivious to them, our quality of life will be better for it. He is concerned to point out that gardens are particularly valuable to us because they are our way into a relationship with the cosmos. You may not have contemplated over your cornflakes recently the importance of a rapport with the rest of the universe and beyond but, since we are cosmological creatures, it is possible that we could be missing out on a whole new dimension to life simply by ignoring the way we relate to our local landscape and our garden.

---

3. *Ibid.*, pp. 131–132.
4. *Ibid.*, pp. 132–133.

I was pleased to discover that the question of whether gardens are places of meaning rather than just aesthetic display was indeed an active debate, and further research led me to York. The 'meaning' debate has been most active amongst landscape designers, rather than in the purely horticultural world, and it was becoming clear that one of the people I needed to talk to in order to understand more was the American landscape architect Charles Jencks who, fortuitously, was giving a lecture in York.

Charles Jencks was born in Baltimore, USA in 1939. He studied English literature at Harvard University and then went on to study architecture and gained an MA from the Graduate School of Design before going on to do a PhD in architectural history at London University. He writes books about the theory of architecture and is known for bringing the concept of postmodernism into the architectural world. He lectures, writes and designs in the UK and around the world.

In 1988 Charles was invited to help design a kitchen garden at the childhood home of his wife Maggie Keswick in Galloway in Scotland, where his parents-in-law lived. In 2003 he was still finishing parts of the rest of the 30-acre site, which is now known as 'the Garden of Cosmic Speculation', and he has gone on to design other landscape areas and gardens in Scotland and around the world. In those 15 years of working on the garden at Portrack, three family members associated with the garden died and with their deaths Jencks realized that making a garden is as much about telling stories and answering questions as it is about aesthetic arrangement and presentation. His book about the garden starts with a chapter entitled 'Three Stories of a Garden' and begins with these words:

> When you design a garden, it raises basic questions. What is nature, how do we fit into it, and how should we shape it where we can? [5]

His answers to these questions over the years have enabled him to formulate his own belief system or spirituality. Chris and I caught up with him in York, where he was giving an illustrated lecture about the Garden of Cosmic Speculation. The lecture was essentially a pronouncement of Jencks's own creed. He began by asking the question, 'What are the deepest things that draw us?' – in the way that cathedrals drew medieval people – and suggested that the evening itself was a speculation on the ties that link us with the universe. His premise was that a 'cosmic passion' underlies all things: it draws the bower bird to make its extraordinary nest and continue its species, it caused the ancient Britons to make stone circles, and it inspires scientists to search for subatomic particles. Clearly it also stimulates gardeners to garden and, to Charles Jencks's mind, the best are those who use their garden to speculate about or critique the relationship between humanity and the cosmos. Ian Finlay-Hamilton in his garden Little Sparta did this by using words and phrases inscribed on various objects such as wooden posts or stepping stones and

---

5. Jencks, C. (2003), *The Garden of Cosmic Speculation* (London: Frances Lincoln), p. 17.

placed all over the garden. They arrest and intrigue the visitor with new possibilities and questions.

In the York lecture, Jencks went on to suggest some of the things that the garden might be. It can be a polemic, in the way that art should be an 'attack' on commonly held ideas. The garden is also a place to go and contemplate or meditate, and he showed a slide of the words *Festina Lente,* which was one of the Renaissance ideals and was found in some of the great Italian gardens. It means 'make haste slowly' and Jencks feels that the whole process of creating a garden is a business of gradual illumination of what needs to be. A garden is furthermore a 'sensorium', which literally connects us to nature through our senses. What the Garden of Cosmic Speculation does is to create a new landscape and a new set of icons through which we may see truth and reality and on which we may build our own creed, using nature to speculate on nature.

It is perhaps not surprising that the Garden of Cosmic Speculation is, on first sight, bizarre. It is probably the best example of how the first visitors to the eighteenth-century gardens at Stowe in Buckinghamshire must have felt. At Stowe Lord Cobham used his garden to display his political views, and in its time it was a radically new way of designing a garden. At Portrack Charles Jencks has used the landscape of the garden to illustrate scientific and cosmological possibilities and to explore how human beings can relate to nature and the universe. At Stowe the visitor walks along sweeping paths past buildings, follies and grottoes, capturing stunning views and reflections in the lake. At Portrack one almost needs to be flown around, perhaps in a microlight, as well as walking at length from one area to the next, in order to appreciate the whole macro picture of waves and swirls; of water, land and wood; of height and depth, as well as the micro details of geometric divisions, subdivisions and intricate sculpture. Everything in the Garden of Cosmic Speculation has been thought about, from the gates and bridges to the plant species, sculpture and buildings. With names such as 'The Nonsense', 'Water Dragon', 'Two Ways to Paradise', 'Devil's Teeth', 'Jumping Bridge', 'Snail Mound' and 'Fractal Terrace', it is a dazzling illustration of biology, humour, philosophy, cosmology and spirituality. It also makes the tacit point that almost anything can be explained through the medium of a garden.

In fact, in the first chapter of his book about the garden,[6] Jencks reminds the reader that gardens have always been analogies of the cosmos, or world picture, as it was understood at the time. Thus, put simplistically, medieval gardens in an age of faith were resonant with religious symbolism and delighted in the joys of creation. They were walled round to keep out pagan evil spirits that might be lurking in the forests. Renaissance gardens, however, opened out and lost the walls, including and manipulating wild nature in their long forest-lined avenues and boulevards. The characteristic geometric designs of these gardens became places where people could wander at length, or sit and debate the issues of the day; places for music and

----

6. *Ibid.*

philosophy 'to cultivate the soul',[7] or sites for the illustration of allegorical themes relating to mythology and the classics. These gardens became opportunities to dominate nature and put humanity, rather than God, at the centre of the universe. Likewise Jencks in his postmodern Cosmic garden is finding spirituality in science. To him the garden is a chance to conjecture about underlying truths and to reinterpret the way we understand the universe in which we are seemingly randomly placed.

One of the foundational concepts of the Cosmic garden is that there are many layers of meaning. In the garden of the senses there are plants that literally smell and look beautiful and perhaps also taste and feel good. There are also other senses explored within this area of the garden such as the sense of humour, the sense of intuition and the sense of fair play (which is the tennis court …). In this part of the garden are the shiny metal DNA and RNA sculpture structures, which refer to those from which our bodies with their senses are literally built, as well as various written signs and symbols that add further meanings, raise other questions or propose riddles (e.g. 'kitchen harmony'/'edible justice').

In our own conversation with Charles Jencks, Chris and I raised the question of whether 'meaning' is important in a garden, and Jencks referred to this practice of creating many layers of meaning:

> I don't just seek an aesthetic end or even a meaningful end, but something that can be interpreted in many ways. I think ultimately what I would like to do is to create a garden that you walk into, a rather magical place that you think: 'Ah, I understand that,' and you slowly learn: 'Oh, there's more to it than that, what's going on?' and you start to get really involved.[8]

One of the many 'messages' of the Cosmic garden is that the universe exhibits both order and chaos. There are many things which are self-organizing and bring beauty and harmony, like the spiral shape which occurs in the pine cone, the hurricane and the galaxy and is found in all sorts of places in the garden such as the Snail Mound, the Willow Twist and the DNA sculptures. Other things speak of disorder, such as the Liesegang rocks, which are naturally occurring rocks from the River Nith that flows through the garden. They are made of sandstone, but the rock has been broken up by circular patterns that score through it. These are deposits of iron, which form concentric circles on and into the stone and are thus an example of 'symmetry breaking', or chaos, rather than order. Soliton waves, however, are waves that can travel through each other but keep their identity, such as the tidal bore waves of the River Severn, or a laser beam. They are an example of order in chaos and are represented in the metal bars of a series of gates in the garden (which, as it happens, also keep out the rabbits). More order is found in the series of equations that have been carved out of the metal on top of the greenhouse roof and illustrate

---

7. Hobhouse, P. (2002), *The Story of Gardening* (London: Dorling Kindersley), p. 122.
8. From the transcript of a conversation with Charles Jencks, 3 October 2006.

the principles and patterns that underlie the material world. Then there are fractal patterns, the crazy paving sort of pattern found in all sorts of places, such as in wet sand on a beach or in oil heating in a pan, or in a pyrite crystal. In the Garden of Cosmic Speculation these ornament a patio area known as the 'Fractal Terrace'. These patterns are a form of self-organization mid-way between harmony and chaos and thus the terrace sits between a stream (raw nature) and a restored barn (culture). Jencks as a designer is very drawn to the idea that although symmetry is always pleasing in a design, the really creative work begins when symmetry is broken, just as in a philosophical sense catastrophes can restructure history in positive as well as negative ways.

Charles Jencks created the Cosmic garden with his wife Maggie Keswick and they enjoyed the challenge of designing together over many years:

> Garden art is a genre close to autobiography because it takes years to achieve, and the events of one's life get wrapped into its meaning. 'We did this and thought of that and then this happened to us which meant that we had to reconsider the whole enterprise from a new angle.' The landscape becomes a record of what individuals do to nature and of what nature does to them: a circular, or, if time is put into the equation, a spiral enterprise.[9]

The garden became their story in many small ways, and in large ways too – as, for instance, when Maggie had a recurrence of the cancer that three years later killed her. At this time of tragedy work on the garden at Portrack stopped. Charles became involved in the garden design and other aspects of the first 'Maggie's Centre', a specialist holistic cancer unit associated with a local hospital. These centres are now independent charities initially founded in Scotland but now found throughout Britain, where people with cancer can trace their own individual path of treatment through the disease. The architecture and the gardens surrounding each Maggie's Centre are carefully thought through, the idea being that art and landscape can positively influence people, especially when the surroundings are part of wider holistic care. Charles Jencks also found that the process of being absorbed in nature in a garden, such as these hospital gardens, helps to absorb the pain and grief that cannot be articulated in any other way. He resolved to complete the gardens at Portrack and to allow the garden there to reflect more of his own and the family's continuing story. Charles explained to us how the inscription *Festina Lente*, mentioned above, is pertinent to this:

> The idea of a garden is a place where you go to get away from the hurly burly of the world, of running to and fro, and that's one of the ideas, it's a Renaissance idea, that in a garden you slow people down, and you do that with beautiful things, sculptural things, things that occupy the mind, make you think.[10]

---

9. Jencks, *Garden of Cosmic Speculation*, p. 18.
10. From the transcript of our conversation with Charles Jencks, 3 October 2006.

First he tackled the project that he had initially been brought in to do: the kitchen garden, the design of which had foundered more than once as he and Maggie had tried to find a way of expressing their ideas. He realized that the basic stuff of life, DNA and RNA, were the unifying elements for this area. It became a garden where the laws of physics were interpreted, and also a physic garden in a literal sense because, apart from any medicinal herbs planted there, working on it provided a tangible way of working through the bereavement experience. It became the part of the garden that demonstrated planned as well as spontaneous creativity in the realizing of a design. The six senses, which were part of the original conception of the design of this part of the garden, remained, because after all it is through our senses that we experience the universe and it is in this way that our bodies, our feelings and our minds are connected. Our senses experience what is around us, and they are inextricably linked with our desire to know and understand the nature and laws of physics that operate the physical world; DNA then links us in with the rest of the stuff of the universe.

In this way the bigger questions began to be answered. 'How do we fit into nature?' was understood through the process of co-creating with nature in a garden and realizing that dialogue with nature is possible. An empathy with and enjoyment of nature is something that Jencks saw more evidence of in the animal kingdom, and perhaps in our own human ancestors, rather than in twenty-first-century humanity; but in the act of making a garden he realized that it is still there. In mulling over how to take things forward when Maggie had died, Charles Jencks decided that the preservation of a garden for its own sake is an anachronism and what matters is the continuation of life and ideas:

> Perhaps in the end neither man nor the universe is the measure of all things, but rather the convivial dialogue that comes from their interaction.[11]

In the same way as a black hole seems initially only to be about destruction, but is also now known to be an agent of change, so a garden is never finished because life goes on and changes and even death can be a catalyst. The answer to another big question, 'What does a garden do?' is also found for Charles Jencks in the process of horticulture. A garden is a place that allows a creative process of working alongside nature in order to understand both nature itself and one's own place in the order of things.

It is quite clear that for Charles Jencks a garden is a place in which to explore deeper meaning, and gardens can be designed to be full of symbols and hints that help to answer some of the larger questions of life and death. Throughout his book about the making of the Garden of Cosmic Speculation there are several direct allusions to the spiritual dimension. His mother-in-law Clare Keswick was a staunch Catholic and he had many discussions with her over the meaning behind the

---

11. Jencks, *Garden of Cosmic Speculation*, p. 245.

universe and our place in it. His wife Maggie was influenced both by Catholicism through her mother and by Buddhism through her experience and love of China. Charles recognizes the parallel between making a garden, and the biblical account of God creating the universe. He also enjoyed the process of naming parts of the garden and allowing words to bring ideas into being, just as in the Bible Adam is given the task of naming (and therefore relating to and understanding) the animals. An area of the garden near the railway line became a specific example of this. There they created a small island in the mode of a Chinese 'island of the immortals' – a symbol of paradise. Charles designed an arched bridge leading to the island which became known as 'The Easy Way to Paradise', and Maggie designed a series of stepping stones which became known as 'The Hard Way', and the area was called 'The Two Ways to Paradise'. Likewise the concept of 'Gaia' or Mother Earth was investigated and Gaia became a sculpture along a wall next to the six senses garden. In the Gaia theory nature is a super-organism with a will of its own and an ability to re-create, reorganize and heal itself. However, in the end it is cosmogenesis itself, rather than a biblical or any other meta-narrative, that becomes Charles Jencks's own expression of meaning and search for faith:

> The cosmogenic view … acknowledges the wonder and mystery of the most powerful and grand thing there is, the ground of being and the basis for existence.[12]

A book that Charles Jencks has written more recently also expresses a concern that there is a lack of meaning in contemporary design. *The Iconic Building* is an exploration into the phenomenon of large and often unusual architecture that is being built around the world. He feels this phenomenon is linked to a decline in solid faith. People no longer know what they believe in strongly, but do know that they want a landmark. The buildings that are being created therefore lack a depth of meaning. Historically, religious icons – which are packed full of meaning and symbolism – allowed for an expression of deeper things, but in a world that shuns faith nothing seems to be replacing these icons. Therefore in architecture we inherit instead aesthetically dramatic buildings which have no meaning.

Chris and I asked Charles about spirituality and he summarized his own creed in this way:

> We live in a universe that isn't just malevolent in the form of killing and competition and chaos, but one in which beauty naturally emerges – the way flowers self-organize and the Fibonacci numbers produce beautiful forms – and so it produces new meaning all the time. So instead of living in the so-called meaningless universe we live in a much more interesting, creative and dynamic universe where meaning is emerging all the time. I have flirted with God, but I am not religious in the conventional sense. I do think there is a cosmic code that both has coherence and multiple directions. I do think there is order in the universe and in this

---

12. *Ibid.*, pp. 247–248.

garden I speculate that it's really the role of the arts to celebrate the laws that we know are there, to use nature to speculate on what these fundamental truths are.[13]

I have used the conceit that at the beginning of my own exploration into spirituality and horticulture I am, as it were, sitting in the gatehouse at the beginning of the path. Here I am drawing together just some of the things that have been written on the subject, and having conversations with some of today's leading garden designers and thinkers. Charles Jencks has shown me, first, that gardens can be a medium through which we explore highly complicated concepts; second, that gardens tell our stories, almost whether we like it or not; and third, that there is much that is helpful in the actual process of creating a garden.

13. From the transcript of our conversation with Charles Jencks, 3 October 2006.

CHAPTER 3

Relational gardens
– Beth Chatto

Beth Chatto has been an iconic figure in gardening in Britain for decades, but her story and contribution to horticulture start long before the dry garden for which she has become famous was conceived.

Just as the decade of the swinging twenties arrived in England, a young boy went with his parents to America. The last few years had not been swinging at all; in fact, Britain was still reeling from the devastation of World War I and, as the boy's mother was American, the family were thinking of going to live across the Atlantic. Among others, they visited an uncle in California. Here the space, the landscape and the sun that was always shining, entranced the boy. He raced outside, delighted, to do some exploring and his questions when he came back inside were botanical: 'How did the orange poppies get here from England?' It was explained that just as blackberries are wild in Essex, so the Californian poppies are wild there. 'So', he wondered, 'do all our garden plants occur in the wild somewhere?'

Eventually the boy, who was Andrew Chatto, returned to England to be educated. He went to horticultural college and learned fruit growing, but the seed that had been planted in his mind on his first visit to California took root, and for the next 50 years he studied and researched the natural habitats of plants, translating when he needed to the French, German and Russian botanists.

In 1943, during World War II, Andrew Chatto married Beth. They had two daughters. Andrew managed his fruit farm and continued his plant studies and Beth, who had inherited a hands-on love of gardening from her parents, also watched and listened to Andrew's discoveries, and with others started the Flower Club movement in Colchester. These clubs held lectures as well as flower arranging classes and brought in all sorts of people from different backgrounds who could contribute ideas of design, including many Japanese with a minimalist approach.

In 1960 Andrew and Beth decided to build a house on the fruit-farm land, and also a garden which could be used to illustrate Andrew's findings. The house site was on land that at the time was a wilderness incubating the worst sort of weeds. It was difficult land to cultivate because it had three distinct habitats: woodland with oaks and dry shade; an area where sand and gravel were the main constituents of the soil and went down to a depth of 25 feet (it became the nursery car park); and a damp boggy area fed by a spring. For many it would have been the worst horticultural nightmare, but because of this it was also the perfect place to put Andrew's research into practice.

The garden grew gradually 'like contour lines going out from the house' (as Beth described it to us) and a small nursery developed alongside it. Initially Andrew was unhappy about the idea of selling plants, as they had made it a practice always to give plants to their friends and acquaintances, but his health was poor (he had emphysema) and after 40 years of farming it was time to retire. A small new business was needed to keep the family going.

This was in the days before garden centres, and Beth was keen to have a place where she could grow on the plants she was using when demonstrating to flower arranging clubs all over East Anglia, whose members often asked where the plants could be found. One thing led to another with the nursery, and between 1977 and 1987 Beth won 10 gold medals at Chelsea for her unusual plants. She was using species that thrive naturally in the right conditions, rather than cultivated varieties with their double flowers or particularly long stems or the like, which were predominant and popular at this time when hybridization was the flavour of the moment.

Andrew and Beth had a friend, Sir Cedric Morris, who was an artist and had a beautiful garden, Benton End, in Hadleigh in Suffolk. He and Andrew shared ideas and experience about habitats, and through Sir Cedric's visits to the Mediterranean Andrew and Beth were able to introduce alliums, euphorbias and other new plants into their garden. Another great friendship, which grew after Sir Cedric's death, was Beth's with Sir Christopher Lloyd. For nearly 30 years she would regularly visit Great Dixter and his very different garden, and she has published a conversation of letters between the two of them called *Dear Friend and Gardener.*

And so the garden at Elmstead Market grew. The combination of skills from Andrew's study and Beth's natural artistic eye produced a unique and beautiful landscape. Her flower arranging experience has been brought to bear on larger subject matter and through the damp, dry and woodland gardens there is always a pleasing balance between the vertical and the horizontal that produces a thousand individual vistas and photographic or watercolour opportunities. Added to this, Beth has always incorporated a future perspective. Before planting anything she asks basic questions such as: 'What will this plant and this combination here look like in ten years?' and 'What will it look like once it has finished flowering?' Her abilities have enabled her to plant the right plant in the right place where it would not only look good and be harmonious with its surroundings, but, with Andrew's advice, would also thrive. It would be wrong to imagine that it all happened smoothly and perfectly, and at the start when they planted the popular asters, delphiniums and campanulas, they also watched them die, especially in the times of drought – something to which Essex is particularly prone.

Visits to different places around Britain and America have brought new plants. Andrew's study did not mean that they only planted species native to this particular geographical area; rather, they planted species that thrive in the conditions produced by the micro-geography of Elmstead. In Scotland, once, Beth noticed a climbing nasturtium which grew in the yew trees and enjoyed the plentiful rainfall. She planted one in the damp garden where it climbs enthusiastically through a tree with its roots in the spring-fed ground.

I want to say that the gardens at Elmstead Market are the horticultural equivalent of a Palladian house, because they have proportion at the centre. However, Beth does not refer to the garden as a classical one, and superficially it is not. It has none of the clipped hedges, topiary and plants enclosed behind box hedging that are typical of so-called classical gardens; neither does it have the obvious symmetry. This garden is part of the landscape around it, in that it has no artificial hard landscaping features that control it or shape it, but at almost every step there is a vista that incorporates the vertical and horizontal in pleasing harmony and provides a combination of open space (grass, water, sky or path) and shapes interrupting that space (the plant groupings). These are principles central to classical design.

Beth explained that at the heart of the creation of this garden is the design principle of the asymmetric triangle, which speaks of earth (the flat), heaven (the apex) and humankind (the steeper side), and which requires vertical spires alongside mound plants. Anyone with half an artist's eye can start to pick out examples of the triangles because they are everywhere: fundamental to the appreciation of the garden and yet overtly invisible. Beth describes herself as a painter, but unlike another well-known painterly garden designer, Gertrude Jekyll, Beth is most concerned with shape, texture and variety rather than colour.

The Chattos were the first ecological gardeners in Britain. Ecology is all about the relationships of plants, animals and humans to their environment and to each other. Ecological gardening has to do with ensuring that plants are suitable for the environment they are put into and that once in it they can be self-sustaining. It is about providing a diversity of plants with a large number of native species, but not exclusively native, because ecology is about sustaining relationships with birds, insects and animals and it also considers the provision of human needs in both food production and aesthetic display. We asked Beth if she felt the garden at Elmstead Market had become her laboratory, in the sense that it is there to serve the purpose of increasing understanding of the natural world and its principles. She agreed that it was, although she preferred to call it a 'living catalogue'. To have gardened in one place in this way for nearly 50 years has provided a consistent educational example and this is what Beth wishes people to remember her by. This is meaning enough: 'I think that what matters is that we sow seeds in our lives.'[1]

At this point she reminded Chris and me of the story of a character from the historical horticultural world: Eleanor Wilmot, who grew eryngiums (sea holly) and was in the habit of taking seed from them in her pocket and scattering it in the gardens of her friends so that when she died they would remember her by the

---

1. All quotes in this chapter come from the transcript of a conversation with Beth Chatto on 31 August 2006.

plants that grew from it. *Eryngium giganteum* is named 'Miss Wilmot's Ghost'. Beth commented, 'I like to think that my ideas might be "Beth's Ghost".'

The gardens today start at the entrance where there is a new tea room building of modern and sustainable design overlooking the famous dry garden planted on the original car park and gravel strata. Standing watch over this is a 300-year-old oak, which provides some shade at the edge. The plants consist of anything that thrives in the dry conditions, such as Mediterranean silver-leafed or aromatic plants like arteme-sia, sedums, thyme, rosemary and lavender, as well as drifts of alliums and poppies. Upright plants include evergreens such as a yew, tall grasses, knifophia and verbascum, to name but a few. The garden then drops down a slope into the damp garden. This is situated at the lowest point of the land where the spring provides for five areas of water. The lakes are surrounded by trees of all shapes and sizes and are filled with water plants: from the giant gunnera to loosestrife and Pontederia cordata, a beauti-ful blue-flowering swamp plant that lines the lakes of Northern America and which Beth remembers paddling amongst for hours on end on a day's canoeing there.

After wandering along the valley floor soaking in the incredible variety of leaf shapes and tones of green, the path leads up to an area of woodland. This is care-fully managed to provide spring bulbs and hellebores followed by small acers and azaleas under the canopy of the larger deciduous trees. Out of the trees on an open slope of ground is an area of ornamental shrubs, roses and bamboos: a kaleido-scope of colour and form interwoven with stretches of lawn; and as you approach the house, there is a collection of alpines in troughs and beds.

I have been to the garden in two seasons of the year so far, and I am really look-ing forward to returning at some point in the autumn. It is a garden where time stops and one senses something of the release of eternity, as well as the colours, shapes and scents of paradise. We quizzed Beth as to whether she feels it has a spiritual side. 'I like to think it does have some spiritual element, the garden here,' she replied. 'My spirituality, such as it is, I find here in the living things, and even in the stones and the earth.'

At this point all three of us were standing at the edge of the dry garden facing the ancient oak tree. Beth was saying how much the garden is part of her family, as she and her children, grandchildren and even great-grandchildren are growing up with it woven into their lives; and the staff, too, are extended family. She reflected that the oak tree has a timelessness about it, having witnessed so much:

> Disasters and good things, wars and pestilences and droughts … and the tree has quietly got on with living there and growing and growing and now in a way I like to think I am its guardian, or I think it is the other way round. I sometimes feel it is my guardian. I can come out here on a moonlit night and stand and look at those great trunks and just feel the presence of it and it's very comforting.

When Chris asked what Beth would like people to take away from their visit to the garden, she said people wrote to her saying that since their visit they had understood something of the joy of gardening. 'I would like to feel that they went away with a happy feeling, that they were refreshed. If they came here in a tense or troubled mood, that that was dissolved, that they did find peace here in the garden: both peace and inspiration.'

A sense of longevity, of the permanent as well as the ephemeral, is built into Beth Chatto's garden. She deliberately puts in plants that have a long life and therefore carry with them a sense of timelessness and stability. This garden is an example of great planting practice: it demonstrates the principles of ecology and it provides an aesthetic masterpiece of horticulture; but it is also about far deeper things. It is about identity ('a book of memories, emotions and ideas', as Beth put it), the people that Andrew and Beth are and were; it is about relationships, of the immediate family, the staff and the visitors; and it is about our connection with that which is beyond us, nature and the forces behind nature.

> Human beings need to define things in words like 'God' or 'Allah' or whatever, because there are no words. We haven't the ability to describe what is inside us, but I think it is partly an awareness of our known smallness, our own vulnerability … I have the same needs as I think anybody else has for something more than the materialistic, but to put it into words is not easy. I think perhaps if I express it in any way, it is in the garden.

My second visitor to the gatehouse, at the start of my journey, has left me with the impression that to create a garden is to weave the natural and the relational world together and in so doing to intuit the spiritual alongside the material.

CHAPTER 4

Journey into identity
– Sir Roy Strong

If I were to compile a list of the most interesting gardens of Britain, The Laskett would certainly be on it. It is the home of Sir Roy Strong, author, broadcaster and initially an art historian as well as a designer. He became well known in Britain as the youngest and then one of the most daring directors of the National Portrait Gallery. He was 32 when he was given the job and in the next six years he rejuvenated its sedate image with an exhibition of the fashion photographer Cecil Beaton's work. Sir Roy elevated the position of photography within the world of portraiture by opening a new department of film and photography at the gallery. He then commissioned Pietro Annigoni to paint Queen Elizabeth II. Annigoni had painted a glamorous and romantic portrait of the Queen at her coronation. His second work, which was visited at the gallery by around a quarter of a million people in the first two months of its opening in 1970, was a much more sober and austere presentation and spoke of the responsibility of her duty alone as monarch.

In 1973 Roy Strong went on to become the youngest director of the Victoria and Albert Museum in London. Here he put on exhibitions that epitomized three pillars of Englishness, the house, the church and the garden, with 'The Destruction of the Country House', 'Change and Decay: the Future of our Churches' and 'The Garden: a Celebration of a Thousand Years of British Gardening'.

Since leaving the V&A, Sir Roy has written books on Elizabeth I, the history, culture and art of Britain, eating, garden history and design, and English country churches. He now concentrates on writing, broadcasting and gardening and Chris and I visited him to talk about his own garden in Herefordshire.

We were particularly looking forward to it because Sir Roy is known for his erudition, knowledge and wit. He is a sought-after speaker because of his ability to educate people on a wide variety of subjects that are of far more than just academic interest, and also to entertain, to challenge and to surprise listeners with his opinions. If I were to sum up my life, having done all he has done, I don't know what I would choose to say. What we were not expecting, however, was the following comment: 'People often ask me what have I done with my life, and I have said: I did two things, I married Julia Trevelyan Oman and together we made a garden. I would say the rest has been irrelevant, and I mean that.' [1]

1. Comments from Sir Roy are all taken from the transcript of our conversation with him in the autumn of 2007.

This is quite a statement from a man who has achieved an awful lot. I think that generally in Britain we tend to value others and ourselves on what we and they do, or what they have done, or even what they might be about to do. It was refreshing to hear someone publicly stating that relationship and what has stemmed from it has been the only truly significant thing in his life.

It was during his time at the National Portrait Gallery that Sir Roy Strong met and married the very creative set designer Julia Trevelyan Oman, who worked in opera, theatre, television and film. They enjoyed 32 years together when The Laskett was their home and the garden became their joint creative expression. Such a project was not their overt intent at the beginning. Initially, finding the house in which they could live and work together was the important thing. Having achieved this, Sir Roy remembers saying, 'Don't talk to me about that garden!' which at the time consisted of 'two flower beds and a lawn' (now it stretches over four acres). Having spoken in such a disparaging tone about the garden, however, he recalls that it was only a fortnight later that he donned wellingtons and found himself working in it.

Julia came from a creative family who grew, harvested and cooked their own produce, and when the removal van arrived in Herefordshire, a quince tree was taken from it that was a sucker from the Oman family quince tree. It was planted in what later became the Christmas Orchard of old Herefordshire apple varieties that Julia collected in enthusiastic quantities, finding species that dated back to the twelfth century. And although Sir Roy pointed out ruefully that one more bottle of apple compote that year might be the one to send him out of his mind, he reflected on the truth of Julia's words that a surfeit is still beautiful as it hangs on the trees. In the end the whole garden developed as an autobiography of the Strongs' life together. New areas were tackled as and when the money was available for them, such as when a design of Julia's was completed, or perhaps Sir Roy's latest book was published.

We stood for the first part of our conversation above what was once a field. This area was mown in 1977 and planted up as the Queen's Silver Jubilee Garden with white and yellow roses and flowers in regal shades of violet, lavender and purple. In the middle stands a sundial bought in memory of Cecil Beaton, who had been a great friend of Sir Roy's in the 1960s, and there is also a white willow herb from his garden and white 'Iceberg' roses, which he loved. The Walls Lectures at the Morgan Library in New York paid for the rose garden, which also remembers Carol Oman, Julia's historian and biographer aunt, with an urn.

It became clear that the whole garden is one of both memory and identity. Sir Muff's Walk conjures up the ghost of one of the Strongs' cats who would stroll up and down rabbiting there. The kindness of Roy's parents-in-law is remembered by poppies, which they had in plenty in their garden in Putney. A pleached lime avenue is called 'Elizabeth Tudor', marking the book that Sir Roy wrote and Julia illustrated on Queen Elizabeth I, after which Sir Roy proposed marriage. A Shakespeare urn was the first serious purchase. It came from a German foundation which awarded a prize to the person considered to have done the most for the arts in the UK, and Sir Roy was awarded that prize in 1980. Unsurprisingly, the garden displays theatricality, drama and wit: an oval plaque of Sir Roy's profile sits between those of Queen Victoria and her consort Albert. It commemorates his time at the V&A Museum, and a 'Temple' was built around it. Sir Roy describes the garden as kaleidoscopic, haphazard, inconsequential and idiosyncratic, but above all it is an anthology of memory. Places, people and things are represented through harmoniously arranged plants and ornaments.

There is no question that two pairs of very capable designers' eyes have been at work in its creation and Sir Roy is keen to point out that good design, with proportion properly at work, creates the sort of atmosphere of harmony that is to be found at The Laskett. To him a garden is about 'placing human beings within architectural space' and proportion is crucial. All the creators of the great Renaissance gardens of Italy, and anyone following the same formulae, understood that the paths need to be a certain width and length and the height of the hedges is important. Only when these are correct is the following achievement possible: 'You stand there transfixed with a feeling of tranquillity.'

Tranquillity is a spiritual quality and thus it follows that good design is one of the gateways that allows in the non-cerebral qualities of a garden. There is no doubt that The Laskett provides many of these. Sir Roy spoke with a shudder of the mid-1970s, shortly after he and Julia had started work on the garden together, and just after he had taken up directorship of the V&A. It was a time of upheaval socially and economically in Britain with the oil crisis, the Cold War and all sorts of things under threat. As director of a large national institution, he was faced with having to impose cuts, make people redundant and battle with political decisions that did not put culture, art and beauty anywhere near the centre of things. In those days, for him it was worth travelling for three and a half hours from London just to stand above the rose garden and drink in the tranquillity that it exhaled, before turning round and returning to the city reinvigorated and energized.

I seem to remember reading that one of the great war efforts of Winston Churchill's wife Clementine was her planting a great spread of bulbs somewhere in London. Initially this sounded a little eccentric and not particularly heroic, until I understood that it was done as an act of defiance – as if she was saying, 'I *will* plant these bulbs which *will* flower in five months' time.' She refused to be thwarted from planting an expression of hope that there would be a future and that future would contain the beauty, colour and scent we have always known and loved. In the same spirit, Sir Roy recalls standing in The Laskett garden in the mid-1970s, beleaguered by the unsettled and destructive nature of that time, and determining that he *would* design and plant this garden: 'This is such a terrible period, but English people have always planted gardens in spite of the fact that they have little money and less labour. We will do this thing; we will plant a great garden. And I can remember doing it as a kind of act of defiance.'

It was an act in good faith, because The Laskett has become one of the most celebrated and most individual gardens of Britain.

However, as we discovered from each of our garden thinkers, the story of creating a garden is also the recounting of the cycle of life and death and rebirth. In 2003

Julia's own coffin, as requested, stood under the trees in the Christmas Orchard the night before her funeral: the most moving scene the garden had been part of thus far. In successive years, recognizing the importance of symbolic acts of closure and moving on in the grief experience, Julia's ashes were buried in a marble urn in the garden; and on another anniversary she was remembered at Hereford cathedral, while back at the garden afterwards Sir Roy read 'The Vision of Paradise' from Thomas Traherne, a moment about which he could not easily speak. Traherne was an Anglican mystic who understood the vital connection between nature and ourselves, something that I realized I was seeing in front of me. 'It's a wonderful way this garden has been knitted into our lives, both in our married life and in our ends,' said Sir Roy.

Mulling on life after death, Sir Roy mused on the fact that some things are simply beyond our comprehension, but that the garden is a place of resurrection: it goes on. He has wrestled with what should happen now at The Laskett. For instance, there were 98 varieties of crab apple trees which Julia had collected. They are particularly beautiful small trees with flowers in the spring and fruit in the autumn, and to start with they were given to friends to remind them of Julia. A large number of spares were still left, but they mysteriously disappeared from where they had been waiting in the kitchen garden. Later it was mentioned in conversation that Shaun, one of the gardeners, had taken to putting them in his car, driving around the Herefordshire countryside and planting them when he saw a lonely country bus stop or some appropriate place that he thought would benefit from a small crab apple tree. It was a gesture that Sir Roy realized Julia would be delighted by, and it formed his own decision to take the garden into a new phase. Thus trees that have grown too large for the space in which they were originally planted have been removed and hedges have been taken out to open up views and let in more light. Moreover, the Vivat Trust has been established to keep the garden in posterity.

After our conversation with Sir Roy, one of the lectures he gave took the form of a conversation with Fergus Garrett, head gardener of Great Dixter, where Christopher Lloyd gardened and subsequently died. Both were putting their own thoughts forward as to how one keeps a garden so associated with a time and a person, and how one balances the tension between preserving memory and allowing a living structure still to have vitality. His own charge to the Vivat Trust's creative gardener is, 'If anything looks boring, take it out!'

The Laskett is a garden of theatricality and fun, as well as privacy and intimacy, an enclosed and beautiful world made over time by two creative individuals working together. It did not start out as a spiritual quest, but somehow along the way it became one. As I listen again to the conversation we had with Sir Roy, I realize that many of the words and phrases he used are resonant of far more than the principles of good design: 'how wonderful', 'fell in love with', 'means a great deal to me', 'great statement', 'great friend', 'he adored', 'the most sacred part', 'the joy', 'spiritual nourishment', 'mystery', 'beautiful'. The Laskett has become the expression of the life energy and loves of two unique people, a record of events that happened in their lives, as well as their purposes, feelings and thoughts, and a source of spiritual benefit – a place where one could, and still can, experience delight and tranquillity. There is a Latin inscription in the garden above the triumphal arch which, when translated, reads:

He who plants a garden plants happiness.[2]

My third visitor to the virtual gatehouse at the beginning of my journey tells me that creating a garden is a profound experience far beyond the telling of it. I am impressed with the thought that to visit any great garden is equivalent to visiting a sacred site. There, anyone with ears to hear will understand that it speaks of love and laughter; tears, sweat and disappointment; satisfaction, triumph and achievement; devastation and serenity.

---

2. This is Sir Roy's translation of the inscription above the triumphal arch in The Laskett garden.

CHAPTER 5

Gardens as therapy
– Joe Sempik et al.

Sitting in the virtual gatehouse as I am, there is another book I must have on the table. In 1759 the French writer Voltaire created a story in which he explored the purpose of human existence in the light of human suffering. The protagonist Candide undergoes many extraordinary and most unlikely adventures with a group of companions, but none of them can decide on the answer to the question they finally put to the greatest philosopher in Turkey: 'Will you kindly tell us why such a strange animal as man was ever made?'[1]

Like everyone else they have encountered, the philosopher is not much help in answering the ultimate question of the purpose of life, but on the way home Candide notices a peasant farmer sitting outside his cottage. The old man suggests that it is work on the land that cures all his ills and keeps him content. The band of hopefuls decide to try this out for themselves. Candide's final words are: 'We must go and work in the garden.'[2]

There are few people who would disagree that gardening is beneficial, whether through its end product on the plate, or its aesthetic achievements, or even its ability to provide satisfying work that is both manual and creative. Allotment gardening, which seemed to have had its heyday during the war years to produce much-needed fresh food, is still in great demand, particularly in urban areas. Garden visiting remains high on the leisure pursuits of a large number of British nationals, whether here or abroad; the 'yellow book' of gardens open for charity is a sought-after reference book each year; and the popularity of the major Royal Horticultural Society (RHS) shows does not seem to have diminished. Britain in Bloom is still a major national competition and many villages throughout the country have 'open gardens' at some point over the summer.

However, do all these simply point to private individual interest, or does horticulture have a wider application? One of my favourite winter reading books of recent years was Robin Shelton's very honest *Allotted Time: Two Blokes, One Shed, No Idea*. This is a wonderfully down-to-earth (quite literally) and very funny account of Robin being rescued from a crisis point in his life. He found himself at an all-time

---

1. Voltaire, *Candide* (London: Penguin Classics), p. 141.
2. *Ibid.*, p. 144.

low on account of divorce, poverty and depression, but came to see light at the end of the tunnel by establishing and working an allotment with his mate Steve. He says in his last chapter:

> Neither Steve nor I was in a pleasant place when we took this project on, and we both feel that the allotment has been, in no small way, the salvation of us ... a venture which has possibly – with the exception of parenthood – given me more cause to care, and has educated me more, than any other.[3]

According to the Federation of City Farms and Gardens, the history of community gardening in Britain can be traced back to the time of the Norman Conquest when land was first taken and given to the invading people. The Enclosures of the eighteenth and nineteenth centuries further diminished the ordinary person's contact with a piece of land, as common land all but disappeared. After the Industrial Revolution had made its mark on the health and work–life balance of the general public, the allotment movement started to come into being, and this was followed in the twentieth century by the City Farms and Gardens Movement, which went hand in hand with a growing understanding and appreciation of human impact on the environment.

In September 2000 an international conference on community gardening was held at the University of Nottingham. It was intended to make people more aware of community gardens and the benefits they bring, with particular reference to their contribution towards global sustainability. The director of the Federation of City Farms and Gardens attended the conference and at that time he calculated there were around 1,000 community gardens in Britain and 63 City Farm projects, with interest in both rising.

All sorts of groups from all over the world attended the Nottingham conference and the subsequent publication is a fascinating insight into garden projects across the world.[4] John Ferris and Carol Norman presented an introduction to how community gardening is defined, through their research into community gardens in the San Francisco Bay area in America. Here the leisure garden is the most common sort of community garden, designed to offer some outdoor recreational space for a large number of apartment dwellers who have no private outdoor space. Typically leisure gardens contain the equivalent of small allotment plots, tended enthusiastically by a culturally diverse group of people, and there is also a picnic and barbeque space. School gardens are popular in the area thanks to active promotion by the California State Education Department. They combine the physical recreation of tending plants with an environmental science curriculum. Health and therapy gardens are a growing form. The AIDS Memorial Grove in the Golden Gate Park is

---

3. Shelton, R. (2007), *Allotted Time: Two Blokes, One Shed, No Idea* (London: Pan Books), pp. 299, 300.
4. Ferris, J., Morris, M., Norman, C., and Sempik, J. (eds) (2001), *People, Land and Sustainability: A Global View of Community Gardening* (Nottingham: PLS).

a 15-acre patch of woodland landscaped to provide a place for those who are affected by AIDS, either directly or indirectly. The San Francisco City Hospital in a poorer neighbourhood has a 'comfort' garden for staff and patients, and a therapy garden for people with mental ill health has been created in Richmond. An example of a citizen-led initiative for what has become known as 'neighbourhood pocket parks' happened in Berkeley, where the Halcyon Commons Park, a relatively small plot that used to be a car park, is now transformed into an area with a children's park, shrubs, trees and flower beds. John and Carol also listed entrepreneurial gardens, urban farms, work and training gardens, crime diversion gardens, quiet gardens, ecological restoration gardens and demonstration gardens as further examples.

Another delegate, Catherine Sneed from the USA, told the story of her move from a role where she was counselling prisoners just about to be released to creating a post-release programme for prisoners, developing and maintaining a garden. Her San Francisco Garden Project has now planted 10,000 trees on the streets of San Francisco and can claim that 75 per cent of its clients do not return to jail.

Krzysztof Gasidlo from Poland spoke about the struggle to keep hold of allotment gardens now the communist regime has fallen. In 1949 an Act went through Polish parliament whereby large companies and municipalities were obliged to provide allotment areas for citizens. However, legislation in 1990 gave the land back to the towns and cities, which have tended to sell the plots to developers. The Polish Union of Allotment Garden Holders fought back, but further legislation in 2000 created more problems. Although initially the allotments had been created for economic reasons, they are seen by the Union to give people back their contact with nature as well as providing a community aspect.

Likewise, the American Community Gardening Association (ACGA) has a vision to build up self-maintaining communities through the provision of community gardens, and in doing so to promote social justice and community cohesion. It believes that the whole quality of life of a community can be improved through gardening because it allows social interaction, reduces families' food budgets, offers exercise and recreation and teaches people about their community environment. Bobby Wilson, vice president of the ACGA, spoke at the conference about a number of major projects in cities across America where horticulture is used in schools, as youth employment training programmes, alongside local government to transform urban areas, and with fringe members of society to draw them back into community. I viewed a website for community gardens in Oklahoma City for 2008 and found 26 listed horticultural projects in operation.

Another raft of people at the Nottingham conference were in some way or another involved in community gardens that promoted health. The UK mental health charity Thrive was one. Elizabeth Hayden from Thrive could report that the charity has a database of 1,500 horticultural projects around the country, which they estimate provide services for 60,000 people each year. Her message was not to forget the positive effect of horticulture on people's well-being, for as well as providing the obvious advantages of exercise, fresh air and, with community gardens, some social contact, there are also the hidden benefits of giving a sense of achievement, providing a contact with nature and raising self-esteem through creativity.

Carol Norman attended the conference from the Queens Medical Centre in Nottingham where she works in the acute psychiatric unit. She helped create a garden in the hospital grounds which serves three psychiatric wards and allows patients there either to absorb passively what the garden offers, or to get actively involved in growing. She talked of gardening as a 'normalizing' activity that provides a crucial link between hospital and home. David Foster, chief executive of Thrive at the time, also talked of the importance of gardening as something 'normal' and therefore appealing and non-threatening to people in all sorts of situations, especially for those who would not take on 'training' of a more abstract or formal nature.

The Lothlorien community in Dumfries is a live-in community based on Buddhist principles where people can find security, friendship, a sense of self-value, dignity and confidence. The community members live on and tend the 17 acres of woodland, pond and meadow and grow flowers, vegetables and fruit. The ordinary daily activities of mowing lawns, weeding, chopping wood, cooking and cleaning restore a sense of balance to the eight-strong community and their volunteer workers.

There was a strong lobby at the conference for children to be involved in horticulture and garden projects. Anna Wasescha from the USA championed the benefits of bringing children and gardens into contact with each other. She argued that gardens could be centres of learning and play, as well as opportunities to develop art and craft skills. Getting children involved in community gardens fosters in them an understanding of the value of community, the importance of things shared and the experience of giving out more than is taken. The educational opportunities of a garden environment are numerous and subjects that can be learned include botany, ecology, sustainability, agriculture, horticulture, work-related skills, food and nutrition. The World Garden Project at the Wilford School in Nottingham has given all these educational opportunities to children there, as well as creating twinning links with South Africa and cross-cultural knowledge through their World Cultural Garden which has plant zones for Europe, Asia, Africa and Australasia. Oliver Ginsberg, an educational consultant from Berlin, also pointed out that conventional playgrounds do not allow for the complex construction play or the social interaction that play in a garden environment can offer. A paper from Robin Moore and Nilda Cosco from the department of Landscape Architecture at North Carolina State University backed him up. Their message was that nature should be made a part of all childhood habitats, whether in the home, school, neighbourhood or church.

A deep love of the planet … must take root early in life … the process … must start in the first year of life to achieve maximum effectiveness. But as an educational process it must continue to develop beyond the pre-school years … to empower children as individuals to create a new, biologically wise society.[5]

5. Moore, R., and Cosco, N., 'Developing an Earth-bound Culture through Design of Childhood Habitats', in *ibid.*, p. 38.

A final strand of the millennium conference in Nottingham concentrated on the value of the production of food in gardening. Producing one's own food provides an individual or community with more than just the immediate economic advantage of not having to buy all one's edible resources, as Joe Sempik from Loughborough University explained:

> Being able to feed oneself, and others, by one's own efforts brings a sense of satisfaction that is second to none.[6]

Vicky Yokwana talked about her role as a field worker in the Quaker Peace Centre that works in black townships around Cape Town. They began food-growing projects in the 1980s after community requests for help in dealing with malnutrition and starvation, which were common problems in the townships. Two workers from the Urban Management Programme for Latin America brought news of small-scale agricultural and horticultural projects in Brazil, Equador, Mexico, Cuba and Argentina. There was a paper on a women's vegetable garden scheme in the Gambia; and Ren Azuma, professor of geography at Mie in Japan, talked about the need in his highly urbanized country for rural allotments where people can escape the pressures of city life. Gleaning is undergoing something of a revival in Washington State, USA; and a local community food garden at Bulwell Hall in Nottingham told its story. But perhaps the last word from the conference needs to be from Michael Littlewood of Illminster in Somerset, who spoke about the concept of ecological and community-supported agriculture. He suggested that if we are to survive as a species, and do more than just survive, we must develop a better sense of caring for all aspects of the natural world.

> Growing and preparing food are integral to the culture, education, joy and spirit of each community.[7]

The message from this millennium conference is that there are numerous benefits conferred by gardening and gardens. Horticulture is therapeutic – physically, mentally, emotionally and even spiritually.

However, most of the delegates were talking from experience and providing anecdotal evidence. Joe Sempik, by contrast, is a lecturer at the University of Loughborough and he has spent the best part of the last decade researching the value of horticulture to people and society. He would be my next virtual visitor at the gatehouse, before I start out on my own journey of discovery. In 2003, in association with Thrive and the Centre for Child and Family Research at Loughborough University, Joe Sempik and his colleagues began a major study of social and therapeutic horticulture in the UK called 'Growing Together'.[8] Their concern was that, although

---

6. Sempik, J., 'Food Security', in *ibid.*, p. 45.
7. Littlewood, M., 'Ecological and Community Supported Agriculture', in *ibid.*, p. 53.
8. Joe Sempik describes the 'Growing Together' project in three publications on therapeutic horticulture (see Bibliography).

the benefits of gardening to individuals and society are implicitly known, there is little hard evidence based on research to demonstrate them.

The first part of the 'Growing Together' study was a review of the literature associated with social and therapeutic horticulture in order to find data offering scientific evidence for the benefits of horticulture. A previous literature review in 1979 (by researchers Markee and Janick) had found 213 references to the benefits of horticulture in a therapeutic sense, although most of these were anecdotal rather than scientific or experimentally based. In 2001, over 1,000 references were found and around 50 of these contained actual scientific data. Clearly the use of horticulture as therapy has increased enormously over the intervening decades, as well as becoming a subject of scientific research.

Sempik suggests that there are essentially two ways of using horticulture in order to benefit people. The first is what occupational therapists have been doing for years and that is using gardening as an activity to stimulate their clients physically or mentally. The charity Thrive defined it thus:

Horticultural therapy is the use of plants by a trained professional as a medium through which certain clinically defined goals may be met.[9]

The second is therapeutic horticulture, which was defined by Thrive as:

The process by which individuals may develop well-being using plants and horticulture.[10]

Both practices quantify the value of horticulture to people, one concentrating on more objective goals and the other on more subjective targets.

What is clear from Sempik's literature review is that horticulture has been found to be of benefit to people in both ways for centuries. A Dr Benjamin Rush published his *Diseases of the Mind* in 1812. In this work he proposes that human beings are designed to be active and that what he terms 'agriculture' provides an excellent cure for depressive illnesses as it gives both physical exercise and mental and emotional stimuli. In 1955 O'Reilly and Handforth first looked at the benefits of horticulture for psychiatric patients and discovered that gardening improved the attitude of the patients (towards caring for their own appearance) as well as reducing their stress and increasing their sociability. A study in India in 1986 with schizophrenic patients also yielded social benefits amongst the group.

In 1997 a pilot programme of horticultural therapy was put in place for patients who had lost the power of speech. Gardening was seen to provide 'soothing and comforting sensory involvement'[11] and patients on this trial experienced enjoyment

---

9. From 'Growth Point', *The Journal of Social and Therapeutic Horticulture* published by the charity Thrive 1999, p. 9.
10. *Ibid.*
11. Sarno, M.T., and Chambers, N. (1997), *Activities, Adaptation and Ageing*, vol. 22 (1–2) (Haworth Press), pp. 89–90.

and satisfaction, a reduction of stress and an environment in which speech returned to some degree. In the year 2000, volume 16 of the journal *Occupational Therapy in Mental Health* reported the project of Perrins-Margalis *et al.*, who formulated seven areas in which horticulture contributed to the well-being of those with chronic mental illness. The seven benefits of horticulture were the 'group experience', the 'sharing experience', the 'learning experience', the 'sensory', 'creative', 'emotional' and 'reminiscent' experiences. They concluded that horticulture, used as an activity in a group setting, had a positive effect on the quality of life of those taking part.

Various projects through the 1990s looked at the benefit of horticulture to people with dementia because of the sensory stimulation, the emotional cogency and the aspect of 'refuge' that a garden provides. This last quality was drawn out in 1997 by Beckwith and Glister, who suggested a design for a traditional 'paradise' garden enclosed by four walls. That model of garden is of particular help to dementia sufferers because it provides a secure environment (something that BUPA demonstrated in their Chelsea Flower Show Garden in 2008).

Children with mental health problems benefit from garden therapy because it provides self-fulfilment, according to McGinnis in 1989, and likewise Smith and Aldous in 1994 found that using horticulture for people with learning disabilities gives the participants self-worth and satisfaction. In a study in 2000, Heliker, Chadwick and O'Connell discovered that horticulture for the elderly produced psychological benefits and they discovered that gardening was meaningful to the participants because it linked in with their own life story as well as providing a spiritual dimension. Thus there are many groups for whom rehabilitation is successfully provided through gardening, which offers physical, psychological, emotional and spiritual benefits.

In the 2003 report *Social and Therapeutic Horticulture: Evidence and Messages from Research*, Sempik *et al.* also take a closer look at the non-physical advantages that therapeutic horticulture brings. Various projects that have brought people into contact with nature through 'wilderness' experiences have shown that deep psychological and spiritual effects are associated with these encounters with the natural world. Studies have also been done in order to see if horticulture reduces aggression and can help offenders, victims of sexual abuse and drug and alcohol addicts. In each of these cases some benefits were found.

Horticultural practice with certain groups therefore brings with it an element of the value of the 'contact-with-nature' experience that Kaplan and Talbot categorized in 1983 as 'tranquillity and peace, integration and wholeness and oneness with the universe'. It is interesting that even listing these values here causes me to reflect that they sound a little 'extreme': many Britons would not put 'oneness with the universe' as a quality of life they were lacking, but if I was presenting this list of the benefits of contact with nature to any indigenous people group such as the Aborigines, Native American Indians or even the Celts of ancient Britain, 'oneness with the universe' would be of unquestioned importance.

Perhaps because it can seem to us to be stretching the point, Sempik *et al.* devote a chapter of the review of therapeutic horticulture to looking at its mechanisms and finding out what gardening actually does in people to provide these emotional and spiritual experiences. Rachel and Stephen Kaplan and Roger Ulrich are the researchers over the last 20 years who have studied the value of nature and horticulture in detail. Rachel and Stephen Kaplan have developed a theory of 'attention restoration', i.e. gardening is beneficial because it provides a particular restorative environment that allows people to recover from mental fatigue. Their research in 1989 found that natural landscapes specifically provide a sense of escape (through peacefulness, quiet and the sensory experience), something to be fascinated by, a world with which one is compatible and a complete ordered 'other world'. Furthermore, their research in 1995 categorized this as 'soft fascination', allowing someone an opportunity to reflect on larger life issues, and Herzog *et al.* in 1997 found that natural settings scored highest for offering the opportunity for attention recovery and reflection.

Roger Ulrich has studied the effects on people of different landscapes and concluded that human beings have innate biophilia: a connection/love/ease with natural surroundings that possibly has an evolutionary root – although the term 'biophilia' was coined by another researcher, Wilson, in the same year that Ulrich was working (see chapter 1). In short, people function better as people when they are in a natural setting. Hence the British Trust for Conservation Volunteers have now set up 'Green Gyms', places where people can work in a natural setting and benefit physically, but also psychologically, emotionally and possibly even spiritually.

The conclusions from Sempik's review were, first, that the literature pointed to several common themes. Therapeutic horticulture is relevant across genders and cultures. It embraces social inclusion and community cohesion, employment, physical exercise and the taking of responsibility. It is shown to control anger and frustration. It provides a metaphor for the process of life as well as a spiritual dimension. Second, Sempik found that although there are numerous anecdotal and 'soft' studies into the benefits of horticulture, a serious amount of 'hard' scientific evidence is lacking.

Thus the team moved on to the second and third stages of 'Growing Together', which involved surveying the gardening project network established by Thrive (which used to be known as the Society for Horticultural Therapy) and studying a number of those projects in order to evaluate the process of social and therapeutic horticulture. Twenty-four projects were chosen and investigated. The team found several features that clients emphasized as beneficial to them. first, social and therapeutic horticulture (hereafter called STH) provides nature, freedom and space. Being in a natural environment builds a bridge between the world of nature and the human world and creates a flow of understanding about the natural world and what it offers. Participants felt they had escaped into a better space, which was more peaceful, healthier, less confined, pleasurable and interesting. Through the process of working with plants it was possible to extrapolate lessons for life, such as it being 'normal' to make mistakes or to have to do something more than once in order to achieve the desired results. The natural environment was for many a healing place where it was easier to talk and reflect and feel connected to the rest of life, as well as to a spiritual dimension. It also brought social contact, a chance to develop social skills, a political involvement and friendship; and it provided training for future employment. Furthermore, the projects also gave people physical exercise and mental well-being. Contributors gained self-confidence and self-esteem and the chance to express themselves creatively.

The conclusions of this study were that STH is of considerable benefit to vulnerable people (the clients of Thrive), providing positive personal, social and political outcomes and promoting social inclusion. There were no negative aspects reported, except that some aspects of specific projects did not suit some clients, but the general practice of STH has no contra-indications.

In 2007 Joe Sempik went on to attend and contribute to the first conference of COST (European Co-operation in the Field of Scientific and Technical Research) on Green Care, which took place in Vienna. Green Care is:

> The utilization of agricultural farms – the animals, the plants, the garden, the forest, and the landscape – as a base for promoting human mental and physical health, as well as quality of life, for a variety of client groups.[12]

The aims of the conference were to find out what research was going on into the health benefits of being involved with agriculture across Europe and to establish collaboration between researchers. Some of the papers were particularly enlightening.

Inge Schenk from Darmstadt in Germany has been exploring ways of putting the UN Decade for Education for Sustainable Development (2005–2014) into practice. She argues that a garden is the first place for learning about sustainability and a school garden is a 'green classroom', which should be central within education as a place of learning and experience of all sorts of subjects, only some of them academic. She suggests that school gardens are vital because parents and grandparents no longer necessarily have garden experience to pass on. The work of German psychologist Dr Ulrich Gebhard has shown that children need to develop personal relationships with nature before puberty, because after this stage they are no longer open to it,[13] and it is only what we love that we protect and maintain – a principle with a clear ecological message. Moreover, children develop properly once they have developed their five senses. They need an environment that offers both familiarity and new stimuli, and a garden does this. It also does it in real time. In a garden setting children learn that natural processes take time, and this is an important lesson when much of their technologically rich world works on instant results and speed processing. A human being, however, also needs time for regeneration, tranquillity

---

12. Gallis, C. (ed.) (2007), *Green Care in Agriculture: Health Effects, Economics and Policies* (Vienna: University Studio Press), from Preface.
13. Gebhard, U. (1994), *Kind und Natur* (Westdeutscher Verlag).

and reflection. Schenck points out that gardens train children in discipline, responsibility, perseverance and patience. Gardening also offers understanding about food production and provides fresh air and exercise. School gardens can offer both knowledge and life skills and therefore should be at the heart of education.

Erje Rappe from Helsinki University in Finland reminded the conference that the benefits of horticulture come through a longer time scale than the benefits of, for example, medicine. Horticultural therapy is more part of health promotion and imparts to its participants coping strategies, life skills and 'health literacy', all crucial elements for conserving and maintaining holistically healthy human beings.

Rachel Hine, Jo Peacock and Jules Pretty from the University of Essex have been examining 'care farming' in the UK, which is much like therapeutic horticulture, but in a farm context, and includes contact with animals as well as plants and nature. They have undertaken research in 2005 and 2007 into what they have termed 'green exercise', i.e. engagement with nature, which could take place at various levels from viewing nature to being in the presence of nature and participating actively with nature, whether through gardening, farming, trekking, camping or the like. They have found that green exercise raises self-esteem and mood, as well as lowering blood pressure and burning calories. It therefore contributes to healthy individuals and healthier communities reduce the cost of public health care.

Konrad Neuberger, from the Association for Horticulture and Therapy in Wuppertal in Germany, has been finding out the micro-processes that occur during therapeutic horticulture. What do plants do for people? His proposal is that there is such a thing as 'phyto-resonance', which is the human reaction to plants. Because of what they are, plants display certain characteristics such as stability, flexibility, beauty or restlessness, which people also have or need to have. Plants are also prone to similar processes, such as the ability to grow, eat and exist in a community, and can provide non-threatening metaphors for life processes. Thus a synergy exists between people and plants. Neuberger goes on to relate the processes of gardening to the human level. For example, with soil preparation, where someone is digging and raking in order to prepare a seed bed, the associated subconscious experience is an awareness of hope and a confidence that, while the experience of being 'dug into' is upsetting, the result will be pleasing. Equally, when someone puts a plant into the space that it will occupy through its growth, subconsciously the person is realizing that they need space – and time – to live, move and develop. Neuberger draws on two research psychologists – Shepard, who in 1994 coined the term 'phyto-resonance' for the relationship between the internal aspects of a person and external plants; and Gallegos, who in 1987 proposed 'active imagination' whereby plants are used to foster developmental abilities. Neuberger concludes that gardening influences people's well-being at a deeper level than just the physical.

The concluding report into Green Care across Europe, from the publication of the Vienna conference papers, was a survey of the educational opportunities for training in Green Care. It was found that Austria, Belgium, Finland, Germany, Italy, Netherlands, Norway, Poland, Sweden, Switzerland and the UK all have some training possibilities, but a more co-ordinated service is needed with more opportunities available. This needs to happen because it is quite clear from the existing projects across Europe that Green Care provides numerous benefits to people.

I was fascinated to discover, through Joe Sempik's work, just how many garden projects are going on around the world, and how horticulture is internationally recognized for the benefits it provides to people of all ages, cultures and abilities. I was also convinced that those who advocate gardening in schools are on to something; it is very difficult to argue against the case for a horticultural education for children, and there are all sorts of good reasons why it should happen. I was further struck by just how many ways people are bettered through gardening and intrigued to read about projects like those by Neuberger, Kaplan and Ulrich that have analysed exactly how the processes involved in horticulture act on people's minds, emotions and spirits. That there is a spiritual dimension to horticulture is without question, although Joe did introduce me to the idea of non-religious spirituality, i.e. an awareness of one's own soul without an accompanying relationship with a deity. I think this could be a helpful concept for many people for whom deistic spirituality is one step too far.

CHAPTER 6

Iconic gardens
– Chelsea

Britain's RHS Garden Shows provide an insight into all things gardening in the UK. As well as garden products and services, the show gardens offer a unique opportunity to understand where garden design is going and something of the current thinking about what a garden is for. The Chelsea Flower Show is seen as the pinnacle of best practice and therefore hopefully the place where forward thinking is happening. I want, at the start of my journey of exploration into the relationship of humanity and nature through gardens to take a trip to Chelsea. For many passionate gardeners, Chelsea is an annual pilgrimage, so I feel I am in good company.

I want to find out whether the concept of 'meaning' is present in the show gardens that have been created at Chelsea in the last two years, but in order to do this it is important first of all to find out the criteria for Chelsea show gardens. As part of our BBC coverage of the Chelsea Flower Show in 2007, Chris interviewed the chief assessor of the RHS, Andrew Wilson, to ask what he felt made an award-winning garden. These are his comments:

> I think the 'wow' factor is a really difficult thing to put a single finger on and say: 'this garden has it' and 'this garden doesn't'. But often you can walk into a garden at Chelsea, or at Hampton Court, at any of the shows, and feel: this is a sensational place to be, or it has drama, or it has excitement – it's got a certain dynamic quality. Sometimes that might be colour, it may be the sheer exuberance of the planting, and it could be sometimes the construction. Sometimes it's all of those things together and when it comes together generally there is a consensus that people feel that this is special or different. Perhaps uplifting is a better way of describing that; it is simply something that attacks you like an emotional wave.
>
> I think it is a very difficult thing to achieve, but often one gets inspiration from the natural landscape around us. People often describe their experience of that landscape as uplifting in almost a religious, a spiritual way, and I think to be able to achieve even a small part of that in one's design work feels just like a fabulous experience and a real achievement.
>
> Certainly there is a conceptual side to design. I think that has been coming through in many designs, not just show garden designs, over the last 10 to 20 years. I think in some ways it brings design closer to art and to experience that

people potentially can gain something from. There is a sort of message within that landscape or that space or that garden. That sort of thoughtfulness and that sort of depth is an experience that comes from living and being in a space – that is a quality that people are looking for in their private spaces and their down time if you like. It is not just about looking at a pretty rose, but actually about a feeling of well-being.[1]

It is interesting that in the judges' minds what makes an inspirational garden is a dimension beyond the visual, physical and conceptual, but to which the visual, physical and conceptual contribute together. The show gardens designed at Chelsea in 2007 did include those with a thoughtfulness and intention towards an 'uplifting' or 'spiritual' experience. The Amnesty International Garden for Human Rights was designed by Paula Ryan. I talked to her as she was building the final stages of the garden, and she felt that there was definitely a spiritual dimension. The Amnesty garden was going to be taken from the show to be installed as a roof garden at Amnesty HQ in London, where it was to provide a haven for people to escape to during coffee breaks and lunch hours. There was a central sculpture by Walter Bailey of the Amnesty symbol – a lit candle surrounded by barbed wire – but otherwise Paula avoided direct and possibly trite symbolism. Instead the garden was a soothing experience of natural materials and soft planting, with a reflective pool, grasses for movement and clipped hornbeam trees for structure.

Three of the larger show gardens demonstrated the concept of a journey through life. The TSB garden designed by Trevor Tooth had this as its theme, although personally I didn't feel it was so clear just from looking at the design. Jinny Bloom created the Laurent-Perrier garden as a place for 'reflection, tranquillity and calm'. This was also a space where the visitor could walk along different levels and paths, up and down stepping stones through the various obstacles of life, from a transparent circular gate at the beginning to a floating lunar gate at the end. Finally, Diarmuid Gavin Designs created the Westland garden, which was a studio garden for an older couple. The garden represented a space of creativity, peace and serenity in which a long-term relationship takes place over time.

There were various gardens that had been designed with a spiritual (in the broadest sense) purpose in mind. Chris Beardshaw wanted his Hidcote Manor garden to be what its namesake is and described it in the show literature as a 'genuine tonic to the body and the soul, a place for weary gardeners to be revitalised'. Lesley Bremness created the 'Through the Moongate' garden, drawing on Chinese Taoist spirituality in which all of nature is imbued with a spirit and a meaning, inviting the visitor into dialogue. The Brett Landscaping garden also invited the visitor to consider humanity's relationship with nature. It celebrated rural life and interdependency with the land.

---

1. Taken from a transcript of the interview Chris did with Andrew Wilson in February 2007.

Many of the gardens reflected a concern for sustainability and the environment. This is a top priority of the RHS and any show garden is expected to have a level of understanding of sustainability; nevertheless, in 2007 the theme was dominant with gardens such as the Fetzer Sustainable Winery garden, the Marshalls Sustainability garden, the Hasmead sand and ice garden which looked at melting glaciers and expanding deserts, and the Chetwoods high technology garden showcasing future environmental technology that could harness light and wind power.

The city gardens were all concerned to provide a retreat from the hectic pace of life. The garden descriptions talk of somewhere to relax, to escape, to 'bring comfort to your soul', to retreat from the 'ever-demanding world', to give a quiet space where it is possible to 'hide away and nurture inner calm'. Interestingly, all the courtyard designs in the Ranelagh gardens were based on an element of nostalgia and represented childhood, a mix of East and West, memories of various bygone ages, or holiday locations and the particular spirit those places impart.

The Chelsea Flower Show accommodates around 600 exhibitors every year, which includes those promoting garden products. International visitors who produce show gardens have come from Australia, New Zealand, South Africa, Trinidad and Tobago, Sweden and elsewhere in Europe. Dominant concerns and thinking of designers will find their way into this milieu.

In 2008 the show gardens once again reflected awareness that a garden is more than a collection of aesthetically pleasing natural elements grouped together. From the main show gardens, the Real Life garden from Geoffrey Whiten was designed to change as its owners' needs did and therefore to take them through their journey of life. The Bupa garden by Cleve West spoke of a therapeutic horticulture agenda. It was there to show that Bupa has a commitment to providing gardens for care home residents as sanctuaries that are particularly good for people with dementia. Clare Agnew Design created the Reflective garden which, as well as its literally reflective pools, also provided overarching trees that created a hidden space for contemplation of nature and relaxation. The *Daily Telegraph* garden by Arabella Lennox-Boyd was inspired by the minimalism of Japanese Zen gardens and was designed to be simple and reflective. The K. T. Wong Charitable Trust had a garden designed by Shao Fan, as an example of a modern Chinese garden linking East and West: 'This garden seeks to calm the mind and the spirit of the observer.' Plants were used for their culturally symbolic nature and the whole garden, built for a scholar, was aimed at providing a 'refuge from society'. Likewise, Diarmuid Gavin Designs' café garden was 'a haven from the hustle and bustle of everyday life'. The Laurent-Perrier garden designed by Tom Stuart-Smith was also created as a 'contemplative space', whereas the QVC garden by Patrick Clarke and Sarah Price was a 'replenishing space of calm beauty' for 'intimate relaxation, quiet reflection and rejuvenation'. The Garden in the Silver Moonlight from Haruko Seki and Makoto Saito was based on a Japanese palace garden where the full moon could be caught reflected in a pool. All five senses were stimulated by a visit to this garden and I suspect the combination of the dramatic contrasts in form, texture and colour brought that intangible quality of 'uplifting-ness' or 'spirituality' spoken of by the assessor Andrew Wilson.

The courtyard gardens of 2008 also echoed a theme of contemplation. The Berkshire College of Agriculture students described their garden as offering a 'quiet intimate sanctuary'. The Mist-Placed garden created for Chessington Garden Centre by Andrew Stevenson and Steve Putnam showed a neglected chapel garden which retains its spirit of peacefulness, allowing for quiet reflection. The SPANA courtyard refuge offered another take on the interdependency of humankind and nature and the spirituality of such a place – a Moroccan courtyard where animals have as much place as plants and humans. It also contained a fountain in the centre, which has a specific religious function of providing water for ritual washing before prayer. The Way Forward garden from St Joseph's Hospice was there as a place of memory as well as looking forward with hope and confidence.

The ideas behind the 2008 gardens of escape, restoration and contemplation seemed to be acceptable to the general public, as the BBC RHS People's Award for Best Show Garden went to the Bupa garden of therapeutic horticulture.

There is no doubt that good gardens are designed to delight the eye with an aesthetically pleasing combination of plants and hard landscaping materials, and the gardens at Chelsea, particularly the larger show gardens, are often able to push the boundaries of style, colour and form. What is interesting to see is the quite marked orientation towards the production of gardens which are there to do more than just stimulate the senses. In 2008 particularly there was a clear message regarding the need for a garden to provide sanctuary and to be a place literally to soothe one's soul.

PART 2

The Quiet Garden Movement

CHAPTER 7

Behind the garden gate
– Philip Roderick

The message from the secular horticultural world is strong. Garden thinkers and designers feel there is both a need for, and proof of the ability of gardens to deliver, an environment with which one can interact physically, mentally, emotionally and spiritually (i.e. relationally). One example of a current network of gardens that do this very well is the Christian charity the Quiet Garden Movement. As part of the 'mYth' project ('meaning through horticulture'), Chris and I visited a selection of these gardens and their gardeners to find out more. Each garden we visited contributed towards a BBC local radio documentary about the Movement and our initial selection of gardens was therefore based largely on their geographical location. We wanted to visit a selection of the gardens spread across Britain and settled on a final list of 17.

The Reverend Philip Roderick is the man behind the Quiet Garden Movement. I wanted to find out not just about the ideas and concepts that had led to its formation, but his own story: how had he come to this point? We met at the Quiet Garden headquarters, a long, low converted garden building within a tranquil English country garden of lawns, beautiful trees and borders in the village of Stoke Poges in Buckinghamshire. Here it was, apparently, beneath the yew tree in the churchyard of St Giles, Stoke Poges, that Sir Thomas Gray wrote what has become one of the most famous English poems, 'Elegy Written in a Country Churchyard'. It seems quite fitting that the place where Gray wrote words which conjure up the spirit and image of rural England at dusk better than any photograph should also be the place where Philip Roderick started a movement acknowledging the spirituality of nature and the essential melding of the physical and the spiritual in our lives.

There is, incidentally, a very good website for St Giles' Church, the introduction to which reminds people that the church has been a place of prayer and journey to over 40 generations of local people. For a millennium the building has signified outwardly the unseen qualities of spirituality, faith, love and searching. Under the curved oak pillars of the porch, which date from the early 1300s, business was transacted and marriages sealed literally 'in good faith'. These concepts of ancient wisdom and community, the blend of the material and spiritual and the natural context are all central to Philip's own thinking.

I don't know what sort of man I imagined I was going to meet that day. Perhaps someone immersed in the church but wanting to open its doors quite literally onto the outside? Possibly someone very obviously spiritual and holy who still wore traditional priestly dress? I learned in the course of my job as a journalist not to be surprised, but with hindsight I realize that actually I *was* surprised to find in Philip Roderick an energetic educationalist. I think it is a comment on our current education system that to find a teacher who was also definitely spiritual was a surprise. Britain's educational system seems to have lost the vision that a person's spiritual side is as important as what they know in their head or can do with their hands; and yet to Philip, a person's journey to faith or spiritual understanding of any sort is also the journey of their life and doesn't happen in holy places alone, but in eating, drinking, talking, loving, working and being part of the world at large.

Philip Roderick was brought up a Methodist, and I have to say I was surprised there too, having tended to put Methodism into the bracket of Protestantism which acknowledges a very practical spirituality and solid teaching, but doesn't have much truck with wandering around under trees being 'present to the moment'. I have a better understanding of Methodism now, especially since experiencing the house and garden of Epworth Rectory where John Wesley grew up, and talking to the curator Joan Sidaway, who has lived and breathed the story of the Wesleys for many years. Philip's grandfather was a Methodist minister and in the early 1900s may well have done much of his work on horseback. He, like John Wesley, had a variegated and dispersed ministry. The church and the local Christian community were therefore an intrinsic part of Philip's childhood. The stuff of everyday life involved going along to Sunday school and church every week in a suit, hearing the conversation of things spiritual as well as practical all around him, watching the priorities of significant family members and eventually also teaching in the same Sunday school from the age of 14 (he chuckled at the memory, and cringed at the thought of what his pupils might or might not have learned).

What Methodism itself delivered was good local community, sincerity, plenty of laughter, small groups who wanted to find God amongst themselves, a love of sacrament, a respect for holiness and an educational dimension which included a call to go out and preach as well as searching for truth within. Philip was always drawn to nature, and wandering alone in fields, woods or by the river or sea was also a major part of the enjoyment and search for his own truth of life. As a family they had holidays in south Wales. On one such holiday in his mid-teens, on a walk out on the cliffs one evening by himself, Philip had what would probably be described as a mystical spiritual experience. At one particular point on the walk he became aware of a new reality and depth to things that he hadn't sensed before. It lasted about half an hour and was something that he carried with him ever after.

However, this was the 1960s and at the age of 18 or 19 Philip came to the conclusion that his traditional spiritual upbringing and its lifestyle was not, as he put it, 'ticking the boxes that my insides need'. 'Felt experience' was the thing to be having in the 1960s, and any and all experiences one could come across, manufacture or experiment with were what was needed. If one was to have God, it had to be a tangible experience of that God. Philip went to study philosophy and English at Swansea University and lived on the cliffs of south Wales, but it wasn't any of the ideologies and concepts of the lecture hall or even experiences of nature that took him on the next big step in exploring faith. It was a person. Ingrid was a Swedish blonde and probably made an impression on many a young searching male! She arrived one day seemingly out of the blue (although it was from London in truth) at a party that was being given in Mumbles for Philip's birthday. Having arrived straight off the train, she disappeared somewhere in the house to meditate. It impressed Philip hugely that someone's first priority, even at an obviously social occasion, should be the practice of one's own spirituality. He chatted at length to Ingrid on the ins and outs of meditation, and this became the next clear focus for his own life. He learned, in the process, about the Indian Vedic tradition of spirituality, was initiated into Transcendental Meditation himself and started the search around the edges for a still elusive God.

This led him to train as a teacher and he worked for a while in a reasonably contented fashion, but the need to look for a tangible spirituality became overwhelming. Giving up the teaching, Philip headed for the Scottish hills in a Mini Moke, met hippies, thoroughly enjoyed himself and then was unexpectedly brought up short on a walk in the hills. A 'voice' spoke to him, whether an inner or an outer voice it was unclear, but the message it spelled out couldn't have been clearer. It was a little odd, and frankly just slightly annoying: 'You need spiritual discipline.' This didn't go down a storm as he was only three weeks out of teaching and experiencing many of the joys of a life of freedom. Spiritual discipline sounded rather prosaic and probably required unpleasant things like stamina and obedience.

Rather than heading for the nearest cloister, Philip recalled visiting a community of Sufis, from the mystical school of Islam, at a place called Peshara in Gloucestershire. He felt sure this was the sort of place one went to in order to find spiritual discipline. Once there, he saw again the diversity of spirituality in healing, meditation, whirling dervish dancing and a genuine and powerful sense of love between community members. However, he experienced it all as a spectator, and after watching their Festival of Religions, where a candle was lit to each of the major faiths, Philip went to bed and slept, still an outsider. While he slept he dreamed, and in the dream a cross appeared, rising from his chest and stretching heavenwards. Perhaps in order to make the point strongly, it was a huge Salvador Dali type of cross, unmistakeably Christian. The next day Philip went along to the community teacher, Rashad Field, and suggested slightly tentatively and in a very British way that he thought, really perhaps after all, he ought to follow Christ. To which the enlightened man replied, 'Wonderful! You have found your path.' The experience of being waved off in love and goodwill as he set off to find a monk whom Rashad knew and who might be able to help was as powerful as any of the more mystical moments he'd had, and informs Philip's own teaching and leading now.

> Openness to God in unexpected places is what it is all about. God is all over the place, we only have to open our ears and our eyes. I have huge respect for other faiths.[1]

---

1. From the transcript of my own interview with Philip Roderick in the autumn of 2006.

A crucifix at St Margaret Mary's Quiet Garden, Huyton, Liverpool

Father Slade was the monk to whom Philip was sent. He belonged to the Society of St John the Evangelist and worked for them in India for many years, getting to know Eastern spirituality. When he returned to England in the mid-1950s he established a small experimental Christian community around him, like an Indian ashram, and in the 1960s they were given a house called The Anchorhold in Haywards Heath. Philip stayed there, met hermits, studied and learned about the monastic tradition and contemplative spirituality. He eventually came out the other end and was ordained in the Bangor diocese. He became a university chaplain, then moved to the Oxford diocese to become principal of a training programme for lay people within the Church.

Fortunately this was not the end of a relationship with the more contemplative and explorative side of Christian spirituality. In 1992 a sabbatical allowed Philip to visit Christian communities in India and America. He realized in the course of all this that he had missed something quite obvious about the life of Jesus. Regularly, as the Gospel narratives point out, Jesus withdrew to places of quiet and solitude, most often places of natural beauty, to be alone and to pray. If this was important for the teacher, it was also important for the follower, and to Philip this became a call. Once back home and sitting in the garden in High Wycombe, he recalled a line from a poem he'd written in his teens, 'a falling flower in the quiet garden', and made a mental connection between the two. Perhaps, for people who can't make it to lakes or mountainsides as Jesus could, a garden could be the place in which to experience solitude and silence?

And so the story brings us back full circle to Stoke Poges, where Philip and I were looking out of the window, over the immaculately manicured green of the lawn, from the office of the Quiet Garden Movement. Noreen and Geoffrey Cooper own the house at Stoke Poges. They were the first garden of the movement, given because Noreen, an ex-rally driver who knew little of gardens or contemplation, nevertheless felt that some Christian group should be using the wing of the house they didn't need. Philip points out that, with his prayer for a building and Noreen's house, they set forth on a wing and a prayer ...

A tiny skeleton staff oversee the 280 other gardens of the movement around the world (all of which are encouraged to have a high degree of autonomy). There are Quiet Gardens in France, Finland, America, South Africa, Australia, New Zealand and Canada. All these gardens are encouraged to be places of celebration, spirituality, hospitality and depth. Philip is concerned that many mainstream churches have lost the sense that 'all of reality holds the mystery of God'.[2]

I would add that the gardens are also places of meeting. They are safe places where it is possible to encounter new thinking, new people and new experiences of God, nature and the interaction between the two. The garden plants reflect two characteristics of God that Philip feels are particularly important: the sense of 'now' and the long term. Both of these are important in the recognition and understanding of who we are and how we relate to the rest of the world. The Japanese maples or classic roses, for example, may have taken a long time to grow but they also encapsulate the moment when the shoot emerges, the flower opens, the bee is poised or the leaf has changed from green to red.

Silence is a crucial aspect of each garden, and jealously guarded. We live in a sound-soaked environment and even in Jesus' time his invitation to his disciples was, 'Come with me to a quiet place and get some rest'.[3]

Philip feels strongly that one of the most important tasks for the Church in the twenty-first century is to recover and validate silence and solitude, because without them we cannot have insight. The Quiet Garden Movement allows that silence and solitude to be accessible, in a non-threatening space of beauty and stillness. The qualities of Quiet Garden Days, such as an openness to all sorts of Christian wisdom about life and spirituality and to all sorts of experiences of nature, as well as the importance of meeting other people, come from Philip's own life experiences and point to the significance of someone's own life story in the creation of their garden.

It is time now to go and find out whether the Quiet Gardens live up to these ideals and do provide the sort of beneficial environment that allows for therapeutic horticulture.

2. *Ibid.*
3. From the New Testament section of the Bible, Mark 6:31.

CHAPTER 8

Arley, Worcestershire

From its own beginnings, and back into the Jewish history on which it is founded, Christianity has always been a journeying faith. The Quiet Garden Movement was formed out of the desire of its founder, Philip Roderick, that people should follow the example of Jesus, who regularly took time out of his physical journeying in order to catch up with his spiritual journey:

> He slipped away into the hills by himself.[1]
>
> Later that same day Jesus left the house and went and sat beside the lake.[2]
>
> One day soon afterward Jesus went up on a mountain to pray.[3]

All the Quiet Gardens in the movement are places where people of any faith or none may stop. They are locations of natural beauty and stillness where travellers, in whatever sense, may gain spiritual refreshment and restore a sense of balance to their busy lives. Every Quiet Garden is therefore part of the journey of its visitors and very often, too, it is eloquent of journey in other ways.

It is impossible to visit Arley Quiet Garden near Kidderminster in rural Worcestershire, for example, without absorbing the travels of some of the early plant hunters and botanists such as Sir Joseph Hooker and David Douglas, or even the lesser-known George Annesley, Viscount Valentia, the second Earl of Mountnorris. Arley is one of the larger gardens of the Quiet Garden Movement and includes a 15-acre arboretum. This was created by George Annesley as part of his extensive planting within the 86 acres of the estate during the eighteenth and nineteenth centuries. The estate lies on a slope of land above the Severn valley. It looks over a sweep of the valley given to fields and woods, which in springtime echo with lambs bleating and in summer and at special weekends with the distinctive sound of steam trains from the Severn Valley Railway. It is situated west of Birmingham just 40 miles from the Welsh border and on the same latitude as Aberystwyth to the west and Southwold much further to the east.

---

1. From the New Testament section of the Bible, John 6:15.
2. *Ibid.*, Matthew 13:1.
3. *Ibid.*, Luke 6:12.

In 1843 Arley House, as it was then, began to be reconstructed into an imposing castle in the Gothic style and, although the castle was all but demolished in 1959, the gateway survives. We entered the paved courtyard of the 1960s Arley House to be greeted by the welcoming handshake of Nigel Goodman, the current guardian of the Quiet Garden at Arley.

George Annesley Esq. inherited the estate at Arley from his Lyttleton ancestors in 1779 at the tender age of nine years old. By the time he was 26, it was clear that the gardens had fallen into the right hands, as he was in that year elected a fellow of both the Royal Society and the Linnean Society on the grounds of his considerable botanic knowledge and skill. Some of his friends were also botanists, including Sir Joseph Banks. Viscount Valentia (another of George's titles) was a plant hunter himself, making a four-and-a-half-year expedition to India via Madeira and the Cape and coming back past Egypt and Malta, sending seeds, bulbs and plants back to Arley as he went. The seeds of these journeys literally established the arboretum at Arley, which was then further increased by members of the Woodward family who bought Arley after the death of George Annesley in 1844. The three Woodwards who then owned Arley were also botanists and came from the family from which there were three successive directors of the Royal Botanical Gardens at Kew: Sir William Hooker, Sir Joseph Hooker and Sir William Thiselton-Dyer.

Things could not have been looking better for the estate, gardens and arboretum, but suddenly family tragedy struck Arley. In 1915, during World War I, Robert ('Bobby') Woodward, the eldest son of the second member of the Woodward family to own Arley, was killed in action on the Western Front. Bobby had first studied at Oxford, then went to the Bar in London where he lived and from where he frequently visited both Kew and Arley. Whether it was the gift of trees from a famous contemporary plant hunter when he was born that gave him his interest in botany, or something that simply ran in the Woodward veins, Bobby had lived up to his horticultural pedigree. His fraternizing with the leading botanists of the time and his enthusiasm for the family arboretum had led him to compile a record of all the plants at Arley in his *Hortus Arleyensis*, which lists over 400 specimens and 300 species that had been planted over the previous century. He was also a practical plantsman and the first to raise a new peony from the mountains of north-west China from seed in 1911. This plant was later named in his memory: *Paeonia veitchii woodwardii*. He supported expeditions of the plant hunter Ernest Henry Wilson and even when he was away fighting he wrote from the trenches asking about the progress of specific plants at Arley.

Nonetheless, Arley is a place of survival and there are one or two quirky stories from the archives. The seed of a Roble beech (*Nothofagus oblique*) was introduced into Britain from Chile by John Elwes, a famous tree expert and author of *The Trees of Great Britain and Ireland 1906–13*. He was a regular visitor to Arley and after the Roble beech seedlings had been raised at Kew, the then director Sir William Thistleton-Dyer sent one to Arley. It was raised in a greenhouse to start with and then successfully planted out in the arboretum in 1904. Sadly there was a severe frost

The soaring tree canopy at Arley Arboretum in Worcestershire

at the end of the year that all but killed the tree, save for a few inches of stem above the ground. It resolutely grew back and was thriving steadily until, in 1906, a dozy cow strayed into the arboretum and ate the leading shoot. Despite all this, the Roble beech reached maturity, died of natural causes and a shoot from the original trunk is now over 25 feet tall. This seems to be a metaphor for the survival of the Arley estate. Despite the death of the most horticulturally-minded member of the family, the fact that the whole family moved out of Arley in 1923, the neglect of the estate grounds through the two World Wars, the Depression and social change following all this; and the selling of the whole estate in 1959, Arley is as thriving a setting now as it has ever been.

R. D. Turner, an industrialist and philanthropist, bought Arley in 1959 and, although he demolished the old castle and house, he restored the gardens and arboretum and established a trust, which now opens the gardens to the public.

Today's Quiet Garden visitors meander through spectacular woodland between champion trees that claim the widest girth or greatest height in the British Isles. There are a number of Crimean pines (*Pinus nigra* subsp. *pallasiana*), including one at 150 feet, which is the tallest, and another with a girth of 16 feet 7 inches, which is the widest. Many of these beautiful tree specimens were originally discovered or given by plant hunters such as David Douglas, who sent seed of the Douglas fir (*Pseudotsuga menziesii*) and a Western Yellow pine (*Pinus ponderosa*) sapling from the Spokane River in Washington State, USA. Sir Joseph Hooker gave two black walnut trees (*Juglans nigra*) on the occasion of the birth of the last Woodward botanist, Bobby, in 1877, as well as some bamboos. There are some of the first examples of tree species in Britain such as Acer griseum, the Coastal redwood (*Sequoia sempervirens*), the monkey puzzle (*Auraucaria araucana*) and a Western hemlock (*Tsuga heterophylla*), as well as the 1964 addition of a Chinese conifer (*Metasequoia glyptostroboides*) unknown in Britain before 1941 from a remote part of western China. There is a monumental cedar of Lebanon, unusually untouched to date by storm damage; many beech trees – including one which has rooted wherever its branches have touched the ground and now covers a space of around a quarter of an acre; a group of three Corsican pines which soar over 145 feet above the ground; and a cathedral-like space with its own apse made of six Incense cedars. (And this is without mentioning the plants that carpet the arboretum floor, such as primroses, bluebells, azaleas, cyclamen, daffodils and a laburnam arch.)

Arley is a place resonant of some of the exotic parts of the world and some of the awe-inspiring adventures of the enthusiastic plant hunters of the past. It is a place

Looking on Pinus nigra *subsp.* pallasiana, *the Crimean pine, one of the champion trees at Arley Arboretum in Worcestershire*

*Bishop of Llandaff dahlia head in a herbaceous border in the
Quiet Garden at Arley in Worcestershire*

of history and endurance. What impressed me most about it, however, was a sense of the presence of the trees. I have visited the place several times and each time I find myself drawn to stand amongst them, as you would be drawn to go and stand in the company of a group of charismatic people. I like trees, but I have not previously considered myself in the 'hugging' bracket of arboreal enthusiasts. Nonetheless, I am beginning to understand that great trees offer more than just a pleasing silhouette. There is something metaphysical in the experience of standing underneath them and looking up over 100 feet, or leaning against the trunks and resting a while. They do have a presence, and offer those who are receptive to it a subtle encounter with something other than ourselves. I would describe the 'presence' of a tree as an understanding that the living thing you stand next to has an incredible history and longevity and this, mixed with the sound, smell, sight and feel of it magnificently inhabiting a patch of land and holding a significant role in the ecosystem of that area, provides a comprehension of something 'other'. That to me is a genuinely spiritual experience.

Individual trees apart, the Quiet Garden at Arley provides a real sense of perspective. Simply to walk in the arboretum and be dominated by the trees' sheer size brings one's own life down to scale, as does the ability at Arley to walk quite a distance and almost literally to lose oneself in the variety of paths and different parts of the garden. As well as the old and new parts to the arboretum, with a small pond area, there is a quiet, formal, paved Italian garden with splashing fountains, vibrant annuals and plenty of seats on which to soak up the sun (and this is not a small space). There are large expanses of green lawn and herbaceous borders that impart a feeling of space and escape. The magnolia garden is a quiet place of its own surrounded by yew hedging so thick that at one point two seats and a table are placed in a carved-out alcove within the hedge. Finally, there is the more domestic feel of the old orchard area and walled garden, which is now the home of a number of rare-breed poultry, a beautiful soft lilac wisteria and an impressive line of brick and glass greenhouses and old bothies, all of which, I confess, I would have been entirely happy to dismantle and take back home with me.

On Quiet Days at Arley, the group of guests gathers over coffee in the house where they relax into the day and meet their fellow contemplatives. There is then a formally led reflection from a visiting speaker, after which the group disperses into the gardens for quiet individual time. In bad weather the village church adjacent to the gardens is open, as is the old castle gatehouse room known as The Barbican, and both of these have their own particular atmosphere to absorb. The group reassembles for lunch, and again for a cup of tea at the end of the afternoon, but otherwise guests take advantage of the freedom and the request for silence to make their own journeys amongst the well-tended garden areas, majestic trees and beautiful English scenery. Arley is a fitting place of pilgrimage, having an atmosphere that exudes a sense of history, adventure and journey, as well as being a place of acceptance and stillness.

CHAPTER 9

Rydal, Cumbria

Rydal Hall Meditation Garden is a centre of pilgrimage in the modern sense of the word. It doesn't house relics, a tomb or a shrine and is not, as far as we could find out, the source of a stream of miraculous healings or the like. It is, however, a retreat centre for the diocese of Carlisle and as such welcomes visitors and staying guests from Cumbria and Westmoreland, as well as the country as a whole, for a bit of 'time out'. Situated as it is just south of Ambleside at the heart of England's Lake District, its location alone makes it worth the journey for many people.

The Retreat Movement was brought into favour in England by the Oxford Movement in the 1830s and has enjoyed a following ever since, none more so than today. Retreats are a way of encouraging ordinary Christian people to take time out, much as Jesus did, in order to stock up on spiritual resources for the next part of the journey. Rydal Hall was leased by the diocese of Carlisle in 1963 and then purchased in 1970 together with its outbuildings and land. Nearly 40 years later, it has gradually been restored and developed into the multifaceted centre it is today.

The building of Rydal Hall was begun in the 1500s by a local land-owning family called the Le Flemings, who seem to have been more concerned with the good use of their resources than with making an ostentatious splash, for the house was constructed gradually over several hundred years as time and money permitted. The Le Flemings actually owned Rydal from 1595 to 1970 and developed it from a modest farmhouse to one of the major houses of the Lake District. William Wordsworth, who lived for 37 years at Rydal Mount, a few hundred yards from the Hall, enjoyed its land and outlook. It is now a fine Grade II Georgian listed building that sits on a ledge of ground between the folds of contiguous fells. The main reception room windows overlook wide, formal parterre gardens and if you stand by the (unusually concrete) balustrades at the furthest side of the parterre, a wooded valley falls away in front of you, revealing the Rothay valley towards Ambleside: yet another perfect rugged Lakeland vista.

On the day we came to see Rydal, the fair weather and brightening skies of the Pennines left us at Keswick and we followed a muddy yellow aggregates lorry past some of the most beautiful scenery in England … if only we could have seen it through the rain and low cloud. Nonetheless, the overall impression of the colours of dark green, mustard and tan, and a sense of moist aliveness, was still an experience worth having. As we entered Rydal's drive, the mist rose from the dripping trees in the valley, and as I walked out under an umbrella to meet Tom Attwood, the head gardener, rain thundered down the drainpipes from the Hall's roofs behind us. We stood in spectacular surroundings while rain ran in rivulets from Tom's hair onto his face and in cold-looking trickles inside the collar of his waxed jacket. He was, however, in the very best of spirits and enthused passionately and at length on all that is good about working in horticulture and particularly outdoors. It was quite contagious!

What Rydal shares with Arley is a link with Kew. Having finished his A levels and still not having any idea where or what he should be doing next, Tom worked for a bit in a plant nursery. He may have been bitten by a number of interesting bugs during his time in the greenhouses there, but the longest-lasting bite was from horticulture itself. He left the nursery to acquire qualifications which culminated in his being accepted for the Kew Diploma, from which he arrived at Rydal, just under two years ago at the time of writing, to take on what he feels is the job of a lifetime. Tom's brief is to restore the gardens at Rydal to their former glory, but within the context of an environmentally aware twenty-first-century Christian culture which pervades everything else at Rydal Hall. He does not embrace faith with both hands, but understands completely the need to provide everyone who visits Rydal with an experience of the beauty, harmony and wildness of the created world that surrounds the centre and gives it identity.

In this restoration project, it is a matter of both frustration and joy for Tom that any documentation explaining the historical development of the garden and the ideas behind it is sadly lacking. Having lived with the garden landscape now for many months, he feels that the original Quiet Garden may have been a Japanese garden, but there is precious little hard evidence. However, if making up the design as you go along and learning on the job is what's required, then Tom is your man. He has launched into the project with a small team of volunteers and a good deal of gusto, although even he admits that as a one-man task it is quite an undertaking! Nonetheless, the formal gardens are clipped and neat, the lovely wide herbaceous borders with the stone walls behind them are gradually being filled and have been topped up, apparently by hand, with myriad barrowloads of manure. The vegetable garden, although not able to cater for the numbers of guests at Rydal in any one month, is nevertheless in production, the summerhouse has been restored and some of the woodland has been managed.

While Tom and I were enjoying the weather outside, Chris was having a much more civilized but, I would argue, less experiential feel of Rydal as he talked indoors to the centre's general manager, who has the apt name of Jonathan Green. Jonathan is another part of the fresh vision for Rydal Hall which has also included a major refurbishment programme that has brought ensuite bedrooms to the pilgrim experience. (What would Chaucer make of that?) The diocese of Carlisle have realized that they are sitting on treasure at Rydal – not that the retreat business brings in vast amounts of capital, but it is an invaluable resource both to the Christian and the wider community. As well as the main retreat house, there is also a conference centre which caters for 200 on a day basis or 60 overnight guests. There are two holiday cottages, a camping field much used by all visitors to this part of the Lakes, and a bunkhouse camping barn for the slightly less hardy who prefer not to sleep as well as walk in the wet. The Rydal teashop (an essential part of the English Lakes experience) is signposted from the end of the drive on the main road, and footpaths cross the estate for the enjoyment of Rydal's temporary walking visitors.

There is another sense in which Rydal Hall and the Quiet Garden are a focus for journeying people. The staff who assist the Rydal guests are themselves a community. They are people of all ages and nationalities, who come to join the team for a specific duration. So although Jonathan is a lay person himself and none of the present staff community are religious in the strict sense of the word, they all share a vocation to serve the multifarious travellers to the centre and operate much as the great religious houses of old would have done. At the time we visited, there were staff there from Brazil, Malawi, Argentina, France, Australia, New Zealand, Hungary and one intrepid adventurer who had made it over from the Isle of Man. As well as working on the estate, in the kitchens, the gardens, the house and the conference centre, they also pray and worship together on a daily basis and, informally within the context of Rydal, share their stories of faith and experience with other staff and visitors. It is an enriching, multicultural atmosphere.

One of Jonathan's managerial visions is to further the environmental emphasis that was begun at Rydal several years ago. According to him, the gardens are the jewels in Rydal's crown and he is keen to develop the kitchen garden further – a passion he shares with Tom. It is not unusual in the Lakes to use the natural water supply as your own and a number of years ago Rydal started reducing its carbon footprint even further by harnessing the power of the water from the beck (which flows through the grounds) by diverting it through a hydroelectric turbine. Jonathan wants to look at the whole concept of green theology and how that can be outworked practically at a centre like Rydal, and fortunately environmental considerations were also high on the agenda of Tom's Kew Diploma.

The gardens are undoubtedly one of the greatest assets of Rydal Hall and Tom took me on one of the shorter walks which winds into the Meditation Garden. Like Arley, Rydal benefits from a large area in which guests can experience a range of surroundings. The top parterre has formal beds, clipped yews, statuary and herbaceous borders to die for. Below and beyond the parterre there are woodland walks. At the beginning of one of these there is an installation that articulates through sculpture the concept of releasing the chains of poverty. It is associated with Christian Aid and has been placed thoughtfully by two still pools. The path to what has been the Quiet Garden leads further on still, winding back on itself and under the road to the house through a rock-clad tunnel and past the fast-flowing beck, flanked with beech trees, mossy rocks and ivy. None of this prepared me for what in my opinion is the diamond at the very centre of this Rydal crown.

Rydal Hall grounds include the beck that creates Rydal Falls – a series of waterfalls of increasing splendour the further up the beck you trek (isn't that always the way?). These are the spectacular falls that placed Rydal Hall at the heart of the English Romantic Movement, much visited as they were by Wordsworth and his fellow poets. What I saw as I came out the other side of the carefully angled rocky tunnel on the path to the Quiet Garden was a view of the last of these waterfalls – pouring a foam of peaty yellow-white water between tight black rocks that then crashed 10 or 15 feet into a dark pool below. Perched on a ledge of rock right in front of the waterfall pool is a hand-built rock summerhouse, complete with ferns growing in the crevasses of the stones and a slate roof. The inside is beautifully panelled with oak benches and window frames and a large removable mullioned window that looks onto the surging water (which apparently in a wet season can lap the sill outside). This is 'The Grot', dating back to 1668 and named by those most articulate of men, the Romantic poets themselves. It is the place where Wordsworth came to sit and write and Coleridge came to paint, and now it is the place where Rydal's Quiet Garden visitors can experience a quiet of a different sort. It is curious that a number of the Quiet Gardens we visited are not *literally* quiet at all. Here in the Meditation Garden at Rydal Hall it can be dreamily tranquil in a dry summer, but in the full flow of a wet spring it gives you the experience of being put in a place where the awesome power of nature dwarfs you and stops you in your tracks. As Tom put it, 'I couldn't create it, not in a million years! When you look at it you just see the power and it's good for the soul.'

Although the two visits described so far, to Arley and to Rydal, may not be typical of the average garden belonging to the Quiet Garden Movement (and in fact Rydal Hall no longer belongs officially to the Movement, though it still maintains its quiet garden as a place of contemplation), they are fantastic examples of two different places where it is possible to sit in idyllic solitude and come to terms with your own relationship to nature.

CHAPTER 10

Epworth, Lincolnshire

Just as Rydal Hall is a centre of international pilgrimage for all those called to the beauties of the English Lakes or lured by the haunts of our Romantic poets, the small but bustling Lincolnshire market town of Epworth perhaps surprisingly exerts an equivalent international pull. Groups of visitors have been moved to tears just by standing in the hallway of one of its older houses.

The Old Rectory at Epworth was home to the Reverend Samuel and Susanna Wesley and their 10 surviving children from 1697 until 1735. In fact Susanna had 19 children in 20 years, all of whom were born at Epworth, most in the timber-framed thatched cottage which was the first rectory. This cottage burned down in a fire in 1709 from which the young John Wesley, aged six, was dramatically rescued. The later, more substantial, brick rectory that stands today became the childhood home of both Charles and John Wesley, who together have bequeathed a substantial inheritance to modern-day Christianity. Charles Wesley, whose three-hundredth anniversary was celebrated in 2007, wrote over 7,000 hymns, a large number of which are still sung in churches and chapels across Britain today. John Wesley was considered the founder of Methodism.

The Wesley parents provided interesting role models for their children. In some ways Samuel Wesley was a negative influence with his aspirations to become a bishop and to live in a style suited to one. His annual £200 stipend should have been enough to live comfortably, but Samuel did not manage his money well and the family lived in poverty in a grand house for the duration of their childhood. However, what John in particular seemed to absorb from the teaching and practices of his father was that the Church of England was not reaching the souls of the people as he felt it should, and neither was it very strong on redressing social injustices. Samuel campaigned for the care of widows and orphans in the small poverty-stricken town of Epworth. He also spoke out against social injustice, and it is possible that those who opposed his reforms deliberately started the fire in the first rectory.

Susanna was the one who instilled a sense of method into John. She learned quite early on that to be a successful mother of 10 she had to get time management right. One of her many methods was to allocate a day a week to the attention of one of the eight children in the house at any one time, with Sunday being devoted to the two youngest. On those days she would seek to educate the children and teach them the values and skills of honest Christian living. She was also famous for maintaining her own prayer life in such a busy domestic setting by putting her apron over her head in order to signify the need to be left alone for a few minutes.

Whatever qualities the Wesley children, including the seven surviving girls, took from their childhood and instilled into their own adult lives is up for debate, but what is quite tangible today is the particular atmosphere of the Old Rectory at Epworth. It is an extraordinarily still and peaceful place. A clock ticks methodically in the hallway and Joan Sidaway, the Wesley museum's current curator, is convinced that prayer oozes from the walls. I understand what she means. The Old Rectory was in fact in use by the Church of England as a rectory until 1954, when it was purchased by the Methodist Church and used as a conference centre for church groups until it evolved into the museum that it is today. The house is run by a board of trustees who represent local churches, the UK Methodist Connexion and the World Methodist Council and it is visited each year by a healthy proportion of the world's 70 million Methodists.

Epworth itself sits on land known as the Isle of Axholme, which is an old Scandinavian word meaning 'raised ground in a marsh'. The Isle is about 17 miles long and five miles wide and lies in northern Lincolnshire. At one time the rivers Trent, Don and Idle surrounded it. At the time of enclosure in the early nineteenth century eight parishes made up the Isle, which was drained to become fen and bog land by the Dutchman Cornelius Vermuyden in the time of Charles I. The king wished to use it for hunting, fishing and shooting. On the positive side, the legacy of this change of use is wonderful, black, humus-rich soil, even if the flatness of the surrounding countryside means that the easterly wind has it easy. (How often are the copper beech leaves still?)

Epworth means 'the enclosure of a man named Eoppa' and is the capital of the Isle of Axholme. It has always had an agricultural history. Two of the original areas of the parish were known as the area of elder trees (Eller) and an enclosure of grapevines (Vine Garth). Oats and rye were cultivated elsewhere, followed after the draining by flax, peas, beans, clover and wheat, with potatoes, onions, rape and hemp coming still later. The abundant supply of water which made all this possible was also a source of historical irritation as people complained that the water was so peaty it made the milk curdle. This doesn't seem to have been a major threat to progress, however, and Epworth developed from a small, poverty-stricken, isolated village whose inhabitants survived by spinning flax and hemp and working in the sacking and bagging trade to today's thriving community known for its annual agricultural show, Plough Festival, and Christmas market. It also has a weekly market, a county primary school, a nearby secondary school, Baptist, Methodist and Anglican communities, one of only two Mechanics' Institutes in Britain (educational establishments set up for working men), a library, and the Epworth Society, a civic preservation and improvement organization. More to the point for hungry travellers, it is also the home of Epworth plum bread, a particularly tasty small loaf packed with dried fruit, delicious eaten with local cheese from the delicatessen just down the road from the Old Rectory.

This is the context for the Quiet Garden at Epworth Rectory. The curator Joan Sidaway is a keen gardener and was herself a member of the Quiet Garden Movement for many years. She felt the garden at Epworth would be ideal as a Quiet Garden and worked towards getting it affiliated. The garden is now being gradually replanted using historically accurate plants and also some of the plants the Wesleys are known to have put in themselves. Rather than being created as a traditional Georgian formal garden, it has remained a typical British family garden with large lawns, trees and flower borders rich with hostas, wood anemones and foxgloves. At the opening ceremony of the Quiet Garden there was circle dancing on the lawn. It is also a garden that welcomes wildlife, including rooks, squirrels and a resident sparrowhawk that perches in view of one of the windows and calmly plucks his prey before eating it. The large copper beech tree is thought to have been there in the Wesleys' time, and the small orchard that once existed at Susanna's request is being put back, including her particular love, a mulberry tree.

Although it is associated with a number of historical English figures such as the poet Milton and King James I, who wanted to encourage the British silk industry, the mulberry tree is not a native of Britain. It was adopted with enthusiasm, however, partly because its leaves are good food for the silkworm, helping to strengthen the silk filament spun by the worms. It is a tree that grows to about 20 or 30 feet with a wide crown of branches and leaves and a relatively short trunk. It produces purple fruits of about an inch long which are extremely juicy and have mild laxative properties, something of which John Wesley would have approved, concerned as he was with all matters of health. In his childhood in particular John was not well and was advised on his health by a doctor from whom he learned a lot. In his adult life his concern for the poor in the face of the crippling cost of medical charges led him to write a book called *The Primitive Physic* which advised on all matters of health and

Spinach leaves in the Physic Garden at the Old Rectory
Quiet Garden, Epworth in Lincolnshire

Onions in the Physic Garden at the Old Rectory Quiet Garden, Epworth in Lincolnshire, the childhood home of John and Charles Wesley

gave many examples of herbal medicine. The most recent development in the garden at Epworth Old Rectory is the Physic Garden at the back of the house, an area that is deliberately cultivated as a quiet space. It is a walled kitchen garden of herbs, vegetables and flowers, many of them mentioned in John's book. There are seats and a water feature where water from the mouth of a stone lion's head flows into a basin shaped like an old horse trough. A blind gentleman from Epworth comes regularly to sit in the Physic Garden, enjoying its sensory stimulation and its peace.

At present, and until the many centenary celebrations of the year are finished with and Lottery grant funding can be applied for, the Quiet Garden at Epworth Rectory is there as an additional space in which visitors can reflect and pause in their own hectic itinerary. In subsequent years it is hoped to provide special Quiet Days for groups to enjoy both the peace and some of the family and even musical atmosphere of the Wesleys' rectory of the past.

However, it is pertinent that, as visitors soak up a sense of peace in both the house and the garden at Epworth Old Rectory, they do so in the knowledge that it was the foundational home of two men who could hardly have travelled more if they had tried. John and Charles Wesley went on from Epworth to study at Oxford where Charles set up the 'Holy Club'. (They were known as 'Methodists' because of the way they systematically studied the Bible.) Both men were ordained into the Church of England in 1728 and Charles became curate to his father for two years. They then travelled to America in 1735 (an epic journey for ordinary people in those days), because John felt he had a mission to convert the Indians and to deepen the spiritual lives of the colonists. Although they learned much in America, that particular mission did not prove as fruitful as John Wesley had hoped and they returned to England in 1738.

Here the brothers' unease about the way ordinary people were excluded from the Established Church led them into an itinerant ministry largely in the open air, as they travelled around England on horseback. They often preached to thousands, including those in their home town of Epworth, where they preached at the market cross. Both John and Charles endured a great deal of persecution for their new ideas, but campaigned relentlessly on social issues such as prison reform and slavery. Charles is said to have preached 40,000 sermons and travelled 250,000 miles, and John achieved something similar. Their journeying spirit is mirrored in the numbers of pilgrim visitors who reach Epworth Old Rectory each year to meditate in the quiet and give thanks for two remarkable men.

CHAPTER 11

Bridlington, The East Riding of Yorkshire

The Quiet Garden Movement exists to provide a means by which spiritual experience becomes part of people's everyday life. Coming away regularly from the pressures and routines of daily life allows the formation of a habit of quietness, and in quietness it is possible to gain perspective – a sense that there is more to life than the structures on which that life is currently built. In fact, as I realize that I exist in the quietness, sitting under a tree at Arley, resting by the water trough in the Physic Garden at Epworth, or experiencing the waterfall at Rydal, this helps me to understand that I am something completely separate from my home environment. I can get off the hamster-wheel of routine as I know it; I could, for example, allow the appreciation of the natural environment to become a greater part of my life, or I could take up tap dancing, study Greek or make new friends.

These were the sorts of thoughts I found myself mulling over having visited the Frank Weston Quiet Garden in Bridlington. Here so many strands came together in one place, so many stories were woven into the one location. In fact, we were so drawn by this garden that Chris and I made a return visit, partly to take more photographs, but also to talk more about journeys and moving on with its owner and creator Penelope Weston.

Bridlington is an old market town situated just under the promontory of Flamborough Head on Britain's east coast, midway between Newcastle and The Wash. It is distinguished today by a small but working port with flocks of gulls, under whose raucous calls and seemingly random circling Chris and I spent a happy half hour early one weekday morning. Chris was pottering around with the camera and I was catching the birds on mike. So entranced were we with all things avian and fishing that we missed the sight of the Bridlington Eye, a new tourist attraction and reminiscent of the one on London's South Bank. For various reasons, it seems, the Eye may not stay in Bridlington for long. Perhaps the Bridlington Tuk Tuk will last longer? This ingenious motorized rickshaw, painted in strident fairground colours and resembling a cross between a land train and an elongated motorcycle, is apparently scarily punctual and will carry its passengers wherever they want to go and by whatever route. We're not used to such flexibility, and I hope that won't be its downfall!

Both the Eye and the Tuk Tuk would have been alarming sights to the founding fathers of Bridlington back in the mists of time. There are various theories as to whom the town has to thank for being there in the first place. It may be named after an Angle called Bretel who came to live in the Old Town, calling it logically, if slightly self-importantly, Bretelston. Alternatively it might have been named after a Saxon chieftain called Bridla whose family (the Bridlings) claimed latter ownership of it. Or its name may derive from the Old Norse word *berlingr*, meaning 'smooth water' – and certainly this particular part of the east coast offers very good shelter for boats. Whatever the true origin of the name, it is a place to which people come at some point on their journey, and that seems very appropriate for the Quiet Garden at Bridlington.

Contemporary Bridlington is in the East Riding of Yorkshire, and was once known as the town of Burlington in the eastern part of the Dickering Wapentake. In 1166, so it goes, the county in which Bridlington (also known as Burlington) found itself was divided into Wapentakes and 'the Dickering' seems to be derived from the Old English for 'dyke circle'.[1]

What is clear is that Bridlington Old Town used to be a very separate entity from Bridlington Quay where we were appreciating the gulls. In 1113 Baron Walter De Gaunt, who held the manor of Bridlington, established the first Augustinian priory in the north of England right next to his manor. It became, in the Middle Ages, the largest and richest monastery of the north, and despite its dissolution in 1537 the nave was allowed to stand. It was used as a parish church (St Mary's) and the Old Town of Bridlington grew up around it. Bridlington Quay, a mile or so away, hugged the shore and gradually spread around the harbour where the Gypsey Race river flows into the sea. Today the two parts of Bridlington have merged to become one town of distinctive areas, drawn together perhaps by the railway that 'happened' between them in the 1800s.

The Frank Weston Quiet Garden is situated on one of the oldest plots in the Old Town. The house here was built in 1673 by a wealthy ship owner with the intention that he could view his fleet coming in and out of port from the cupola (now sadly removed) on the roof. Should he, on any of these inspections, have also cast his glass over the town itself, he could have followed the toings and froings of what was then a large community of Quakers in Bridlington, established in 1652. After 20 years and probably much religious persecution, the large community was seriously depleted when many of them literally threw all to the winds and sailed with the boats of the Pilgrim Fathers in search of a new and more tolerant land. In 1677 a ship called *The Kent* took around 200 pilgrims from Yorkshire and London. They landed in America near the site of present-day Philadelphia and in time established a settlement there, which they called Burlington. The remaining Quakers in Bridlington maintained their quiet spirituality through to the twenty-first century and lend a precedent to places of quiet reflection such as the Frank Weston Quiet Garden today.

---

1. My thanks to Gwendoline Hirst, author of *The Bridlington Guide*, available online (*www.ba-education.com/for/travel/guide/bridlingtontown.html*).

A sense of history pervades the garden in other ways, too. Frank Weston, Penelope's husband, latterly the Bishop of Knaresborough, previously served at Christchurch, Oxford, Edinburgh Episcopal Church's Theological College and the missionary training College of the Ascension at Selly Oak. Missionary blood ran in the family. Frank Weston's namesake, his uncle Bishop Frank Weston of Zanzibar (1871–1924), was a leading and sometimes controversial Anglo-Catholic, famous and loved for working with native Africans and against slavery, and also well known for defending some of the finer points of theology to do with the incarnation and person of Christ. His spirituality seemed to encompass clear doctrinal thinking and practical action and he was very highly esteemed. His biographies reveal a man utterly dedicated to the African people among whom he worked: someone remembered for his passion for God and people, a man capable of great courage and sacrifice who commanded his own unit of native troops during the war, but who insisted even with them on the importance of prayer. Frank Weston, Bishop of Zanzibar, was a truly holy man.

Frank Weston, Bishop of Knaresborough, seems to have inherited some of his uncle's attributes, although he was a different character. There are books, pamphlets and biographies galore concerning the African bishop, but only a few snippets of information about the English one. Tellingly, one of these is an article in the *Evening Press* in the summer of 2000 drawing attention to Frank Weston's plea that the countryside and farmers become a major focus of Christian concern. The then Archbishop of York spoke of Bishop Frank as demonstrating 'an enormous pastoral capacity, and (the) remarkable concern, care for and interest in people from every walk of life'. The Latin phrase engraved on the back of his Episcopal cross, *Omnus amandi*, 'all are to be loved', was his *raison d'être*.

Frank Weston served the Church faithfully, wisely and with a warm and loving spirit for 40 years. Being Bishop of Knaresborough was his final job and, looking forward to retirement as he and Penelope were, they turned their thoughts to buying a house somewhere in Yorkshire. They chose Bridlington and over the next two years worked together, when the bishop was free, and separately, when he was not, to sort out house and garden and create a place of hospitality. It became more and more of a focus in their life: they had a family Christmas camping there under renovation conditions, and at the end of April 2003 Penelope and Frank held their ruby wedding celebrations in the town with a service at the priory church and a party in the house and garden.

Just two days later, Frank suffered a stroke and died within a few hours.

Picking up the pieces of one's life when a partner dies suddenly is a daunting process. I imagine that being caught a little between two locations doesn't make it any easier, but it didn't take long for Penelope to realize that Bridlington had already become home. When she arrived in the garden to do some tidying up a few weeks later, she found that all the new small plants she had established in early spring were now completely engulfed by annual poppies, and by weeds a little higher than the will to remove them. She pressed on.

It helps to have empathetic friends and here Penelope could not have done better than Jean Parker, a sculptor, very good friend, fellow Quiet Gardener, and someone who had just created a series of sculpted busts called 'Bald Statements'. These are a collection of heads with faces and particular expressions. They were created while Jean herself was undergoing treatment for cancer. Articulate beyond words, these stark sculptures take the viewer through a range of emotions and subtleties of feeling that belong to the state of grief.

Unsurprisingly, it was Jean whom Penelope commissioned to produce a memorial of Frank for the garden. The diocese of Ripon had generously made a gift at Frank's retirement and Penelope decided to use it to create a unique focus for the Frank Weston Quiet Garden. Under her direction and with the aid of clay models, a block of Portland stone that had to be craned over the wall into the garden and a collection of power tools, Jean created a statue in memory of Frank. It was 'some sort of hug', as Penelope put it. The finished work stands about 4 feet high on a plinth in the centre of the herb garden and shows two figures, one held unequivocally in the arms of the other. Originally white, but now weathering to a gentler hue, it is carved from the one block of stone. Jean was still recovering from cancer when she undertook the work and so used an angle grinder to cut slashes in the rock and then prised out the slices with a chisel. The stone is thus left deliberately rough and marked, a beautiful and telling contrast to the powerful sense of tender enfolding that looking at the statue brings.

Above all else, the Frank Weston Quiet Garden is a healing garden.

It is also a garden of three parts. First, nearest to the house, is the knot garden, which is surrounded by an old wall and equally ancient wisteria and comprises box hedges filled with lavender and slate chip paths. Knot gardens came to being in the late medieval and early Renaissance period, being most popular in Britain in the 1500s. They were part of the thinking of the day which put man at the centre of the picture. In garden design terms this meant arranging things around him in his house, into a united whole, using geometry, symmetry and mathematical proportion. Moreover:

> Renaissance man believed that to know God's world was in fact to know him … Gardens in which nature had been re-arranged by the hand of man into geometry were an expression of divine order. [2]

The Quiet Garden Movement would echo the first statement, that nature is a means by which to understand something of God, but would not want to limit an expression of divine order solely to the geometric. Here at Bridlington the knot garden with the statue does particularly express something of the nature of God, but visitors benefit equally from the other two parts of the garden.

---

2. Strong, R. (2000), *Gardens through the Ages* (London: Conran Octopus), p. 26.

Through the central arch in the clematis-covered trellis that divides the herb garden from the rest, one follows a brick path from the knot garden onto a circular lawn surrounded by traditional herbaceous borders that spill flowers and foliage onto the clipped green edges. Blue, pink and purple perennials sit alongside sculptural Miscanthus 'zebra' grass, Crambe cordifolia, hostas, roses and a Grissolina hedge. In the centre, on the brick path, is an Ali Baba urn with water just overflowing from it onto the stones below. It makes a gentle sound in a tranquil area.

The third part of the garden is partly sheltered by a large old copper sycamore tree that allows a small woodland patch of ferns, foxgloves, cyclamen and snowdrops to flourish, before the potager opens out. A potager was originally a French style of ornamental kitchen garden where flowers and herbs were planted in amongst vegetables for aesthetic and sometimes also culinary value. It tends to have a vertical aspect with climbing plants (often beans) making their way up hazel stakes, as well as clearly defined beds for lower-growing plants with permanent paths in between.

Dividing the potager in half in Bridlington is a spectacular living willow tunnel. Penelope now studies horticulture to increase her knowledge and smiles ruefully at the memory of the first summer after planting the willow when the new willow shoots of up to 15 feet sprouted randomly from the neat arching structure and waved threateningly at any visitor like an old-fashioned sci-fi triffid. Gardening wisdom, Penelope found, is developed 'with a wry smile and a large pair of secateurs'.

On either side of the tunnel are beds of carnival colour. Climbing beans and purple-podded peas are set off by a mass of vivid yellow and orange marigolds and nasturtiums with bright green parsley and chive bundles bristling at the edges. It is difficult to decide whether the vast wigwam of sweet peas rising from a bed of citrus splendour on the other side of the tunnel is more overwhelming for its scent or its colour. I can understand why people spend several hours on a conveniently placed seat there, just drinking it all in.

All the historical, aesthetic and horticultural nuances would be enough together to provide any visitor to the Quiet Garden at Bridlington with a baptism of nature and a larger perspective on life. But it is the statue of the hug which endows the Frank Weston garden with as tangible an experience of the spiritual reaching out into the human world as any object is likely to provide. Loss of any kind is a process by which we are often tongue-tied. Experiencing the natural beauty of the garden at Bridlington provides the visitor with a tangible sense of having been given something special. Contemplating the statue hones this down to the understanding that by being there one has been held and loved, even in loss, and given the strength to carry on with the journey.

CHAPTER 12

Petworth, West Sussex

In order to experience a random sample of the Quiet Gardens in Britain, my rather unscientific method was to scan the directory and choose the gardens with the most interesting names, as long as they fell in the right part of the country. Sometimes when I made the initial phone call people would not wish to be sampled. For some the Quiet Garden really is a very quiet affair, for small numbers of people just once or twice a year, and I think occasionally my phone call conjured up visions of coach-loads of tourists arriving unannounced. It is important to note that all the Quiet Gardens are private gardens which their owners have chosen to share in a particular way. They are open to anyone who genuinely wishes for some peace and quiet in a beautiful space, but it is always by appointment.

The sign for Iris's Bible garden in Whitland, Carmarthenshire

Sometimes, too, it was the case that the Quiet Garden had been operating for a while but the numbers of visitors had dropped and the future was slightly in question. Others, however, were going from strength to strength, like Limbo Farm in West Sussex. Given my selection criteria, somewhere with such an intriguing name was just asking to be investigated.

Ian and Sheila Cole have farmed for 30 years at Limbo Farm just outside the walls of Petworth House estate on the edge of the town of Petworth in West Sussex. The town is small but ancient (to be found in the Domesday Book), with a current population of around 3,000 people. It is difficult not to look on it as anything other than a privileged place, situated on the edge of the rolling green of the South Downs and bristling with shops full of expensive antiques – for which it is a centre in the south. In fact, the area around Petworth is known locally as the Golden Triangle, with winding lanes and well-preserved old buildings on every corner. A prestigious country house stands literally on the doorstep, containing a significant collection of Turner paintings, essentially because this was where they were painted, as well as Van Dyck paintings and Grinling Gibbons carvings which also feature in a major way inside. The house was given to the National Trust to manage in 1947, although the Wyndham family who own it still live, as they have done for the last 250 years, in the south wing. It is still home to the Petworth House Real Tennis Club, and helps to host the Petworth Festival of world-class classical music and literature each year. Capability Brown landscaped the 700 acres of deer-filled parkland around Petworth House, which includes a 30-acre woodland garden and the largest herd of fallow deer in the country.

It is a place of superlatives and you could be drawn into the idea that all is rich and well and always has been. It is a helpful balance, therefore, to find Petworth Cottage Museum, the home of Mrs Cummings, a seamstress and wife of a drunken husband who was a blacksmith for the Royal Irish Hussars as well as for the Petworth estate. The museum is there to show what the lives of poor estate workers were like and has been sealed in time at 1910. A century or so earlier, rural poverty was a serious problem and a clergyman in Petworth at the time, the Reverend Thomas Sockett, was part of a movement that assisted poor rural people to emigrate. With the help of the Earl of Egremont, who provided money, Thomas Sockett organized the Petworth Emigration Committee that chartered ships and sent emigrants to Ontario in Canada from 1832 to 1837. People went from almost 100 parishes in Sussex and around 1,800 of them arrived in Toronto from Portsmouth assisted by the Petworth committee. It is perhaps some credit to Thomas Sockett that while the emigrants to Ontario were generally middle-class settlers who didn't adapt very well, the Petworth travellers blended in so well that it has proved difficult to trace their fortunes, although books about the project are now being published.

The Coles of Limbo Farm have likewise not found it hard to blend in to their locality and over the years have developed both the use of the farm and their own faith locally. Sheila describes herself as a cradle Catholic: she went happily through the motions of the faith for many years without any real individual engagement. Her own faith began when she started visiting Lourdes. Faced with Our Lady in a more personal way than she had previously experienced, Sheila asked her if she might know her Son better, and her own journey of faith started. Meanwhile, Ian was part of a neighbouring family and courtship between them was a healthy development of their more casual relationship. However, an uncle of Sheila's was scandalized to discover that Ian had never been christened and forever after referred to him, in the way that only family members seem to get away with, as 'the Limbo boy' (Catholic teaching at the time included an idea that unbaptized children went to a state called 'Limbo' – it being deemed unfair to consign them to hell). Sheila and Ian married and when the farm that Ian was managing was due to be sold, they set about looking for a farm of their own. Limbo Farm near Petworth came up as a possibility and they felt that with a name like that it had to be theirs! From local history records, it seems that it refers to a lime copse which grew there – 'Limbo' being an evolution of 'Lime Hoe'. However, for a practising Catholic family with a prayer room and a quiet garden, I rather think that 'Limbo', meaning 'an intermediate place between two extremes' (from the medieval Latin for 'on the border of'), is quite apt. Visitors to Quiet Days at Limbo Farm can feel secure in the knowledge that they rest for the day in an intermediate place from which they may choose upon one course of action or another.

For many years the Leconfield Estate, associated with Petworth House, provided something of an income for Sheila alongside the farm. She used to cook for hunting groups who would come to shoot on the estate, although her real interest was more and more to do with her faith, something Ian has always encouraged and actively participated in. For 14 years Sheila worked in Lourdes with the Arundel and Brighton Pilgrimage Group, and she became a prayer guide in Sussex. Pilgrimage formed a regular part of the Coles' own life and it was during a visit to the Holy Land, when Ian had retired from a job he had been doing with Sotheby's, that the pair of them were challenged by the chaplain of that pilgrimage to start up a retreat centre on the farm. This evolved into the Eremos prayer room (named after a cave they had visited in the Holy Land and converted, echoing the parable of the Prodigal Son, from the old pigsty), where groups or individuals could come for some peace and quiet for an hour or two or even a day of prayer.

Shortly after starting this venture, Shelia heard about the Quiet Garden Movement and felt it would be an excellent partner project to the prayer room. She hasn't looked back. Groups come and, after a reflection in the Eremos room to start them off, they are free to wander the paths and fields of the farm, to the bluebell woods and back, or to sit in Our Lady's Garden, where a white statue of Mary presides in the laurels. In the vegetable garden, a surprising number of people like to sit and contemplate the courgettes or nibble the ripe raspberries, or they can wander to the copse where a handmade cross is a focus of attention.

Numerous letters of appreciation from Quiet Day participants and a bowl full of folded prayer requests in the Eremos room are testimony to the fulfilling experience of being in limbo for a day.

CHAPTER 13

Clehonger, Herefordshire

The curfew tolls the knell of parting day,
The lowing herd wind slowly o'er the lea,
The plowman homeward plods his weary way,
And leaves the world to darkness and to me.[1]

The Quiet Garden Movement was founded by Philip Roderick from a house in the village of Stoke Poges, where Thomas Gray composed his poem *Elegy Written in a Country Churchyard*. The elegy was written after the unexpected death of a friend of Gray's and therefore at a time when the poet felt obliged to re-evaluate the human condition and journey. In the churchyard he was surrounded by the graves of young and old, many of whom were not, in our terms, celebrities of any sort, and he spends the elegy trying to understand the idea of the significance of 'unknown' people:

> Far from the madding crowd's ignoble strife,
> Their sober wishes never learned to stray;
> Along the cool sequestered vale of life
> They kept the noiseless tenor of their way.[2]

Journeys and journeying are an integral part of, and a rich metaphor for, our human experience. Some thinking, like the Greek myths of Odysseus or the search for the Holy Grail, leads us to believe that ultimate truth, beauty or meaning is something to travel towards and, if we are fortunate, courageous, wise or holy, we may attain it and find the reward at our journey's end. Many of us may feel lacking in most of these virtues, but we go along with the Western thought process in which we travel linearly with a beginning and an end. St Gregory of Nyssa, an early Christian Father of the fourth century, saw things differently. He too understood that we are on a journey, but believed that the journey itself is the prize, because it is in the process of journeying that we find the answers. The ultimate 'whatever' is gradually pieced together along the way and only because we are on the way, rather than it being collected as a trophy at the end. This more circular thinking is something to which Eastern faiths have held for millennia.

Many of the Quiet Gardens are 'far from the madding crowd', as Gray's *Elegy* puts it, and in that sort of location they can stimulate reflection. This is certainly true of

---

1. The first verse of Thomas Gray's *Elegy Written in a Country Churchyard* (1751).
2. The last verse of Gray's *Elegy*.

Philip's and Sue's garden in the tiny village of Clehonger in Herefordshire. Sue in particular shares with Thomas Gray that experience of standing back and reflecting on a certain stage of the journey. She has had her busiest professional working period, and being a mother is now more of a long-distance role. She and Philip have set up Priors Mead as a Quiet Garden in mid-life and are hoping that others will also benefit from the experience of taking time out and gaining perspective on their own stage of life.

Philip is a Church of England minister, currently chaplain at the hospital in Hereford, and he sees the therapeutic side to the space and quiet that Quiet Gardens offer. His favourite spot in the garden is by the small pond carved out of the patio, in which swim several pink goldfish. Not having met a man who speaks quite so warmly about fish before, I felt obliged to meet them, and certainly there is an instantly calming effect from the gently trickling water, the soft colours and the liquid movement of the fish. The garden itself has a large, smooth, well-mown lawn surrounded by trees and herbaceous borders. Some older trees have been removed in order to open up the view, as the distant hills and valleys of both Herefordshire and Wales surround the garden.

Together Philip and Sue have always been actively hospitable and currently run a thriving bed and breakfast business. So their garden, to which Philip retreats with a spade or hoe at regular intervals for some 'switch off' time, was an obvious extension to what they already do. Having always been on the sharp end of a working mother's lot, Sue feels keenly that today's culture requires a woman to have it all but also to do it all, and she wants the Quiet Garden to provide an oasis for busy women. Fittingly, Clehonger has always been well supplied with water, both from the River Wye to the north and Cage Brook along its western boundary. In fact, it has been so well endowed that there were once four water mills that served the area. Tuck Mill remains, having been in operation as a corn mill since the early 1800s.

Priors Mead house was built on a piece of land that once belonged to a local monastery and the name is possibly derivative of 'Priors meadow'. There was a small statue of a prior perched slightly oddly on the front wall of the garage when Philip and Sue arrived, but his rather skeletal form didn't offer much hope for anyone about to partake of Sue's good cooking, so they took it away and replaced it with a more replete-looking St Francis. Priors Mead was completed in 1939 just as World War II began. It has a beautiful and typical late-1930s look about it, with white walls and a dark tiled roof. The garden leads out around the house and beyond the lawns, rhododendrons and trees to the fields grazed by black Welsh and Ryland sheep, and beyond them to views of the Golden Valley in the south-west and the Black Mountains of Wales. The gardens were designed and laid out by Hilliers, a famous Winchester-based firm whose choice of trees in particular has been exemplary. There is an organic vegetable garden to the side of the house, which supplies the bed and breakfast kitchen and lunch on Quiet Garden Days.

We visited Priors Mead in the first year that the Quiet Garden was operational, so there was little to report on how the Quiet Garden Days were organized or appreciated. Sue has now completed a local diocesan course for women's ministry and is looking forward to building up the Quiet Garden work gradually, according to the perceived need. For both of them this is a new part of the journey that promises both fresh insights and rewards.

The St Francis statue at Priors Mead in Clehonger, Herefordshire

CHAPTER 14

Exmouth, Devon

We saw at Clehonger that there are different ways of understanding journeys. In Eastern thought it is acceptable to go in circles, looking for the layers of meaning that are revealed gradually along the way. Charles Jencks talked of feeling uneasy with a straight correlation between God and the universe, and he felt more comfortable with the latest scientific concept of the universe as parallel layers of being. This idea of progressive enlightenment was furthered in our thinking by a fascinating element that we found in several of the Quiet Gardens that we visited.

The labyrinth is a rich and ancient symbol and phenomenon. The most famous example from our own cultural reference is that of the Greek Minotaur legend. Minos, son of Zeus, became king of Crete and the first king to control the Mediterranean Sea. However, his rule was blighted by the murder of his son Androgeus by the Athenians. In response Minos placed a monster, the Minotaur (and you don't want to know how the Minotaur came to be), in the centre of the Cretan labyrinth, and every ninth year he ordered the Athenians to send seven maidens and seven youths to the labyrinth where they met their doom. Theseus arrived in Athens just after the summons had come from Crete for the third time and offered himself as one of the youths. When he went into the labyrinth, he took with him a magic ball of thread from Ariadne, the daughter of Minos (who had fallen in love with Theseus), and once he had slain the Minotaur, Theseus emerged triumphant to go on to more daring deeds elsewhere. It is a fantastic story, containing everything a good superhero tale should, but the labyrinth imparts some depth to an otherwise superficial narrative of fighting and seduction. The point of the labyrinth is that one must make the journey along its paths to get to the centre, where something is conquered, and one emerges again triumphant over that particular manifestation of evil. The labyrinth is the journey, and the full journey involves going in, overcoming and coming out again.

Incidentally, it does seem fairly clear that in fact the Cretan labyrinth was more of a maze, otherwise Theseus would not have needed the ball of thread from Ariadne to find his way out. From the labyrinths we visited, we found that they are not to be confused with the maze, or indeed with any old serpentine prayer walk. A labyrinth is one path that takes the traveller to its centre and out again, and it is the process of travelling the many twists and turns of the path to the centre and back out which provides the unique experience.

The labyrinth has been included in a number of Quiet Gardens because of its symbolic qualities. It is the perfect tool to aid meditation and prayer in a quiet and natural setting, because it can be a means of freeing the walker to encounter and possibly overcome their current inner struggles. Or so we had heard, and therefore, once we realized there was a Labyrinth and Quiet Garden in Exmouth, Chris and I were keen to meet Maureen Douglas, the owner and creator, as she had not only made the garden but also studied labyrinths in some depth. A BBC meeting in Bristol early in the year seemed the best opportunity to incorporate a trip to the south-west. At least, it was a good idea until five o'clock that cold and frosty morning. We queued endlessly on the M25 and then the M4. Tranquillity was not to be ours for a little while, but in the end the leafless lanes beyond the M5 promised something more ancient and mysterious.

Exmouth is a port and seaside town situated on the east side of the River Exe and therefore bounded by both river estuary and sea, although it did not boast a serious settlement until the eleventh century, when the ferry port was established between the two small parishes of Littleham and Withycombe. By the end of the seventeenth century it was known as a seaside resort and attracted many visitors, including none other than Horatio, Lord Nelson (whose wife is buried in Littleham churchyard). Lord Byron also paid a visit; he no doubt wanted to check out the swimming conditions. Mass tourism developed apace after the railway arrived in 1861.

The Exe estuary is a site of special scientific interest for bird-watchers and like-minded naturalists, and the town is situated at the far western end of the Jurassic Coast World Heritage Site. In February the modern-day tourist attractions were boarded up and hibernating and the beach was deserted and blowy, but there were signs enough of the commercialism of the summer holiday culture. The Quiet Garden, however, is not out of place in a town of around 32,000 people which has 14 churches, including Roman Catholic, Anglican, Methodist, United Reformed, Brethren, Community, Baptist and Salvation Army, as well as a Spiritual Awareness Centre (more interested in clairvoyance than worship) and a spiritualist group. I particularly liked the sound of St John in the Wilderness, which has a Sunday service at the rather civilized hour of three o'clock in the afternoon.

Maureen's home was tucked into a pleasant suburb of Exmouth, not so far from the sea. Our rather tight timescale made it a necessity as well as a treat to go out with Maureen and walk the labyrinth while she explained some of its qualities. All through her working life she has been involved with dance and movement education, and so has always been 'body conscious'. The Quiet Garden was set up in 2000 and it seemed an obvious opportunity to create a labyrinth and start to understand the effect it has and how to use it. Below is an explanation of the labyrinth in Maureen's own words.

The labyrinth offers those who walk it a single winding pathway to the centre. It is not like a maze, there is no choice of pathway or false trail, but the path is tortuous.

Labyrinths have existed through centuries and across continents. Archaeologists and historians have found evidence of them in the ancient civilizations of Egypt, Greece and Rome, as well as in the South American continent and Scandinavia. The design appears in different forms; most are rounded, but some rectangular Roman mosaics have been found. The ancient labyrinths have seven rings and are generally described as 'classical'. Different cultures have different labyrinth stories. Western Europeans are most likely to know the Greek myth of Theseus and the Minotaur.

In medieval Europe, cathedral masons created pavement labyrinths. One of the most famous was placed in Chartres cathedral where it can still be seen and walked. This was described as *le chemin de Jérusalem*, 'the road to Jerusalem'. It has been surmised that those unable to make a pilgrimage to the Holy Land walked the labyrinth. Medieval manuscripts give limited evidence of the ways in which labyrinths were used. It is recorded that in Auxerre, it was used in the Easter rituals. By the eighteenth century the use of the cathedral pathways seems to have declined and some were removed. This happened at Rheims, where the children were found to make too much noise as they played on it.

Turf labyrinths can be found in parts of England. It is known that they were used for games on festivals such as May Day. One tradition is that the paths were run as races. My own experience is that when a large canvas bearing a labyrinth is out in front of the West Door of Exeter cathedral, young children enjoy running and playing on it, as they do in the Quiet Garden.

The later part of the twentieth century saw a revival of interest in labyrinths. The interest has not been confined to those found in Christian contexts. In Devon, at Seaton, a labyrinth was created as a millennium project. In Chartres there are regular opportunities to walk the ancient cathedral pavement. In the Christian community there is also an interest in creating labyrinths as aids to prayer. These do not all follow the medieval 11-ring design. Some place prayer stations along the winding pathways. Here people may pause to reflect or engage in some symbolic action.

Listening to those who have walked the labyrinth, I have gained an insight into the richness of image and symbol that people find in the 11-ring design. The circular shape has been seen as a symbol of the world we live in. A circle is sometimes described as a perfect shape, and has a particular wholeness. The uninterrupted curve of the perimeter gives a strong sense of the boundary enclosing what many have described as a sacred space. The pathway winds to the centre and out again. Although complex, with many turns, it is like a spiral, a never-ending line that speaks of eternity. The whole design is built around a cross, the most powerful of Christian symbols. The centre is the heart of the labyrinth and is the focus of the journey. It may represent the centre of all things, God, the centre of our own being, or the still place of meeting with God. For some, it is simply the centre, the special place because it has been attained. Stepping onto the pathway is to leave the general space, the rest of life, and to enter a sacred space. This becomes time and space set apart from the everyday activity. The walk is a journey to the centre, retracing the same pathway to leave and rejoin the world outside. This, like other journeys, has the capacity to create change as we engage with the experience. We may emerge and re-enter enriched, rested, or with some other insight from that time apart.

I have seen that walking the labyrinth can be a powerful experience. For some it is moving and even profound, for many it is prayerful. Initially I thought that it was the movement that was the key to the meditative mood. The attention has a single focus, the narrow path to the centre. The mind does not engage in decisions about the route. There is no distraction, just walking. The pace tends to be steady, especially on the shorter sections where the turns are more frequent. A rhythm of stepping develops and patterns of managing the turns. I thought that the slow rhythm had the same effect as attention to slow breathing can have, a stilling of the mind and the whole person. With no great variation of speed, energy or action, the body and mind can settle into calm. However, I have come to recognize that this is only a part of the impact on those who walk. The form or the pattern of the walk is highly significant and makes an important contribution to the affective nature of the experience.

The pathway has many turns and this has been related to facing new things and turning one's back on the past. Some have found the frequent turning confusing, or irritating, raising the question, will I ever get there? The walk demands trust as it moves through the four quarters of the labyrinth in a way that can seem at first unpredictable. The sudden move towards the centre, the focus of the inward journey, and the short distances between turns, are a contrast with the long outer sweeps of the path. Some people respond to the short and long distances between turns, enjoying the freedom of the outer tracks. The centre can become a special place. It invites pause and offers stillness. It has been said that it is not easy to leave and on the outward journey there is a sense of the centre calling you back. This, like the other responses I have recorded, is an individual response. It is particular to one person and also to one walk, but the many references to the importance of the pattern of the journey indicate the significance of the form or the pattern of the walk.

The context of the labyrinth also contributes to the experience. In the garden I have, I know people find significance in the light and the shade they pass through. Flowers, scents, sounds, birdsong and the rustle of leaves can all bring joy to the experience.

I have suggested that the style of the movement and the pattern of the labyrinth are important, and the Quiet Garden provides a Christian context for the walk, which can bring a prayerful stillness. The 11-ring design holds fascinating mathematical patterns, beyond the scope of this chapter, but I believe they too contribute to the sense of balance in the whole walk. Above all else, people describe the walk as an experience of peace. The labyrinth can be a tool of prayer; it is a dynamic tool inviting us in. As one visitor wrote after walking, 'Past, present, future laid out, but only experienced in the moment. The eternal now – but only available in the present.

Maureen is particularly interested in how the action of walking the rhythmic turns and curves of the path acts as an aid to stilling the mind and freeing the soul. In this way, walking the labyrinth does become a non-verbal form of prayer. Maureen described the experience of coming to walk the labyrinth in terms of time 'set aside' as a fallow field is set aside. It does give the walker time – time which could be used to wait on God or at least to become comfortable with one's own skin. And possibly the more you do relax into the rhythm, the more you may perceive. 'We are embodied people,' she points out to me as we walk, 'and we can process experience through movement.' Paradoxically, the physical movement of walking *La Lure* ('The Way') can still our souls, much as moving fingers rapidly over rosary beads can lead to prayer.

Here, in the labyrinth and Quiet Garden in Exmouth if anywhere, is an example of the experience of the journey itself being valid in its own right.

CHAPTER 15

White Waltham, Berkshire

It could be said that Quiet Gardens are another manifestation of a much older tradition of hospitality to travellers such as pilgrim hostels and coaching inns also were. They are there for guests to have a chance to pause on their life journey and perhaps take stock. As I also discovered at the Quiet Gardens of Exmouth and Waltham Place, however, sometimes the visit is not a pause within the journey, but, like the labyrinth, itself becomes the journey.

Waltham Place is another garden within a larger estate, this one being 170 acres in all. There has been a manor on this land since Domesday times, and the house, which became Hill Farm and then Hill House, had many owners. One of these was William Neile, an astronomer and mathematician who built an observatory at the house, but sadly died there in 1670 of a broken heart after an unhappy love affair. Tragedy has been replaced over the centuries by energy and vitality. It is now the home of Mrs Oppenheimer and her husband, whose mandate for the English estate is both that it embodies a strong ecological and sustainable philosophy, and that the community shares the land.

Waltham Place lies just outside the village of White Waltham near Maidenhead, and these days sits between the M4 and the M40. Under Mrs Oppenheimer's direction, in 1999 it became a member of the Soil Associations Organic Farms Network, because it is still a working farm with rare breed sheep, pigs and cows, arable and grazing fields, orchards, vegetable gardens and ornamental gardens, as well as woodland and a lake. It is open to garden visitors during the more seasonable times of year and in 2003 it became part of the Quiet Garden Movement, opening four times a year to today's pilgrims.

Chris and I approached Berkshire for our visit to Waltham Place on a most unpromising autumn afternoon with dark grey clouds hovering overhead, a suspicious wind stirring the trees and dusk seeming to approach, even in the middle of the afternoon. Chris disappeared to do plant talk with head gardener Beatrix and I talked to Vinnie, who co-ordinates the Quiet Days and works on the White Waltham estate and farm. He is a man with a strong feel for nature and it is his intention, on a Quiet Day, to help at least some of the guests understand 'the atmosphere thing', as he put it. I wanted to get a feel for the estate, and nothing was going to keep me from communing with the Berkshire pigs, so we set off in our wellies.

It became clear quite soon that the combination of White Waltham, with its emphasis on working *with* nature not against it, and Vinnie, with his affinity for all things living, is a unique and productive partnership. Waltham Place can be a chance to come to terms with our own identity. This may not be the question we think we want answered as we arrive, but that, I am beginning to understand, is the nature of pilgrimage.

Vinnie grew up in the Wicklow Mountains outside Dublin. He was more than happy as a teenager to take the bus into town at every opportunity and do the street thing, but he was also raised on the mountains. As an Irish Catholic there was no question that Vinnie was to be educated at a boarding school, in his case run by Carmelite priests who had a very strong sense of direction. It was also the case, as Vinnie explained, that as soon as he was able to, he ran as fast as he could in the opposite direction. He worked for a bank in London for a while, but disliked it intensely, realizing that he needed an outdoor life. After training at a horticultural college near Derby, he worked for a couple of years for the Duchy of Cornwall before being drawn to White Waltham 'to milk cows'.

White Waltham has been organic for eight years and now the estate is working towards becoming biodynamic. It is a thriving community of domestic animals, plants, wildlife and people and it is in this context that Vinnie feels 100 per cent at home. He has made the journey of discovering who he is and so now – and only now, as he is keen to point out – he can go and enjoy life, relate to others and perhaps, through the Quiet Garden experience that White Waltham offers, help others to find out what is around them and what they are made of. Whether it was the old trees we were walking between, or the natural mud paths that in places were completely and magically carpeted with bright emerald moss, or the fact that I was talking to someone who was completely at home, I don't know, but it was an atmosphere in which it was very easy to talk. In a very un-British fashion, I found I had strayed completely from fact-finding, and even from extracting a biography from Vinnie, into asking questions about what spirituality was and how and where we might start our own journey of finding out. Every day at Waltham Place a 'soap opera' (Vinnie's words) of daily life is played out between the trees, squirrels, badgers, birds, sheep, chickens and foxes. It is a good environment in which to start a search into the relationship of nature and spirituality.

We walked along the wide mossy paths through the woodland area, past the fields with the breeding flock of Jacob sheep, and on to the lake edges. 'If you were to meet somebody who didn't have a spiritual side to them, they would be more or less empty and characterless,' Vinnie suggested. 'Everybody has a spiritual side, but maybe that's not what they call it. After all, to express your own personality, that's showing your spirit; it's what you are, it's that little light that glows.' We came to an agreement that choosing to understand one's own spirituality is probably the hardest thing to do: to understand who we are and how the processes of our lives have shaped us. Vinnie quoted the example of Nelson Mandela, who, he feels, would not be the man he is were it not for having been locked in a room for 27 years. In some ways the journey to find your spirituality is a very selfish journey: 'But if it's not done in a lifetime, it's probably a waste of that lifetime. If you don't do the journey, you haven't lived, and I'm not talking about religion. I'm not even talking about finding out the answers to life. I'm talking about finding out the person you are.'[1]

For the water voles, deer and pigeons around us at that point, life is all a matter of instinct: they listen to their bodies and their environment and respond accordingly. What we as humans perhaps need to recover, it seems, is a similar listening to our own instinctive drives, and finding out what our bodies and souls, and the surrounding environment, are telling us.

These were profound thoughts, but profundity is clearly not a bad thing, as 80 per cent of visitors to White Waltham Quiet Days have been before and will be back again. Many of them literally breathe a sigh of relief as they come through the gates, for they feel at home. At the end of my conversation with Vinnie, leaning over the pigsty wall enjoying the contentedly grunting Berkshire pigs, I realized that it had been a very satisfying experience. I had asked questions I actually wanted to ask and together we had formulated answers that made quite a lot of intuitive sense. We had walked probably no more than a mile, but in my thinking I had travelled a lot further.

When I talked to Quiet Garden Movement founder Philip Roderick, he said, 'Giving permission to people to stop is the biggest part of what we're doing.'

---

1. Vinnie's own words, taken from a transcript of the conversation with him in the autumn of 2006.

CHAPTER 16

Charlcombe, Bath and North Somerset

It takes some courage deliberately to break rules that are drummed into you from an early age. As a driver, ignoring 'road closed' signs is a case in point. A road is obviously closed for a good reason – perhaps it's dangerous to drive along it and to do so would be to risk death? Notwithstanding such sensible thoughts, in February and March the first thing that daytime visitors to Charlcombe near Bath are told by locals is, 'Take no notice of the "road closed" signs.' The reason for this cavalier attitude is that the road is closed for the sake of frogs and toads and their nocturnal amorous wanderings. The Charlcombe Valley has been denoted the most important site in Bath and North Somerset for breeding amphibians, but numbers are declining. That's because the frogs, toads and newts come down off the hills full of ardent intent and get trapped in Charlcombe Lane (where the houses are all surrounded by high walls). Each night of the mating season, volunteers armed with buckets come to rescue the love-struck amphibians and help them on their way to Toads Reunited. The last year anyone counted, 1,754 toads, 136 frogs and 266 newts were able to make their annual migration across the lane in this way.

By some strange omission, Jane Austen failed to mention amphibians when, in a letter dated 2 June 1799, she told her sister Cassandra:

> We took a very charming walk from six to eight up Beacon Hill, and across some fields, to the village of Charlecombe, which is sweetly situated in a little green valley, as a village with such a name ought to be.[1]

Of course, by late summer, when the novelist visited, the romantic encounters of early spring were just a distant memory, even for the frogs. But is it perhaps fanciful to conjecture that Jane was able to use, in some of her writings, the knowledge of the difficulties of successfully finding a mate that she gained at Charlcombe?

The other literary connection that Charlcombe boasts is that of Henry Fielding, the author and playwright. He was married in the village church of St Mary's in

---

1. From Jane Austen's letter to Cassandra dated Sunday 2 June 1799, as reprinted in Hughes-Hallett, P. (ed.) (1990), *My Dear Cassandra: Jane Austen, the illustrated letters* (London: Collins and Brown).

1734 to his first wife, Charlotte Craddock. It may sound as if his first marriage was a thing lightly taken on, the bounds of which he sought to escape as soon as possible. Nothing could be further from the truth. By all accounts, this wayward rake loved Charlotte dearly, and for the first three years of their marriage he took her to the relative obscurity of his childhood home. Their marriage only ended because of her untimely and tragic death, which left him devastated. His second wife was Charlotte's maid. The family link with Charlcombe continued through Henry's sister, Sarah, who died in 1768 and has a fine memorial on the west wall of St Mary's nave.

We knew none of this literary history when we drove past the forbidding signage to access Charlcombe church, its holy well and its Quiet Garden. It was mid-morning, so the frog elopement was over for another day. We had arranged to meet Richard, and despite the privations of the M25 and M4 at rush hour, had managed to arrive within a few hours of the appointed time (something that would certainly have impressed Miss Austen). Richard had served as churchwarden at St Mary's for over 14 years, and on retirement switched to the ministry of licensed reader. In this role he had served 13 years when we met him, and he had agreed to introduce us to the garden and the well of the church that has seen so much of his devoted service.

St Mary's well has a distinguished history. In *Somerset Holy Wells*, a monograph by Dom Ethelbert Horne published in 1923, it says:

It is situated in a bank, now covered with ferns, and the water flows through a pipe into a small natural basin. The village people used to take away the water from this well, as it was reputed to be 'good for the eyes', and the font in the church is filled from the same source.

In 1986, perhaps when Richard first became warden, a fairly elderly rector lived in what was then the Rectory, which had a rambling garden. When that august clergyman retired, the central church authorities took the opportunity to sell the rectory. But the rectory garden, as well as (no doubt) being used in the traditional manner for church fêtes and garden parties, also contained the source of the water – a spring – for St Mary's well. Loss of the parsonage meant consequent loss of the aquifer. This distressed many local people, but none more so than 'bearded 42-year-old artist Alan Broughton', to quote the *Bristol Evening Post* at the time. He took up residence as a hermit in a makeshift home under a tree, and only left when the bishop got a court order to eject him.

A letter-writing campaign was mounted against the church commissioners, and they were prevailed upon to pipe the water from the spring into that part of the garden that was to be retained for church purposes. Persistence succeeded, and the house and garden were sold minus the perpetual right to obtain water from the well. A large wall divides what is now a private house from the public gardens. Charlcombe is in the aptly named diocese of Bath and Wells and the present site of the well was rededicated in 1989 by the then Bishop of Bath and Wells, George Carey, just before he became Archbishop of Canterbury.

The next reverse for the well was that the council insisted that a 'no drinking' sign should be put up, because they claimed the water was not fit for human consumption. People would come with plastic bottles to take the water away (no doubt leading to a consequent loss of income for local ophthalmologists), and anxious local government officers were afraid they would catch something more than a cure for weak eyesight. Richard dutifully put up a notice saying 'no drinking water', but somebody tore it down. However, the council later reversed its decision and now the water is approved as being perfectly drinkable. Richard told us that a chap who used to be local but now lives in Bristol regularly rides out on his bicycle, fills up his water bottles and rides back to Bristol again.

It was ever thus. Charlcombe has always been a place of pilgrimage, and water of religious significance is a big feature of the area. The village is just outside the city of Bath, which the Romans inherited from the ancient Britons. In this place, the legendary Bladud was cured of leprosy in the warm swampy water and founded the nascent city of Bath in 863 when he became ninth king of the Britons (as well as allegedly being the father of King Lear). Just over 900 years later, the Romans developed Bath (or Aquae Sulis, as they called it) for recreation and relaxation, a sort of turn-of-the-millennium Las Vegas. Like Las Vegas, it was seen as a bit naughty, Tacitus in CE 80 describing the taking of the waters as 'one of the those luxuries that stimulate vice'. There was, however, also a temple dedicated to Aesculopius, suggesting healing and not just relaxation. After the fifth century CE, the baths gradually fell into decline and the elaborate buildings into disrepair. There was a revival in Saxon times and various saints became associated with the healing springs. In the Middle Ages the baths were claimed for Christianity, and people came from far and wide throughout Europe to wallow in the waters. The church building at Charlcombe, as we see it now, was part of a much larger abbey, possibly even the original Bath abbey. The fact that the church is near a well suggests a very old date for the site – perhaps even preceding Christianity.

When we arrived, St Mary's, Charlcombe was no longer a parish in its own right, but part of a team, linked with a bigger church building nearer the main Bath road. It makes a lot of sense to bishops and diocesan boards of finance, faced with lack of clergy, ageing congregations and parishes with falling incomes and rising costs, to rationalize. Like most businesses in the service sector with a nationwide spread of branches, it is logical to concentrate resources on where there are most customers to be served. Unlike in the commercial world, however, the passionate devotion of someone like Richard can tip the balance. In the world of the Church, it's the branches that command the greatest loyalty which have the rosy future. Those that are in the most strategic place, but generate no allegiance, turn out to be simply a drain on the resources of the rest.

Churchwardens have a duty to take certain services if no authorized minister can be found, but Richard went beyond that obligation to accept a wider call on his retirement. His vocation was to be a licensed reader. The men and women who answer this particular call are a sort of halfway house between clergy and lay people. They

St Mary's Church Quiet Garden and holy well, Charlecombe in Somerset: the wellhead

are not ordained, but they do take church services and preach sermons. In many areas, they are the catch-all for funerals and even the weekly Sunday service. At Charlcombe, the church is the oldest in Bath in current use and can trace its origins back to Anglo-Saxon times when Abbess Bertana founded a religious community of 100 virgins in the area. It has about 50 members with a regular weekly attendance of about half that. Thanks to Richard's faithful ministry, there are services almost every week. The latest booklet, *Charlcombe Parish Church of the Blessed Virgin Mary*, published in 2008, has a photograph of the congregation of 31 people at the Mothering Sunday service in 2008 with the eldest member, Mrs Margery Berry, aged 102, and the youngest, Eve Collins, aged 1. There is also a wonderful picture of a baby boy being baptized in the holy well, rather than the font, in 2004. There is a sense from this brochure of a vibrant community very committed to their church and garden.

Charlcombe is a Quiet Garden near a church building and its guardians and gardeners are also the churchwardens. Because of the holy well and its constant stream of visitors, there is an obvious reason to develop and retain the ministry in this particular place. But Charlcombe is by no means unique – most churches are surrounded by at least some land. God's 'acre' may actually be only a few square metres, but we have seen Quiet Gardens created in the most unlikely places.

Every church building could be set in a Quiet Garden if the congregation paid more attention to the situation in which they find themselves. Only too often, church land is a wasted resource. It should not be seen as a burden to keep tidy and presentable, but as something that could help ameliorate the alienation that local communities often feel from their religious buildings. With appropriate design and a well-thought-out maintenance regime, church gardens could draw people in and develop a much wider community, rather than forming an additional physical barrier to keep them out.

Many of the Quiet Gardens we visited have had the concept of 'journey' at the heart of their *raison d'être*. Charlcombe like White Waltham is a community garden. This village church and garden are open for the worshipping community, the village community, who regularly picnic in the garden, the taking-the-waters community and the Quiet Garden community, who may be none of these. Richard's commitment to keeping the church alive in its community is admirable, and the Quiet Garden here is an excellent outworking of that vision.

Looking across St Mary's Church Quiet Garden (and holy well), Charlecombe

Storm clouds over the meadows at The Elms Quiet Garden, Draycott, Derbyshire

Through the garden gate at the edge of Arley Arboretum

An atmospheric autumn morning at Rydal Hall formal garden, Cumbria

The potting shed at the Elms Quiet Garden, Draycott, Derbyshire

The pond on the edge of the Quiet Garden at Arley in Worcestershire

'Rhus typhina' the Stags Horn Sumach in its autumn glory in The Pureland
Japanese garden, North Clifton, near Newark

Our Ladys Quiet Garden, Stainforth, South Yorkshire

The Catholic Church in Stainforth

'The Hug' in the Quiet Garden at Bridlington

The 'Hands of God' in Iris's Bible garden, Whitland, Carmarthenshire

The insect hotel in a quiet garden belonging to the Glass Onion community centre, Peterborough

Wheelbarrows

CHAPTER 17

Musgrave, Westmoreland

It was becoming clear that a Quiet Garden doesn't have to be any particular sort of garden. One question that was very interesting was why people were attracted to the Quiet Garden Movement: what was the story behind their decision to join?

Joy retired with her husband to Westmoreland. She grew up there in a small labourer's cottage, which her mother bought in the 1950s. She remembers planting the damson, Worcester apple and white cherry trees, and her brothers training the pears along the wall of the cottage. They are still there, and Joy is back living in the cottage, although she has substituted a border edge of step-over apples which are able to hide from the prevailing winds. She and her husband have also added a garage and study, bought another small strip of land and put in a gazebo from which one can shelter out of the wind and admire the stunning views west over to Helvellyn and the Lakes. The cottage is in the village of Musgrave and looks out east towards the A66 a mile or so away, and more picturesquely to a limestone Pennine ridge which catches the sun on fine days, lighting up the rock with a blaze of glory. It is also less wet in Westmoreland than in the national park to the west, so I imagine watching the rain clouds over the Lake District could sometimes be a consoling pastime.

For Joy gardening is something she has always done. Gardens, she feels, like nature itself, are places where people can be brought closer to God without trying. 'You can lose yourself gardening,' she says. 'It's something outside yourself that when you focus on it, you become completely absorbed by it.' She likens it to art in this way, like painting or sculpture or music, or, for that matter, prayer. Having (like Penelope in Bridlington) been a bishop's wife for the last part of her husband's working life, she has probably seen a lot of people over the years trying to reach God in a church setting, and perhaps not always succeeding. In her own working life, Joy was a psychotherapist working with groups of people, and gardening was her hobby and relaxation. She obviously did it wholeheartedly, because, much to her amusement and surprise, she found herself as Country Life Gardener of the Year in Exeter. She tells me this almost apologetically, feeling that the four-acre garden with Exeter cathedral as a backdrop and a man to do the day-to-day tidying jobs were significant factors in the award. But gardeners are a very modest bunch and the photographs I saw of that garden were stunning.

Back in Westmoreland, as we wandered around the small fellside garden surrounded by fields of sheep and heard tractors carrying on the agricultural cycle just over the dry-stone wall, I asked Joy about her past and present roles in the church and in this village. She has really enjoyed being involved in the communities they have lived amongst on a parish level. In a parish, Joy explained, you are part of the whole community. Then, as a bishop (or bishop's wife), you meet so many different people you wouldn't otherwise encounter. Both were moving experiences for her of connecting with people and seeing how people connected their experience with God.

Here in Musgrave, the church is one of the few surviving village assets. At one stage they had a shop, a pub, a school and a station, but now there's just a 'tin institute' and the church. So for Joy it is all the more important that the church has genuine connections with the people in the community it serves. She is therefore a trustee of a new village project called the Musgrave Church Field Trust, which recently bought an old four-acre field that leads to the church. The diocese no longer wanted it, but the thought of this beautiful piece of land – with its avenue of horse chestnut trees and the River Eden attracting curlews, oystercatchers, dippers and sand martins – being bought by a developer was too much to bear. The trust has ensured that the field and its barn can now be used by the community. Through the summer it is inhabited by village families for picnics and barbecues, and dog-walkers make use of it all year round. This sounds very much like the Quiet Garden space at Charlcombe and could, in Musgrave, equally be a Quiet Garden in its own right.

Four times a year, the tiny church at Musgrave is filled to the brim for events that are significant to the people of the village. A rush-bearing service, which looks back to the time when the church floor was mud and rushes were cut and scattered on it once a year, brings a procession of children accompanied by a band through the field into the church. The boys bear rush crosses and the girls wear flower crowns. After the church service the field is used for sports and tea. The church is equally full for harvest festival, the carol service and a spring thanksgiving service for the lambs, which are blessed. 'It's so important that we find the connections between people's experience and the church,' Joy says, and here farming is still at the heart of the community.

It is this concern to bring people as they are to a place of quiet, which may allow spiritual connections to be made, that is at the heart of Joy's desire to set up the Quiet Garden. A friend of hers who visited the garden in Westmoreland as a Quiet Garden said recently, 'This is heaven!' and that, for Joy, sums it up. It is only a small space that has been divided up naturally with dry-stone walls into about six areas, including a bed of 'hot' coloured perennials, a vegetable area, roses and fruit bushes or trees all over the place. There is also a plaque that Joy and her husband were given on their wedding anniversary. It is inscribed with a Latin phrase which, translated, reads, 'I will lift up my eyes to the hills' and refers to a commitment of King David in the Psalms to be always looking for God in his surroundings. It is particularly appropriate in this Quiet Garden setting.

The garden is open to anyone searching for any sort of spiritual dimension and the Quiet Garden Open Days that Joy runs from it are very low-key. In Exeter she ran prayer schools. These were an opportunity for adults who were interested in understanding and experiencing ways of praying that got beyond the 'Our Father' to get together and try things out. The Quiet Garden Days held once or twice a year at the cottage in Westmoreland are also exploratory and very individual. They start with a meditative thought of some sort (and Joy is a fan of R. S. Thomas's poetry). This leads the small group into a period of silence, from which they can go out and sit in the garden, or walk some of the local footpaths, or read a book in the gazebo. There is a little more input at lunchtime and a prayer or two at the end of the day, but the whole point is that the background setting of the small cottage garden surrounded by the fell scenery becomes the main event, the trigger to move someone on in their understanding and their relationship to the bigger picture.

CHAPTER 18

Canterbury, Kent

Pilgrims have been wending their way to Canterbury ever since the knights of Henry II performed their dark and shocking deed and cut down Thomas à Becket at the altar. I suspect pilgrims travelled in this direction even before then, since this was the place where the slightly nervous St Augustine announced himself in CE 597. He was sent by Pope Gregory, not once but twice, to bring Christianity to the terrifying woad-bedaubed Britons of the time. One cannot really blame him for turning round the first time: reports of naked blue beach-dancing warriors must have borne some resemblance in his mind to the devil incarnate (some of us would feel the same about landing on Ibiza today). Moreover, he was not to know that the Irish saints in their coracles had already brought the good news much further north and were busy converting the kings and kingmakers in Britain so successfully that Celtic Christianity was actually thriving. Fortunately, Pope Gregory possessed persuasive faith as well as authority, and so Augustine became the first Archbishop of Canterbury.

In view of all this spiritual history, I was very keen to visit the nearest Quiet Garden to one of the great pilgrim capitals of Britain, feeling sure that here we would happen upon some of the secrets of a decent faith odyssey. Kent didn't disappoint either, holding in its folds of countryside both Burrswood, a Christian hospital and centre for healing (see page 111), and, closer to Canterbury, the Quiet View Quiet Garden in Kingston.

Kingston is a small village situated about five miles south-east of Canterbury. In the 2001 census it had a population of 444 people who all live surrounded by countryside designated as an area of outstanding natural beauty. The village church is dedicated to St Giles, a Roman saint of the seventh century who lived in France and was most famous for being wounded when protecting a deer from being shot by an arrow. He is consequently patron saint of cripples, lepers and nursing mothers, as well as blacksmiths (why not?) and he demonstrates the connection between ourselves and all created life. He seems an eminently suitable saint for a village in which there is a Quiet Garden where people seek to establish more of a relationship to nature. The village itself has an active parish council which sends out a welcome pack to newcomers to Kingston. They also spend their time, as do many parish councils, making decisions on planning applications, tree removal, dog litter bins, where to put 'Kill Your Speed' signs, how to replace the post bus and how to cope with the effects of extensive flooding.

Interestingly, Kingston has some claim to a connection with its larger neighbour Canterbury and its first archbishop Augustine. In 1771 amateur archaeologist and curate of the parish the Reverend Bryan Faussett was excavating Saxon graves on the Downs above the village, when he came across the grave and coffin of a small woman who had died around CE 630, in the time of Aethelbert. It was Aethelbert who was Augustine's right-hand man in converting Kent to Christianity. The woman was wearing a beautiful gold brooch about 8cm in diameter and set with garnet, blue glass and shell. It is still the most valuable individual Anglo-Saxon treasure yet discovered in Britain. The piece of jewellery seems to have done its own pilgrimage, resting as it now does in the Liverpool City Museum, but it will always be known as the Kingston Brooch.

The old Pilgrim Way through Canterbury can be seen from Kingston on the high ground above the Dover Road. Both the old trackway and the fields where the Kingston Brooch was found can be seen from the Quiet View Garden, but it's not the geographical and historical setting of Britain or British Christianity that is the inspiration behind this garden. John and Lizzie have lived here for 35 years. Lizzie started gardening when her children were small and found it an absorbing pastime. She became more and more enthusiastic and was keen to share what she had created with others. She and John were not active Christians at the start of their life in Kingston, but through Lizzie's singing interest they gradually found themselves attracted to things spiritual. It was the children, though, who started seriously to shape their parents' own spiritual path. They insisted on being taken first to a Taizé service in Canterbury and then to the Taizé community in France. From subsequent regular visits to Taizé, John and Lizzie became interested in spiritual journeying and in the idea of a community that is welcoming to all people of all faiths and none. This has become the creed that has gradually shaped the Quiet View Garden.

The Taizé community was in the news in our own times for a very similar incident to the death of Thomas à Becket. Brother Roger, its founder, was stabbed to death while at prayer, though not this time by a pack of godless knights. It was an ironic and tragic loss for the Taizé community, who base their lives on providing a space where anyone and everyone, including the mentally ill, can come from around the world to experience a Christian community and an attractive, meditative style of worship and prayer. It is deliberately a community without walls.

Roger Louis Schutz-Marsauche (later Brother Roger) was the ninth and youngest child of a Protestant family with a Swiss father and a French mother. He was born during World War I at a time when his grandmother in France was helping people whose lives had been blown apart by the war. Roger was an invalid for years, suffering from tuberculosis, but in 1937 he was well enough to study reformed theology in Strasbourg and Lausanne. He finished his studies in 1940, aged 25. With World War II raging, he rode his bicycle from Geneva to Taizé, a small town just inside unoccupied France. His motive and calling was to set up a community of simplicity and kindness. The pressing needs of the war drew him to this place where he could offer help to refugees fleeing across the demarcation line that cut France in half. Joined by his sister Genevieve, and having bought a house with a small loan, the two siblings sheltered Jewish and other refugees for two years before they were warned by a retired French officer to flee.

Two years later Brother Roger returned to Taizé to found a community which, despite his own Protestant background and study, was based on the monastic principles of simplicity, celibacy and a sharing of resources. On Easter Day 1949 the first monks took their vows and from then on the message of reconciliation and community has spread in an extraordinary way, far and wide, causing thousands of pilgrims, many of them young, to flock to Taizé. The brothers themselves go out from the community to live with the very poor and disadvantaged all over the world. They also seek to establish what they call 'a pilgrimage of trust' where people who first meet God through worship and prayer at Taizé then also meet others around them and agree to overcome barriers of difference and share with each other. A powerful example of this came at the Taizé meeting in Zagreb, when Croatian families welcomed into their homes some of the young Serbs who had come for the five days of prayer and sharing. Since the death of Brother Roger in 2007, his named successor Brother Alois leads the community and Taizé goes on encouraging its pilgrims to continue providing places of meeting.

The Quiet View garden in Kingston is one of these many places of meeting. It's a fascinating, eclectic garden with many quiet and hidden spaces where individuals or groups can come and spend hours, or even days, seeking a bit of solitude and wisdom to inform their own life journey. Chris and I arrived there one afternoon at sunset and had an atmospheric tour from Lizzie and John. There is a water garden to which many people gravitate initially as they enter the garden. It contains rocks that came from a friend's house in France and is bordered by a Provençal-style sunflower patch for the benefit of both those who visit and those who can't – but who may be given a sunflower in season.

The first of the garden's hidden spaces to be set up was the 'Thinking Place'. John created it one afternoon when he was mowing the usual path around their newly acquired field. This time he went further than usual, to a space under an ash tree by the fence. Visitors to the house started to use this spot for a bit of peace and quiet. The area immediately around it is now deliberately kept a little wild, in order to maintain privacy. The attraction to people of this 'Thinking Place', and a comment from their young son that he felt God was more present in a garden than anywhere else, led Lizzie and John to carve out more spaces. A fragrant place was created for a friend who was blind. It includes rosemary, honeysuckle and a small tree known as a toffee apple tree. In the autumn, when the leaves of this tree are just turning, they can be scrunched up and smell just like toffee apples.

Two static caravans given by friends offer places for people to stay overnight, and one of these has been given its own private garden. The original Taizé-style open shelter sits in the centre of the garden. It provides shade from the sun in the summer and a place for youth groups to congregate. The youngsters tend to divide their time between that and the camp fire further on. There is also a woodland walk and a shady glade in the ancient blackthorn thicket where you can sit and listen to the strident calls of blackbirds, as well as the dawn and dusk chorus of many other birds. John has also seen buzzards and badgers, jays and magpies, swallows, swifts and an occasional hunting hawk. A Middle Eastern prayer tent has been erected to one side of the thicket and a log cabin is being added at the far end of the field thanks to a legacy from a friend who died suddenly in a car crash.

There are in fact several plants, trees and artefacts placed in memory of people, and the garden has a strong feel of involvement with a much wider community. There is a fir tree on which the widow and young daughter of a man who died young hang Christmas decorations in his memory each year. In this sense, as well as being a journey garden and a community garden, Quiet View is also a healing garden.

These days Lizzie is chaplain to the local hospice, and life, death and journeying are very much the bread and butter of her everyday work – something that has been increasingly reflected at Quiet View. A more recent addition to the garden is a labyrinth, built with the help of family and friends one weekend. Lizzie is a keen exponent of the benefits of walking a labyrinth. Many visitors have walked under her guidance to find calm in the walking, transformative experiences at the centre, and a sense of liberation on leaving. The centre can be seen as the centre of ourselves, she explained to me – a place where we may need healing, or where we need to face whatever is dark within us, or where we can perhaps find God. Walking back out of the labyrinth, we take that experience of transformation with us into the wider world. One exciting prospect for the future in the garden is the use of the labyrinth as a meeting place for local faith leaders and groups from all faiths.

As we left the garden, dusk was rapidly approaching. It seemed very fitting, as the inner silence of the Quiet View had stolen into our souls.

CHAPTER 19

Stainforth, South Yorkshire

When I first came across the concept of the Quiet Garden Movement, it conjured very particular images in my mind. In a Quiet Garden I would wander dreamily along paths where greenery and flowers of all sorts blossomed and flourished on each side. Overhanging trees dripping with ripe fruit would offer just the right amount of shade. Foliage would brush against my feet and as I dawdled through the daisies I would hear the sounds of birds and water trickling from a nearby brook, while a breeze gently rustled through the leaves and wafted the scent of warm honeysuckle and roses across the garden. Idly I would crush lavender leaves between my fingers as I passed by, my head tranquil with vague thoughts of the beauty of creation, backed with a bit of Mozart.

All this is part of what Quiet Gardens can and do offer, but the Quiet Garden Movement is more than a sentimental pass at God, tendering country-cottage or grand-park nostalgia of an old English kind. What I was less prepared for, but I'm more than glad to have found, is a movement which is grounded in contemporary situations. Such situations don't come more gritty and real than that of Stainforth in South Yorkshire, where Our Lady's Quiet Garden has been created beside the town's Catholic church.

Clouds scudded across the sky on the day that we visited Stainforth, bringing variable periods of brightness and gloom. Our small blue car hastened along narrow green lanes, over wooden canal bridges and past low-lying white houses (as usual we had been slightly optimistic about exactly how long it would take us to reach our next destination) until we dropped into the top of Stainforth. From here onwards the neat houses of the edge of town gradually stood closer and closer together and became beige or grey and sometimes scruffy. Here and there, sandwiched between the housing, there was a working men's club, a small supermarket, video shop or a pub with boarded windows. Greenery and nature had disappeared under concrete and paving, until we rounded a corner into an estate of council houses and maisonettes that had seen much better days. They stood unceremoniously on an area of flat green grass. Behind the estate we saw the steady incline of a huge shoulder of rough brown earth, looming behind the town like a mythical sleeping monster. It appeared to be a flattened slagheap. In front of it, the higher-than-wide architecture of the Church of Our Lady of the Assumption rose strikingly from what looked like a neighbouring area of demolition. The broken tarmac of a former car park was coated with a layer of weeds and glass and surrounded by grey metal security fencing with spikes on top. I tried to pretend I had never heard of Gertrude Jekyll.

Stainforth is an ancient settlement built up around what was in Saxon times the only crossing of the River Don, hence the name, meaning 'stony ford': stones were placed in this naturally low part of the river so that people could cross. The river flooded each year, especially with the spring tides, and silt washed over the flatter plain around Stainforth creating fertile land, which has been farmed for centuries. The villagers worked the cycle of the seasons, carrying on sometimes unwittingly through political upheavals such as the Battle of Hatfield just two miles away, when the Christian king of Northumbria (Edwin) was slaughtered by the pagan Cadwalla of Mercia, and the rise and fall of their King Harold in a certain battle of Hastings much further south.

Making the most of commercial opportunity, in 1348 Stainforth residents lobbied Edward, Duke of York, who asked King Edward III for a charter to hold a market. From then on, every Friday Stonyford bustled with its own market. The traders, who had arrived by river, then travelled on to the Saturday market at Doncaster. Fame has continued to represent Stainforth throughout history with names such as Mary Simkinson, who became the mother of William Brewster, the elder churchman who sailed aboard the *Mayflower* to America and led the Pilgrim Fathers to New England. In 1927 William Moores became the world middleweight wrestling champion, and in the 1930s Jack Pye was a heavyweight wrestling champion. Dr Anderson, a prominent town figure who once dived into the canal to rescue a lady, played rugby union for Yorkshire in the 1940s. In the 1950s and 60s Alan Poskitt was Stainforth's champion clay pigeon shooter. The Nobel Prize winner for chemistry in 1967 (George Porter) and the junior British taekwondo champion in 2003 (Jessica Deakes) both came from Stainforth. Stainforth has, moreover, long been a musical place, with a choral society, a musical society, a male voice choir, a brass band and a concert society, most formed in the early decades of the twentieth century.

The feel I get from Stainforth is that it has always been a place of spirit, with men and women of determination in many areas of achievement. This is perhaps just as well, because since the early 1900s Stainforth has been a mining town of varying fortune. Around the turn of the century it became known that the land to the northeast of Doncaster was rich in coal reserves, if only the local geology would allow access. In 1908 the first shaft-sinkers arrived in the area. The problem was that a layer of Old Red Sandstone lies above the coal seams. This is porous rock and when a shaft was sunk through it, water poured in from the layers above and neatly filled the shafts as fast as they were bored. It took nearly ten years to solve, but a combination of a particular chemical process (which effectively seals the sandstone with a gelatinous layer) along with pumps at the bottom of the shafts proved sufficiently successful and interesting for Thomas Blandford to present a special report about it to the Midlands Institute of Mining in 1917. By 1921 Hatfield Main was in full production.

The future was bright, with the railway, the canal and river waterways to take the coal away, and a seemingly endless supply of migrant workers, largely from further north, as well as all the local population to take the jobs that were offered. In 1920 there were 700 workers, but by 1938, 2,700 men worked these seams. In 1930 there was a freak accident in one shaft when one lucky miner (Fred Dunham) and one unlucky (Harry Sutcliffe) slipped while working on top of the cage. Fred somersaulted to safety, but Harry was killed. Then in 1939, just before Christmas, another cage accident caused the death of one man and serious injuries to 58 others. During the war the only changes were in personnel, when POWs worked at Hatfield Main. Sadly, a greater war was to come with the miners' strikes of 1969, 1972, 1974 and finally 1984. In the latter, particularly, the community was torn apart by the violence and strength of feeling on the picket lines (dramatized by the BBC in a docudrama called *Faith*, shown first in 2005). The community bears the scars of these years in many ways and the colliery was essentially in decline after 1985. It was bought by the previous management with a workforce of 205, but closed in 2001 when Coal Power took it over from the Hatfield Coal Company. They had big plans for a new future, but these were deemed to be financially unsustainable and the pit eventually came to a standstill in 2004.

To those outside a mining community it is hard to appreciate the effect of something like this, except to visit and see for yourself. It is noticeable in the physical deterioration of the community buildings and housing of the town, and in the closure of businesses and amenities – the chicken factory closed in 1983, the swimming pool in 1989. Tellingly, one of the first successes of the following 20 years was the Stainforth Drug Project in 2004. People talk about these years using few words, and the silences between their words are eloquent.

Stainforth's spirit refused to be beaten, however, and one or two other projects also came to succeed. Stainforth Methodist Church was at this time down to just 11 older members and its premises were in need of renovation. At the same time, the Citizens Advice Bureau acquired government funding and together with the Methodist Church they built a HOPE centre: the church buildings were completely renovated and extended to provide rooms for the CAB and the Job Centre, as well as a joint kitchen and lounge. The congregation is still small, but it is back at the centre of the community and looking forward.

Likewise, the Catholic church had reached an all-time low. The stone grotto at the back of the church, in the style of the one at Lourdes, had at one time housed two statues, running water and piped music, but was now vandalized beyond repair. The piece of land in front of the grotto was a mass of huge tangled shrubs and abandoned three-piece suites and mattresses. It was the prime hidden space in Stainforth where locals could get hold of their next drug fix. The windows of the church hall had all been smashed, as had those of the church itself, and the priest who now lived six miles away was powerless to do much about it.

It took around £25,000 and five years to repair the buildings, demolish the grotto and put up the six-foot-high security fence. Only then, in quite unlikely surroundings, could the vision to create a community garden take place. However, the church family were determined to be back in the centre of Stainforth and making a positive contribution to their community. Many helped to manage the project, including Frank, a former head of the local Catholic primary school, and Tony, who was a policeman in Stainforth for 20 years. On 15 May 2004, the Right Reverend John Rawsthorne, Bishop of Hallam, formally opened Our Lady's Quiet Garden.

Chris and I arrived three years later to take a look at this extraordinary Quiet Garden. The church hall still has bars on the windows and the security fence seemed a little forbidding at first sight, as did the broken glass carpeting the old pub car park next door, but Frank greeted us with the information that the noise we could hear was that of the pit being opened up again. Just a few months prior to our visit, Hatfield Colliery had been taken over by a Russian mining company. As we walked past the church hall, Frank explained that it rang again to the sound of the women's bingo club three times a week and that not since its opening had the garden suffered a stroke of vandalism (although more than once he did add, 'Touch wood').

A 'Blessings' rose gets the better of the security fence at Our Ladys Quiet garden in Stainforth, South Yorkshire

It still felt odd having the garden gate opened with a key in a padlock, and even the leaves and blooms of a yellow rambling rose curling through the bars didn't take away from the severity and size of the security fence. However, once inside, the garden felt quite different. The old stone grotto had been completely demolished and the rubble used as a basis for the rockery. On the concrete foundations of the grotto, a gravel garden has been established with pots of grasses and bamboo. The lawn area next to the church building has island beds of herbs bordered with old railway sleepers that allow the school groups who use it to sit down at lunchtime and get up close and personal with mint, thyme and a central eucalyptus that is kept pruned as a shrub. The borders between the lawn and the fence are filled with perennials and roses and are a mass of colour and scent. In spring the rockery blooms with over 200 daffodil bulbs as well as miniature tulips, and alpine perennials take over in summer. The borders are regularly weeded and mulched with the grass clippings by a working party.

Our Lady's Garden in Stainforth welcomes visitors from the local community, and many from the church community have their own keys so that they can come and enjoy the quiet whenever they like. Frank spoke of one elderly lady who said to him, 'I feel OK here, Frank, I feel I'm all right.' Simple words that spoke volumes of the years spent living in a community racked with violence, distrust and disillusionment, where people only felt truly safe behind locked doors. The garden provides this sort of haven. It is a memorial garden in the sense that all the roses are dedicated to people from the community who have died, and there is a book that records each name next to each rose. However, the active and living spirit of Our Lady's Garden is uppermost. School children from primary, secondary and sixth-form colleges come to have days of quiet here when they are encouraged to experience the plants and flowers – how they look, sound, feel and smell – and to reflect on creation and their place within it. Prisoners come from the local prison every three weeks or so for a Saturday of work outside the restraints of their normal existence.

There is a deliberate policy of community involvement and the garden has 40 pairs of gloves, plus rakes, forks and hand tools. Frank is passionate that the garden is inclusive and he recognizes that asking people to come and sit in silence and ponder the wonder of God might be taking things a few steps too far for many of them. However, if you give the same group some tools and a patch of ground to work, the result is quite different. Many of them, particularly the men from prison, speak of gaining a sense of peace, achievement and affirmation from being in the garden. One man, who was on his last visit because he was about to go back into the outside world again, thanked Frank and Tony for the church community who treated him with dignity and respect, something he thought he'd lost for good. And Frank mused over the lad who had asked him repeatedly one Saturday if he was doing all right with his patch of ground. Receiving approval for his digging was worth more to this individual than any number of hours of contemplation. At the end of the day the same lad looked at what he'd done and recognized that it was a good day's work.

With the low border seating, the beds of sensory plants and the deliberate policy of including everyone in the local community who wants to come, this is a truly catholic garden. The sheer beauty and increasing variety of the plants themselves, and the luxury of being able to appreciate them in a secure environment, is perhaps just a small taste of paradise itself. This is a beautiful garden. Even when we returned in the summer of 2007 in the teeth of a thunderstorm and widespread flooding, the roses were thriving and the grass had never looked greener, even if it was a little damp underfoot. On our first visit, we had stood surrounded by the physical signs of a community that had lived under stress for too long, talking to two members of that same community who had lived through the hardest years there. Nevertheless, they were talking less about those years, and more about this new project and what it offered. When we returned during the storm, a new house had been built on the outside of the garden. This time Tony was enveloped in a raincoat and commenting with good Yorkshire pragmatism on surviving the effects of the deluge that had been their great British summer. On 9 January 2008 Stainforth resident Ethell Higgins celebrated her one-hundredth birthday. Her daughter put her longevity down to a healthy lifestyle in which she kept active, particularly with gardening, and devoting her time to her family, her home and the Salvation Army. Likewise, Our Lady's Quiet Garden in Stainforth may be just a garden, but it is also a significant symbol of health and hope, of renewal, healing and the desire for community in a place that has never yet turned its back on these things.

CHAPTER 20

Witham, Essex

We have found many times in the course of meeting garden makers that sometimes the place they start at, when the creation of the garden begins, is not at all the place they end at. Making a garden is likely to take you to the most unexpected places.

At some point in their marriage, Val in Witham qualified for a disabled person's bungalow because of her aggressive bouts of arthritis, and her husband Reg nursed her through those difficult times. Having learned gardening from her father, it was natural for Val to set about making a garden of her own, directing Reg where to put the plants and even which way round to put them. The garden progressed slowly, as Reg was a lorry driver and Val a training officer with an international company, which involved her in frequent trips abroad. Then in 1999 their world fell apart. Val's father died, triggering in Val a debilitating arthritic reaction that spread to her skin and heart. Then Reg collapsed, unconscious, and when he came round his brain – in the words of his GP – had simply shut down. Reg lost both his memory and most of his adult abilities, sleeping for 22 hours a day. Val could hardly get out of her chair. Working was out of the question, and they both required extremely demanding care.

Seven years later, it was a gloriously sunny mid-September day in Witham when we visited Val and Reg. Witham is a small town in mid-Essex, whose main claim to fame is a connection with Dorothy L. Sayers. As well as writing religious plays and detective novels, she worked with the poet T. S. Eliot and the mystic Evelyn Underhill to improve spirituality in the county, and perhaps Val and Reg are part of the fruit of this collaboration nearly half a century later. The bungalow where they have lived for over 20 years is on a small corner plot. Getting to the front door involves a short walk from the road between other similar bungalows. On Tuesdays, a plaque by the door announces 'The Quiet Garden'. But it doesn't prepare you for what comes next, because apart from a few carefully planted tubs out front, there is little to suggest what kind of garden this might be. Entering the house and going down a short dog-legged passage, you come to the living room. The window overlooks the garden to the north – or rather, the garden overlooks the window. The tiny house has a tiny garden, but it is so well planted that it is impossible to comprehend its size at a glance.

Val and Reg welcomed us at the door, like any other long-standing married couple. Reg stood in attendance, passing the time of day, while Val fussed around to make us feel at home. There was nothing on the surface to suggest the traumas they had been through. What was clear, however, was the justifiable pride that they have in their garden.

Unlike most gardens, which are laid out on a horizontal plane, Val's garden is full of vertical accents. Every wall and upright surface is clothed with climbers. Val is a flower arranger and knowledgeable plantswoman, and this is reflected in the horticulture. There is no lawn, but there are fruit trees, artefacts, water features, paths, seats and at least two quite different garden rooms. To give you some idea of the fecundity of the place, on the lunch table (and, yes, we did stay for lunch) was a bowl containing figs, grapes, apples, plums and berries, all picked that morning from the garden. And all this happens in an area that would more appropriately be measured in feet rather than yards. Despite its small size, the garden has been opened for Witham in Bloom, when it was described as a sensory garden and was very popular among visitors. The limited area and its sheltered nature mean that the scent of the flowers and shrubs is intensified.

The garden was the focus of the couple's recovery from illness and has also become a tangible memento of the steps along the way. After their collapse, they were both forced into effective early retirement and spent their days working on the garden bit by bit.

Val's father was a very keen gardener, even though they moved house every seven years because of his job. She remembers very clearly the garden that he made a few years after the war. In 1950 they moved down south from Val's native Yorkshire and she helped him with the new garden even though she was only seven years old. When her father died, 50 years after he made that garden, she went back to see it and was comforted that so much of what her father had done was still there as she remembered it. In Val's garden today is what she describes as something of a family heirloom. When her father got married, his grandfather gave him a piece of peony. Every time they moved house, he always sliced up this peony and took a bit with him. Val and Reg have it in their garden, and when she went back to the garden that she and her father had made half a century earlier, she found the peony, still blooming.

As she slowly regained her mobility, Val spent many hours just sitting in a local church. Amongst the church literature she found a leaflet from an Essex Quiet Garden and, although there was no way she could make the journey to see it for herself, she phoned the owner and the idea of it sustained her through that dark time. Meanwhile, Reg was slowly regaining his mental functions and confidence. The church in question was near their caravan on Mersea Island and became an important part of their recuperation. Singing hymns, for example, helped Reg to learn to read again, and simply negotiating the route to their second home in the car was an important mental feat for him. The garden back in Witham went from strength to strength, and just over a year after their illnesses they opened it to visitors to raise money for local charities.

The idea of a Quiet Garden still weighed on Val's mind. She kept the leaflet pinned up on the noticeboard in her 'office'. When they were beginning to get themselves sorted out, she kept returning in her mind to what she thought of as 'this quiet garden thing'. She says, 'It wasn't really for us – I mean, we're not that sort of people, I didn't think.' But she sent off for more information. Meanwhile, their personal spiritual journey continued and they got more and more involved in the church. Val had always been fond of writing, and then one day, out of the blue, she started writing a pilgrimage, based on their garden. With great clarity, she could see how a journey through the garden could be a metaphor for a journey through life, with its ups and downs, and frequent stops for reflection and contemplation. 'You step down off the patio and go through the rose arch onto a path that goes all the way round the fruit garden. This path bends and turns, and you are asked to reflect on your life.' At each bend and turn, Val has put words to make people think of their life, from birth, or even from conception, right the way through to the point when they are in the garden. 'Then they step back up onto the patio through the arch, and their journey of life has come to an end, and Christ is waiting for them.' Eventually, they asked their vicar to be a referee for them to join the Movement and open as a Quiet Garden. He agreed, but suggested that Val go on an Alpha course, which she did, finding great spiritual comfort in some of the sessions.

They now open their garden, usually on Tuesdays. Val has identified eight points to start the pilgrimage, and she has made printed versions that start in the eight different places. This means that people doing the walk aren't in a queue or tripping over each other, but are walking in all directions. The theme of physical movement in the garden as an aid to prayer and reflection is one that we find recurs again and again in our conversations with the Quiet Gardeners, and no less here.

Visitors arrive in groups of up to eight and are welcomed into the living room. There they are helped to relax, given refreshment, and allowed to absorb the familiar surroundings of the domestic hearth. Encouraged by the sense of security that this brings, they are then ready to step out into the unfamiliar: both the unfamiliar world of the garden and the unfamiliar world of communion with the 'other', that is, with God. Some people walk in bare feet, because the paving slabs are smooth and they like to feel the warmth or the coolness of the slabs, depending on the weather. People are also encouraged to run their hands along the plants and release the aromatic odours.

Along the pilgrimage path are artefacts and plants to help people reflect on their own life's journey, and which also echo the journey of Val and Reg. There is a statue of St Francis, for example, and an octagonal birdbath, reminiscent of a font, which they bought for their twenty-fifth wedding anniversary. The walk through adulthood is in the fruit garden, and there are places to sit. The path does not provide a single route. There are diagonal stepping stones across the fruit beds where Val suggests people think of the things they have done that have been wrong turnings in their life, and they can't get through at the other end because it's blocked, so they have to turn around and come back. At one place where visitors might reflect more on their life because they have reached retirement, there's a seat and a wooden cross they can hold in their hand.

Since their problems in 1999, Val and Reg have bonded together through the need to work with each other to regain their health, and the garden has been the pivot around which that work took place. Opening their garden as a Quiet Garden has enabled Reg to be as confident as he is today, able to speak to visitors and hold a conversation. Val says he could not do that four years earlier, before they opened for the first time. They now feel as though they are through the worst, and that they have become the people they are today through the church and through the garden. As Val says, 'It's a very spiritual thing. I am very mindful of the fact that it's God who has given us this wonderful world. There is a skill, of course, in putting one plant next to another, but it is God who made all that. It's God who made the bees that we have on the blossom today, and of course gave us Jesus his Son. It's here somehow, I feel it very, very strongly here.'

Reg agrees that there is more to gardening than just the physical. 'I feel that when I am planting things, it is not just a matter of digging a hole and putting it in the ground. I feel there is something more to it and I do stop and ponder and look at the plants and I feel close to the spiritual. I feel that just by being in the garden I am at peace with myself, and it's just a matter of sitting down and enjoying the peace and quiet. I find that very rewarding.'

Val looks back on the past and sees meaning in all that has happened. 'It has been an enormous journey, it really has. If you had asked me in March 1999 where we would be eight years later, I could never, ever, have envisaged that we would be where we are now. We were broken, we truly were broken. But by being broken that much, we were able to heal and be repaired and fulfil a plan. It does say in the Bible – and I have a little note of it stuck in the office – that God said "I have a plan for you", and it all may have been part of that plan.'

CHAPTER 21

Glastonbury, Somerset

If we are to take to heart Tim Richardson's ideas about 'psychotopia', or the interaction of a person's psyche with the psyche of a place such as a garden (see chapter 2), it is clear that the context of each Quiet Garden is an important element. Behind the garden of Val and Reg in Witham lies an incredible story of personal suffering, determination and healing, and we found that many of the Quiet Gardens, including Bridlington, Charlcombe and The Quiet View in Kingston, Canterbury, incorporate a healing element, because of who and what has been involved in their creation. I was, therefore, particularly interested to visit a Quiet Garden in Glastonbury which offered a context of spirituality going back for centuries or even, as we discovered, millennia.

Glastonbury is a small town in the Somerset Levels with a unique and powerful reputation which, I'd like to suggest, seems to have come about because of its surrounding landscape. Originally the Isle of Avalon was literally an island: right up to late medieval times people came to the town by boat along the old River Brue. The river has since been rerouted and the Levels drained for cultivation. If you look at the panoramic views across the Levels towards Glastonbury, it is easy to see that the Tor, a pyramidical hill standing 522 feet above the surrounding flatlands, would have been an obvious place for settlement during the area's wetter history. There is indeed some evidence of community around the Tor even from Neolithic times. Lake villages were built here in the Iron Age around the third century BCE, and the burial ground was known as Ynys Witrin, an old English name meaning 'Isle of Glass'. 'Avalon' could equally be derived from Avalloc, a Celtic god who ruled the underworld. Or it could refer to the 'isle of apples' and the Somerset cider-making tradition would bear that out. A Druidic college with a choir that sang around the clock seems to have been established close to the Tor between 200 and 100 BCE, and Roman pottery kilns have been found nearby, though it was not until 166 CE that settlement actually takes place on the Tor in the form of what was probably a Celtic Christian hermitage. Until that point, the hill seems to have been visited and objects buried on it, but it is possible that it had always been a sacred site which was therefore not inhabited. It was not unusual for hills to be seen as places of connection between heaven and earth, or even as gods in themselves.

A closer view of the Glastonbury Tor reveals that it is in fact a hill with terraced spiral earthworks around it, and these earthworks are thought to have been created in the prehistoric period. Various explanations exist. Around 1935 Katharine Malt-wood, a resident of Glastonbury and a mystic, declared that the earthworks mirrored the shape of the star constellations, bringing together terrestrial and celestial energies in a zodiacal harmony. In 1964 Geoffrey Russell, an Irishman, realized that the earth-works bore a startling resemblance to the Cretan labyrinth pattern. Geoffrey Ashe took up this idea in his book *The Glastonbury Tor Maze*, and started to link the labyrinth to the concept of ancient goddess worship, something Kathy Jones does more explicitly in her book *The Glastonbury Goddess*. She explains another theory: that the larger topographical picture of the Glastonbury area with its hills and hollows resembles a reclining goddess. The Tor would in this case be her left breast, and Neolithic historians do allow the possibility that a religious cult of earth mother/goddess was prevalent in the area.

Russell, however, had initially connected the labyrinth with the early Welsh Caer Sidi, which was the dwelling place of the goddess Cerridwen, an enchantress who possessed a cauldron of wisdom. Caer Sidi was a spiral castle and a point of entry into Annwn, the Celtic otherworld. The Tor is known to have underground passages and caves that were often mentioned in local legends. The Celtic fairy legends refer to Glastonbury Tor, where Gwyn ap Nudd became king of the fairies and established his court in the magically hollow Tor. (At this point you need to imagine a fairy more in terms of Viggo Mortensen acting as Aragorn in the *Lord of the Rings* films, rather than Cicely Mary Barker's flower-dwellers.) Gwyn was a mediator between the otherworld and the human race. He seems to have gone permanently under-ground following an encounter with St Collen, a devout Christian monk, and some holy water – although the Tor 'Fairs', originally selling magical or 'fairy' wares, were established in 1127 and carry on today in the form of the town's psychic fairs.

Glastonbury Tor is situated on what is known as 'St Michael's line', which stretches from Land's End to the easternmost point of East Anglia and takes in important Neolithic and spiritual sites such as Burrowbridge, Avebury, St George's Ogbourne, and the like. *The Sun and the Serpent* is a book written by Paul Broadhurst and the Scottish dowser Hamish Miller, who walked the length of St Michael's line and describe the presence of a geomagnetic energy channel on the course of the line.

Whether it is this sort of energy, or the attraction of spiritual people to sites where other spiritual people are already settled, or, more pragmatically, the existence of lead mining nearby, something (according to legend) drew Joseph of Arimathea here in the first century CE. He was, it is said, a rich metals trader and so would have heard of the lead and tin supplies in southern Britain. He may well also have heard of its reputation as a spiritual place and therefore felt it was somewhere that might be friendly to him as an early Christian. It is believed he alighted from his boat with his companions, found a resting place for the night somewhere on the Tor and stuck his staff into the ground next to him. When he awoke the next morning, the staff had sprouted branches and leaves, which in biblically symbolic terms means a recogni-tion of divine power and presence. Certainly there is a species of hawthorn known as the 'sacred Glastonbury thorn' (*Crataegus monogyna praecox*), which is said only to grow in the few miles around the town. The thorn tree became a focus for pilgrimage in the Middle Ages. The original tree was cut down in a fit of holy fury by a Roundhead soldier during the Civil War, but it is said that he was blinded by a splinter from it and the wickedness of his action was thus made clear.

Joseph of Arimathea is believed to have brought with him to Glastonbury the cup from the Last Supper, which was also thought to have been used to collect some of Jesus' blood from his crucifixion. This cup travelled under the name of the 'Holy Grail', and is the subject of another mass of legends from Saxon England. It was said that Joseph buried the chalice just below the Tor at the entrance of the underworld, and that shortly afterwards a spring started to flow there. The Chalice Well in Glastonbury has a spring whose waters have never dried up, not even in the droughts of the early 1920s or 1990s. Every day 25,000 gallons of water surface and fill several man-made subterranean rooms. There are also associations between the Chalice Well and the goddess beliefs, in that the healing waters of the spring are seen to be from the earth mother, and the reddish tint to the water suggests her blood. Another holy thorn grows next to the well. The wellhead was made by the resident archaeologist of Glastonbury Abbey, Sir Fredrick Bligh Bond, as a thank-offering for peace at the end of World War I. It has the *vesica pisces* symbol carved on it, consisting of two interlocking circles from which the proportions of the Golden Mean are taken and on which a number of stone circles are based. With just a little bit of stretching, it is possible also to create from it the fish symbol of early Christianity.

Glastonbury is rich with symbolism and, because of its sacred and healing reputation, it was the place to which King Arthur was brought before he died. Arthur is supposed to have been King of England before Saxon times. He was born illegitimate and raised by the wizard Merlin, who clearly conferred more than knowledge upon him, as was seen when Arthur withdrew the magic sword Excalibur from the stone in the Isle of Avalon. Arthur then took up residence in nearby Cadbury Castle and, it is said, spent a great deal of time around tables and on pilgrimage for the Holy Grail. It seems unfortunate that Arthur didn't apparently link the Grail with Glastonbury, where he was himself eventually buried.

There is much faith, experience and legend in Glastonbury, but it is not a place of hard fact. The natural elements of earth and water, and their local manifestations, are at the centre of spirituality in and around the town, and spiritual seekers have always felt at home here. From the Christian tradition alone, Glastonbury was reputedly visited by St Patrick, St Benginus, St Bridget, St David, St Paulinus and St Dunstan, which is not a bad pedigree for any town, and there has been a Christian presence here ever since those days of the early Celtic saints. Ine of Wessex originally founded Glastonbury Abbey in Saxon times, around the seventh century. His stone base still forms the west end of the nave. The church was then enlarged by its tenth-century abbot St Dunstan, who became Archbishop of Canterbury in 960. After 1066, Norman abbots took over and by the fourteenth century the abbey at Glastonbury was second only to Westminster Abbey as the wealthiest monastery in the land. In its medieval heyday, there was a chapel complex just outside the abbey, known as the St Mary Magdalene Hospital. The chapel is believed to have been founded by St Margaret of Scotland, who was a refugee from Hungary, daughter of the exiled Saxon prince Edward Atheling. Despite really wanting to be a nun, she married King Malcolm of Scotland, raised eight children and became a benefactor of the Benedictines. This latter duty involved her establishing many chapels across the whole of Britain, including the one at Glastonbury.

The hospital complex attached to St Margaret's Chapel was a gift and foundation of the abbots of Glastonbury for the care of 10 poor men. After the dissolution of the monastery, the hospital was recognized as an important social institution and allowed to continue. Two parallel lines of almshouses were created with upper and lower floors and a dining room at one end. In the early nineteenth century these were considered unfit for 'decent persons' and converted into five dwellings plus a washhouse. In 1958 they were once again derelict and one row was demolished. The other row and the chapel were repaired leaving a narrow strip of wasteland. On this spot 30 years later, I came across one of the smaller manifestations of the Christian presence in Glastonbury: the Quiet Garden. The ground on which the garden grows belongs to Mendip Housing and the old buildings associated with it belong to English Heritage. In theory they could at any time be taken for another purpose. For a while the ground was under the care of the Quest Community but, when it was no longer feasible for this group to operate, the Friends of St Margaret's Chapel was established to do the day-to-day work under the authority of St Benedict's Parish Church Council. In practice, Pauline, who lives nearby and loves this place with its history and current visitors, created and tended the garden on the shallow ground on top of the foundations of the demolished row of almshouses. It is a small paradise just off the main street. Thousands of Glastonbury's pilgrims from all over the world visit the chapel of St Margaret's each year and happen upon the garden as well. Alas, when I tried to re-visit a year or so later, I found that the curse of the alternative lifestyle that flourishes in Glastonbury, with its associated carelessness or vandalism, has brought official opening and closing hours to the Quiet Garden here (in line with most other Quiet Gardens), and the garden has another caretaker. If they book ahead, visitors to the chapel can not only enjoy the extraordinary tranquillity of its simple whitewashed space, but can also sit in the garden afterwards.

Plants thrive in the Quiet Garden, because the Chalice Well runs underneath and, although the ground is shallow in places, it is also moist. Pauline kept the hospital theme by planting many herbs and plants that were used at one time for healing – rosemary, woundwort, evening primrose, marjoram, St John's wort, cistus, marigolds, comfrey, yarrow, tansy, sage and dill, as well as roses, lavender, honeysuckle, cowslips, buddleia, lily of the valley and one lupin that struggles with the onslaught of the slugs. St Mary Magdalene (for whom the hospital was originally named) is represented with a thriving red rose. The resident frogs that fall off the wall between the old almshouses and the monks' garden on the other side are kept cool under the leaves of ferns in the shade of the wall, and are provided with small bowls of water to rehydrate themselves.

I loved this place. It is a garden built in a location soaked in spirituality and nature and the connections between them. Pauline was convinced of its ongoing healing properties in its gift of tranquillity to any who are open to receive it, and I for one believe her. Of the thousands of people who flock to Glastonbury every year for the music festival. I hope just a proportion of them, the true believers, find the Quiet Garden.

CHAPTER 22

Burrswood, Kent

One of the elements that never ceased to surprise us as we visited Quiet Gardens around Britain is their variety – from the arboretum at Arley, planted by some of Britain's most famous plant hunters, to the back garden of a tiny bungalow in Witham, via everything in between. The Quiet Garden experience at Burrswood is no exception.

Burrswood is a small country-house estate in the village of Groombridge in Kent, four miles south-west of Tunbridge Wells. The village has always been an estate village, with many of the original houses now Grade II listed. It lies on a steep south-facing slope, noted for its beech woodland. The slope leads down to the Grom, one of Britain's shortest rivers, rising in Tunbridge and feeding into the Medway only two kilometres from Groombridge. Groombridge Place Gardens are quite well known and popular with the garden tourist, and their entrance lies almost opposite that of the drive leading to Burrswood. If you resist the pull of Groombridge Place, however, and turn the other way, you will find yourself travelling down a different but equally long drive, past small lakes and woodland, with occasional vistas across fields and rolling hills, until a building of the old English country house variety meets the eyes.

There has been a significant house on the site of Groombridge Place since Saxon times, but Burrswood was a farm and tannery for the early part of its life. The notable resident of this farm was one Henry Camfield, whose father owned it. Henry followed his sister and brother-in-law's family to Western Australia in 1829 where he became resident at Albany and named the area 'Burswood' after his family home in Kent. A plaque stands to this day in Burswood Heritage Gardens in Albany commemorating Henry's life and struggles, which were typical of those faced by the English gentry in the colonies as they came to terms with a very different landscape and agriculture. Back at home between 1831 and 1838, Burrswood House was designed and built by Decimus Burton on land belonging to the farm, which then became the gardens and estate grounds. Burton was an English architect famous for his work at the Royal Botanic Gardens in Kew, designing there the Palm, Temperate and Water Lily House. He had Burrswood House built for Sir David Salomon, who was to become the first Jewish Lord Mayor of London in 1855, although he sold Burrswood prior to this in 1852. The house still retains its looks and charm, with its unusual Italianate chapel, although its use has changed considerably over the years – and hereby hangs another tale.

Dorothy Kerin was a young woman living in south London. In 1912, aged just 22, she lay dying of a combination of tubercular meningitis and peritonitis. Either one of these conditions is enough to kill the average human being in a relatively short time, even today. The doctor visited her for what he considered the last time, breaking the news to her gathered family that she would not survive the night. Inexplicably, at a quarter past nine that evening, Dorothy sat up, declared herself well and walked downstairs to the larder where she prepared herself supper. The next morning the doctor found her completely restored to health, with no signs on her body of the disease that had so nearly consumed her over the previous few weeks.

Dorothy tells her own story in her book *The Living Touch* and describes the visions she experienced while in a coma. She says that God asked her if she would go back, charging her to 'heal the sick, comfort the sorrowing and give faith to the faithless'. For 17 years after her recovery, Dorothy went about life as the adopted daughter of an Anglo-Catholic priest and his wife, while she honed down her vision and prepared herself for what she must do. She established Chapel House, her first healing home, in Ealing in the 1920s and 30s. By the end of the war years, Dorothy owned seven properties. She settled in one in Speldhurst in Kent, but later moved to Burrswood where she lived in the current guesthouse with her nine adopted children, while the main house, under her supervision, became a Christian hospital.

Dorothy's is the sort of story that, littered with miraculous events as it is, starts to make anything seem possible, and hence anything anyone then says about what happens at Burrswood today seems entirely in keeping. It is still a Christian hospital, registered as an independent hospital with the Health Care Commission for non-surgical care, and with an emphasis on caring for the whole person, body, mind and soul. Burrswood is a registered company and charity, administered by the Dorothy Kerin Trust. Miraculous healing does apparently still happen, but it is not lauded from the rooftops; rather it is the accepted culture that God heals, whether through conventional medicine and care, or through a combination of this and prayer, or really in any way he wishes to.

As I reflected on the fact that we were in Kent, the pilgrimage county of old, where once upon a time Christian monastic communities were the only source of medical or hospital care, it seemed odd to find a Christian hospital an anomaly, and yet it is. I was intrigued. Passing through the main door, I followed signs to Reception that led into the previous baronial hall porch area. Eggs, honey, Christian cards and trinkets were on sale, while people on crutches or a little short of breath sat back for a moment on a windowseat. It was a little like a cross between a National Trust shop and an outpatients department, but not in a bad way.

Wisely, the director, head gardener and administrator had offered lunch from Bocky's Tearoom first and as they cook using fresh produce from the 220-acre estate, this was not a disappointing experience. Over the meal I learned about the resources and care available from Burrswood. It is a 35-bed hospital specializing in medical, post-surgical, palliative, terminal, respite and convalescent care, with a growing reputation for the holistic care of chronic fatigue syndrome, as well as counselling and rehabilitation. It has a physiotherapy department and a hydrotherapy pool. I was a nurse in a previous life, and it all looked encouragingly just as it should. Where Burrswood differs from any other small private hospital is in the way it brings together medical knowledge and treatment with Christian wisdom and prayer. At the centre of the buildings, which include a conference centre and guesthouse as well as the hospital, is a chapel: the Anglican Church of Christ the Healer, built by Dorothy Kerin. Here healing services are conducted twice a week and it's always open for individuals to have their own time of quiet reflection.

I spent the afternoon, rather bizarrely, driving with the head gardener, Richard, in a golf buggy around the considerable acreage of Burrswood grounds. He pointed out to me the unique water system, pumped up from a spring, filtered naturally and subsequently piped to the Burrswood complex. We chugged contentedly through the woods, visited the Shetland ponies, fed and walked among the sizeable flock of chickens, and I tried to remain neutral at the sight of a field full of burgeoning green-houses, cold frames and a huge kitchen garden to die for. There is a tree sponsor scheme in action – where people bequeath a tree in thanks for family, friends or even pets who have benefited from Burrswood. A fine coppiced woodland can be viewed across the valley lawn, and walking along the terraces just below the main hospital building is a vivid experience of azaleas, rhododendrons, acers, rockeries and croquet. I heard all about the St Francis Pond Quiet Garden where people lose themselves regularly with a book, or in their own thoughts, sometimes for hours on end and occasionally forgetting to come in for meals.

Richard is in one sense not a paid-up member of the whole thing; he is an inter-ested outsider to Christianity, seeing what goes on at Burrswood in terms of genuine healing experiences and the practical love which staff show in many small ways to patients and visitors, and weighing everything up over the years. 'Miracles do happen,' he says to me almost as an aside, 'no doubt about it.' Dorothy Kerin would approve, I am sure. Richard's task, meanwhile, is to care for the natural environ-ment in such a way as to provide patients and visitors with beauty, vistas and constant small surprises, and he's more than happy to be disturbed as he does so and chat to any of the guests who feel the need. I had the impression that the kitchen garden, which supplies the hospital kitchens with as much organic produce as it can, as well as eggs and honey, is one of his particular favourites.

Burrswood is a business as well as a charity. It has things to do, rather than just being a place to 'be', unlike many other Quiet Gardens we visited. It is also very much a living, breathing community made up of the staff, current patients, volun-teers, previous patients, friends and those who live in the neighbourhood who enjoy walking and playing in the extensive grounds – and we did bump into a young band of Robin Hood and his merry men en route through the woods who were thoroughly enjoying their freedom. There is one specified quiet area at Burrswood, but people are free to wander in all of the grounds, all of which have their own sense of restfulness. Here the emphasis is unashamedly holistic and the gardens and plants are as much a part of this as the physiotherapy or counselling. In this place the spiritual and the physical are on an equal footing, and this philosophy and the practical outworking of it benefit greatly from the wider natural environment in which they are placed: ground gained in any area is ground gained in all.

CHAPTER 23

Journey into contemplation – Metropolitan Kallistos Ware

I started this part of the book, which explores the Christian Quiet Garden Movement, with the thoughts and ideas of the movement's founder, the Reverend Philip Roderick. I want to end the section with the thoughts and ideas of one of Britain's contemporary spiritual leaders who is particularly associated with the movement.

Metropolitan Kallistos Ware is a member of the Eastern Orthodox Church. He is one of Britain's religious figures who teaches and lives out the importance of the relationship between human beings and the world of nature. He was asked to be a patron of the Quiet Garden Movement when it was formed in 1992, chosen because of his commitment to the theology of nature. I met him at one of the celebration days for the movement's fifteenth anniversary and, fittingly, talked to him sitting on the terrace of the garden at Arley House, overlooked by the majestic trees of the arboretum. He is a gifted communicator who is able to avoid over-complicating issues. The simple phrase that will always stick in my mind from the conversation I had with him is his observation about living today in our technological age: 'We are losing our roots in the earth.'[1]

The Eastern Orthodox Church is the second largest Christian group in the world, after the Roman Catholic Church. It traces its lineage back to the time of the first apostles, following the death and resurrection of Jesus in the first century, and is very conscious of that continuity with the past. As well as preserving the traditions and teaching of the past, however, it recognizes the need to develop them. Thus it will adopt ideas that clarify original teaching within a new context, as well as rejecting others that are deemed theologically incompatible. It is characterized by an emphasis on worship; by monastic communities, which are still a thriving part of Orthodoxy; liturgy; icons; and, importantly for the purposes of this book, a spirituality of the unity of all things, not only spiritual but also material.

His Excellency the Most Reverend Metropolitan Kallistos Ware, who is most usually seen in traditional black full-length robes and sporting a decent-sized white beard, is also known by his lay and birth name, Timothy Ware. He was born and brought up in an Anglican family and was always taken to church. However, when he began boarding at school in London, he started to explore different spiritual paths, which

---

1. From a conversation with Metropolitan Kallistos Ware in May 2007.

ultimately led him to the Russian Orthodox church in Victoria. Standing there in the congregation, surrounded by physical and musical beauty, Timothy found himself almost overwhelmed by a strong sense of the unity of heaven and earth, and of being caught up in an event and an experience that was greater than the sum of its constituent parts (i.e. himself, the congregation of which he was a part and the building in which they were gathered). Subsequently he also visited the Greek Orthodox cathedral in London and experienced again the presence of the eternal world 'so close to us here in the visible world'.

However, new pilgrims were not encouraged to step onto a path that was so different in language and culture, and Timothy's journey into Orthodoxy was a slow one. He went to services, read, prayed and studied and felt increasingly that in Orthodoxy he would not be rejecting his Anglican roots but finding a fulfilment of them. He was drawn by the sense of tradition and continuity with the past – not just the past of the Reformation, but also the past of the Early Fathers, the Great Councils and the Early Church. Although there are mystics to be found across Christianity, the mystical tradition was particularly flourishing within Orthodoxy, and accessible to anyone through practices like the 'Jesus prayer'. It was the 1950s and, although the war was well and truly over, Stalin was in charge in Russia and Timothy was deeply impressed by the faithfulness of ordinary Orthodox believers who were willing to suffer and die for their faith.

Finally, in 1958 Timothy Ware was received into the Orthodox Church. In the 1960s he went travelling and in 1965 he went to live at the monastery of St John the Theologian on the island of Patmos in the Aegean. He stayed there for a year and at the end of it took monastic vows and a new name: Kallistos. He was a solitary Englishman amongst the Greek brothers, all of whom were natives of Patmos. However, in 1966 Kallistos did feel the pull of England and returned to Oxford University where, remaining a brother of the monastery of Patmos, he taught Eastern Orthodox Studies until his retirement. He served simultaneously as a priest at the Greek Orthodox Church in Oxford.

The sense of journey is intrinsic to the Quiet Gardens. Creators, caretakers and visitors alike recognize that they, like Kallistos, are on a path and the garden environment can be a catalyst for a change of direction, or an oasis of calm on that journey.

At the fifteenth anniversary celebrations at Arley, Metropolitan Kallistos spoke to participants about the relationship of humanity with nature. He related stories and sayings of the Desert Fathers, who lived in the wilderness in very close communion with the elements. He also quoted the words of more recent poets such as Gerard Manley Hopkins and R. S. Thomas, whose words demonstrate a harmonious relationship between humanity and nature.

In my own conversation with him, I asked Kallistos how his own love and theology of nature developed and he said, after a characteristic pause, 'Gradually and organically.' Although he has always lived in an urban setting, he cannot remember a time when he did not love the world of nature into which he regularly set foot, especially on holidays in the Lake District. Walking the hills became a habit and a pleasure most enjoyed when solitary. At those times, surrounded by such examples of natural beauty and experiencing the elements in all their variety, he received what he called 'moments of disclosure'.

He recalls one particular day, walking up to a high pass. It was quite a climb and squalls of rain fell in rapid succession, followed just as suddenly by intervals of brilliant sunshine. Finally, reaching the top, for the first time he turned to look back and saw spread out in front of him across the fells and valleys not one, but a whole series of rainbows, stretching into the distance. The very tangible experience of hope which was at the heart of that moment has always remained with him. Kallistos describes such moments as times when nature becomes a sacrament of God's presence. I know enough about the Church to understand that to describe nature as having a similar function to that of taking communion is to elevate the experience of communing with nature very highly. I had only previously come into contact with the notion of the natural world being enmeshed and entwined with our own consciousness in the Celtic Christian tradition, but I was reminded that it is very much part of universal Christianity, and therefore a quality also to be found at the heart of the Christian East.

Metropolitan Kallistos believes that this organic relationship has been overshadowed in the West: 'Christianity has become too intellectual and too moralistic.'[2] In effect, our Christian faith in the West is in danger of being simply an ideology or a moral code, whereas the Christian East has kept a greater emphasis on the value of immediate personal experience and of God's presence with us in the physical world around us. There are many examples of early Christian leaders for whom nature was inextricably part of their life. We are in danger, I was warned, of forgetting universal Christian truth in exactly the same way that, in the cacophony of noise that surrounds us today, we are in danger of forgetting silence.

It became very obvious that one of the reasons why Metropolitan Kallistos Ware is a patron of the Quiet Garden Movement is that the movement allows people to experience silence as well as the natural world. He had this advice on entering a Quiet Garden:

Simply sit, or walk slowly.
Let the feeling of the place sink in.
Stop.
Look.
Listen.
Be present where you are.
Listen to the wind in the leaves of the trees.
Listen to the sound of the birds, or perhaps little animals, or insects moving among the grass.
Then listen to the silence beyond those sounds.

---

2. *Ibid.*

Don't be afraid.
Don't feel it is making a demand on you.
Just be open to it.
Let it speak to you.
Just be present where you are.[3]

Metropolitan Kallistos is a contemporary theologian and I want to take a short look at some of his best-known writing. His book *The Orthodox Way* (originally published in 1979, revised in 1995 and reprinted many times since) is a delightfully simple account of what being part of the Orthodox Church means in one's life, and describes the Orthodox theology of nature. The prologue immediately draws the reader's attention to the idea that we are on a journey. Christianity was initially known as 'The Way' and all of us who embark upon it are travellers, of the kind who are called to be nomadic and live in temporary dwellings, rather than occasional trekkers with a permanent base. Our destination is to find out for ourselves the truth of what we have been taught, or, as the Bible puts it, 'to work out our own salvation'. That includes the way in which we relate to the natural world.

In *The Orthodox Way*, Metropolitan Kallistos explores concepts of God through some of the many natural images and metaphors used by the Greek Church Fathers: 'Encountering God is like walking the mountains in mist.'[4] At any moment in our spiritual journey we might find something unexpected below our feet. But, he suggests, God will always be below our feet, and above us and around us and beyond us: closer to us than we could imagine.

Likewise, the theological doctrine of the Trinity is described through the natural images of wind, running water and fire. Kallistos uses experience of the natural world to illustrate what would otherwise be an abstract and intangible concept. He also suggests some implications of the doctrine of the Trinity, which informs our understanding of the natural world. For example, the idea of a three-in-one God brings diversity to the table, as well as unity – in the same way that genera, species, varieties and 'sports' (one-off and sudden changes in a species) are all found in the plant world. The love and common purpose shown to exist between each person of the Trinity also serve as an example to us: together, humankind can pursue what is for the highest good – an idea that, in other writings, Kallistos applies to ecology.

The Orthodox Way underlines the significance of God as Creator. We are told that to go about without a sense of joy in God's creation, and without offering thanks to God for the natural world around us, is to have progressed only a very short way on our Christian path. Creating the world was not simply an activity God indulged in out of a sense of mild boredom, or conversely even from an excess of energy. The creative act was an act of love, and an act of sharing that asks for reciprocation: 'I have made this for you, come and enjoy it with me!' Furthermore, creation is not

---

3. *Ibid.*
4. Ware, K. (1979) *The Orthodox Way* (New York: St Vladimir's Seminary Press), p. 13.

something that happened in the past that we simply acknowledge, but is an ongoing relationship here and now. Humanity's highest vocation is to be a mediator between the natural world and the spiritual world. We are made of body, soul and spirit — both material and spiritual stuff — and our role is to bring these together in order to demonstrate all their possibilities. Kallistos teaches that, at the Fall, this highest purpose was perverted, and instead of bringing unity we put division between ourselves and everything else, including the natural world – a division we see today in the problems of climate change.

The book goes on to explain some of the fundamental doctrines of Christianity, which I explore in later chapters. At the conclusion of *The Orthodox Way*, Metropolitan Kallistos brings our attention back to the idea of the Christian life as a journey. He suggests that it consists of three stages: *praktiki*, or the practice of doing good; *physiki*, or the contemplation of nature; and *theologia*, or the contemplation of God himself. The three stages do not necessarily follow one another; in fact, they are much more likely to be happening at the same time: three deepening but parallel levels of understanding and experience that draw us closer to God.

What is important to note is the insistence that a fundamental part of being a Christian, according to Kallistos, is to appreciate nature. He gives practical advice on how to do this, including the concept of learning how to live in the present moment. I spend a lot of time either planning ahead, or mulling on what has been. Kallistos suggests that to inhabit the present, where we are, rather than where we were or where we would like to be, is fundamental to our development as human beings. Like nature itself, or 'church' activities such as communion or baptism, the present moment is also a sacrament: something that can bring us nearer to God. We are to contemplate the natural world around us as we stop, look and listen to our surroundings; in doing so, we start to appreciate our own place in the natural order, alongside other sacred things, and in the presence of the Divine, who is both in all these things and also beyond them.

We are encouraged to understand that we should not be trying to transcend the physical in order to attain a higher spirituality, but rather that this higher spirituality incorporates the physical here and now. What is more, in the hereafter, when the new heavens and the new earth become a reality, Kallistos says, 'There is surely a place not only for man but for the animals: in and through man, they too will share in immortality, and so will rocks, trees, plants, fire and water.'[5]

Metropolitan Kallistos is a treat to listen to. His easy way of explaining difficult concepts, his active sense of humour and an obvious delight in life in all its fullness embody his teachings. In 1999 he delivered a series of talks to the Orthodox Peace Fellowship in the ancient French pilgrimage centre of Vezelay (where St Bernard preached the Second Crusade), and at this conference he also had something to say about the unity of all things physical and spiritual. One of the conference organizers, who wrote an account of the week, said he had felt uplifted by listening

---

5. *Ibid.*, p. 137.

to him: 'His sense of awe and wonder, of sacramental living was vividly communicated to us.'

The theme of the retreat was 'The Sacrament of Healing' and Kallistos started by looking at the nature of human beings who stand at the 'centre and crossroads of creation'. He spoke later of the need for Christians to go out from worship in church into the world to serve, not just our fellow human beings, but also the whole created order by getting involved in the environmental lobby.

Metropolitan Kallistos Ware is not mistakenly or accidentally a patron of the Quiet Garden Movement. He is one of the few spiritual leaders in Britain today who comprehensively embraces a relationship with nature as central to our existence as fully human and spiritual beings. He is 100 per cent behind any pilgrimage that is intent on searching for this relationship, and the stories of the Quiet Gardens illustrate the same commitment to journeying, community and healing within a natural context. Kallistos sees all people holistically at one with all of creation, and gives me to understand that gardens should be cherished as one of the many ways in which we can develop our latent relationship with nature. The people who have created the Quiet Gardens, and the people who have visited them, often speak of the spiritual satisfaction they have experienced in the process. For me that would seem to validate the truth of the Orthodox concept of the unity of heaven and earth; perhaps it can spur us on to 'go and work in the garden' as Voltaire's Candide suggests, so that we don't, as Kallistos warns us, 'lose our roots in the soil'.

PART 3

Journey across Cultures

CHAPTER 24

Baha'i gardens

Gardens and gardening are seen to be beneficial in a physical, mental, emotional and even a spiritual sense by some of our leading horticultural practioners and garden designers, in the widespread secular practice of therapeutic horticulture, and in the thinking and practice of the Christian Quiet Garden Movement. From my own work for the BBC with people of all faiths, I realized that gardens feature largely in the theology and practice of many world faiths. A large part of the 'mYth' project involved exploring how other faiths viewed gardening and how horticultural projects might be an excellent way forward in interfaith dialogue. This next part of the journey, into other cultures, brings the results of that exploration.

The Baha'i faith is the youngest of the nine recognized world religions. Its founder, Baha'u'llah, lived in Iran from 1817 to 1892, and is seen as another in a long line of 'messengers from God' which includes Abraham, Moses, Buddha, Krishna, Zoroaster, Christ and Mohammed. The central message of the Baha'i faith is one of unity. Humanity comprises one people who need to live together as one global society, upholding peace, justice and equality. Nowadays Baha'is live in more than 100,000 localities around the world and come from every background and culture imaginable. Their World Centre is in Haifa in Israel, on Mount Carmel, which has strong religious associations for Christians and Jews as well as having been visited by Baha'u'llah in 1890. He marked out the site to his son Abdu'l-Baha as the place where his martyred forerunner, the Bab (founder of Babism, recognized as a precursor of the Baha'i faith), should be laid to rest, and this was done in 1909.

Since then, the grounds around the original mausoleum on Mount Carmel have gradually been developed into gardens. Nine terraces below it were constructed in the 1930s, and in 1953 Abdu'l-Baha's successor Shoghi Effendi had a golden-domed building built over the Shrine. Fifty-four years later, the Baha'i community were able to open 19 terraced gardens that stretch almost a kilometre from the base to the peak of Mount Carmel, surrounding and complementing the Baha'i World Centre buildings. Many speak of these spectacular gardens in terms of the eighth wonder of the world, and draw parallels with the Hanging Gardens of Babylon, which are also thought to have been terraces like these. They have won international acclaim for their architectural and landscape design.

It is apt that Baha'u'llah also taught using natural metaphors. One of the images he used for unity is that of a tree, where humanity in all its diversity is nevertheless just like the fruit of one tree or the leaves of a branch. For Baha'is, who believe that religion and science are complementary and that the natural world is the context from which human unity can come, a garden is a perfect symbol and expression of core Baha'i truths. The gardens in Haifa represent a vision of confidence in the future and are a big draw for visitors who love gardens as well as pilgrims of various faiths.

The barren mountain slope has also become a natural sanctuary. Ecology is very important to Baha'is and each terrace is divided into three parts that become increasingly 'wild'. A central formal section is planted with lawns, annual flowerbeds, clipped hedges and pruned trees. To each side of this there is a more informal section with perennials characteristic of the Middle East such as rosemary, oleanders, olive and jacaranda, as well as succulents and flowering trees, which are underplanted with wild flowers and bulbs. A third section at the very edge of each terrace has been left to develop into natural forest. This third part has become a wildlife corridor and native animals such as mongoose, hedgehogs and reptiles have returned to populate these areas, along with wild birds, including blue kingfishers, Palestinian sunbirds, hoopoes and owls. Insects have been introduced to provide natural pest control, rather than relying on pesticides. A mixture of old practices such as mulching, drought pruning and using drought-resistant ground-cover plants carefully controls water use, while new methods such as computerized irrigation systems controlling under-lawn drip irrigation are used to lessen evaporation loss, along with recycling the water in the fountains.

The gardens have been landscaped into nine concentric circles (nine being a number of unity for the Baha'is) and these illustrate the aesthetic principles of harmony, symmetry and order, which delighted Abdu'l-Baha and which allow the Baha'i optimum of beauty, peace and harmony to be established in this place. Bridges allow the visitor to walk the length of the gardens without interruption from the city around, and the gradual merging of the gardens into the natural landscape at the edges models the idea of bringing order out of chaos. The noise of the city is masked by the water that splashes in the fountains and flows in channels down the side of the central steps, and also by the birds that are attracted to the water and add their song to the sound mix. Water is a rich religious symbol speaking of the grace of God flowing to humankind, as well as being the source of life. It's not hard to see the gardens as a life source situated at the heart of 24 square miles of the urban city of Haifa.

In a telephone interview with Gustav Niebuhr from the *New York Times* in May 2001, the architect Fariborz Sahba said, 'My aim was to create some spiritual feeling, not just some beautiful gardens, because there are beautiful gardens all over the world.'[1] He wanted to bring about a sense of the spiritual through the water,

---

1. As published in the *www.nytimes.com Religion Journal* for Friday, 1 August 2008.

but also through light and colour. At night the Shrine is illuminated and by day the sunlight reflects from the water and filters through the leaves.

The Baha'i gardens at Haifa speak of unity in diversity; they express the precedence of spiritual values within the material and the value of beauty; and, because they are open to the public and free, they are accepting of all peoples and cultures. The Baha'i founder Baha'u'llah didn't have the benefit of the Haifa gardens, but he rented the Ridvan garden outside the city of Akka and visited this many times, especially during the last part of his life, and drew strength from it.

I discovered that Baha'is have been very active in the last decade when environmental issues have come to the forefront of the political agenda. In 2007 the Baha'is organized a panel discussion on the ethical dimension of climate change at the meeting of the UN Commission on Sustainable Development – and by then they had been active in this area for some considerable time. In 1995, the Summit on Religions and Conservation held in Windsor Castle was attended by representatives of the nine world religions, including Baha'is. The delegates agreed that protecting the environment was a religious concern of all faiths. Immediately following on from that summit, the World Food Summit was due to be held in Rome in 1996. Thus the July–September online newsletter of the Baha'is that year reminded the community that Abdu'l-Baha, in his vision for a global society, upheld the central importance of the farmer and had said in 1912, 'The fundamental basis of community is agriculture, tillage of the soil'. [2]

It was not surprising to find that, in the late 1990s, the small Baha'i community in the isolated village of Erdenbulgan in Mongolia was developing a local vegetable garden. It had come to be a matter of concern for the United Nations Development Programme in 1997 that Mongolians were suffering health problems because of a traditional diet largely composed of meat and dairy products. That year, at the end of the summer festival in Erdenbulgan, the community garden provided vegetables and salads on the tables alongside the meat and dairy dishes.

The Baha'i emphasis on the relationship of humanity and nature also influenced a unique garden project in Fiji called the Coral Gardens Initiative. An American marine scientist, Dr Austin Bowden-Kerby, who was a Baha'i, lived in Fiji and studied the coral reefs there, concerned with the problems of both over-fishing and dynamite fishing. He now heads up a team dedicated to restoring the reefs with the help and advice of the local communities who fish there. His work has attracted funding and won awards over the years, but for him it is a living example of Baha'i thinking in practice. It demonstrates the importance of consultation and community participation as well as working ecology:

A lot of conservationists seem to have deified nature, holding it to be perfect, apart from humanity, and viewing humanity as a plague on the planet, but the Baha'i teachings speak of man as being 'organic' with the world. [3]

2. As quoted in *One Country*, July–September 1996, *www.onecountry.org*.
3. From *One Country*, October–December 2002.

I was keen to know if there were any horticultural projects run by Baha'is in Britain and I was put in touch with the Burnlaw Centre in Northumberland. Late one autumn afternoon, we made a visit to this hidden delight to find out more.

Burnlaw is a small upland farm in the north Pennines. It is roughly centrally situated between Carlisle on the west coast and Newcastle on the east, in that part of the country where the roads wind from moorland down into woodland and you are more likely to see a pheasant or a fox than a human being. The land used to be deer forest belonging to the prince bishops. The current buildings of the Burnlaw farm date from 1547, when it was first established, and in this section of the forest livestock replaced wild deer. The Catholic family who owned the farm for 300 years became Quakers in the 1660s when Quakerism became a vibrant presence in Britain, and one of the farm buildings became the Meeting House for the local community. However, the last Quaker farmer died 'without issue' and the farm was sold to someone who also bought a large amount of the surrounding land. In the 1980s, when Baha'is Garry and his wife and another family were looking for a place to establish a spiritual community, the owner had also decided to sell some of his outlying property and they bought the farm building complex and 45 acres of land.

More families and individuals came to join the community, which developed a public face in the form of a retreat house in one of the barns. This is used as a centre for creativity, spirituality and education on all sorts of subjects and for all sorts of people. It is let out to groups locally and nationally, and the centre runs its own courses centred on the arts, music and dance. Garry's dream was to be a gatekeeper to paradise: offering facilities through which others are inspired to become more themselves and perhaps also to experience their inner spiritual world.

Burnlaw is certainly a sort of paradise and during our conversation with Garry he walked us up to a top field where they have built a circular, tent-like 'earth temple' with nine windows, a roof and canvas walls, which flapped energetically in the northerly winds. This is a dedicated spiritual space used by youth groups who attend the annual Earth in the Spirit festival, and was also on one occasion host to an extraordinary summer wedding, when the bridal party and friends processed up the hillside carrying lanterns, accompanied with music and chants.

More circles awaited our attention and we gradually moved down the hillside to the labyrinth, created by a student group one summer and used as a meditative exercise. Like all good labyrinths, this is illustrative of our life journey and the idea of reaching a centre of illumination. Below this is the Vikram Garden, created by the friends of a young lecturer at Newcastle University. Vikram loved the outdoors and regularly visited Burnlaw, appreciating the many different aspects of nature and friendship it offered. Tragically he died one summer, walking in the hills outside Rome. His friends expressed their grief and their celebration of his life and personality by building a garden to his memory at Burnlaw. The Vikram Garden is encircled by a hedge and has a cherry tree in the centre known as a tree of peace, which produced fruit the first year it was planted and has been a centre of stillness and delight to visitors ever since. Many other trees have been planted across this part of the hillside in and around the labyrinth area and outside the Vikram Garden. The farm buildings are found at the bottom of the slope on which the labyrinth and temple sit, and also the converted barn retreat house with a fantastic all-wooden interior and views out across the valley behind.

According to the Baha'i tradition, the will of God is expressed through nature and anyone who interacts with nature will understand more about himself or herself. Garry sees working the land as a form of worship. One of the community families has Buddhist leanings and created a garden of the spirit, in the form of a Japanese garden. Beyond that is a wildlife pond. Garry talks about the pond in terms of a metaphor for the many people who come to 'drink' at Burnlaw, are enriched and move on. Further into the grounds there is a bird hide and another tree plantation including a very ancient gnarled hawthorn tree which it is difficult not to see as sacred. The community farms the acres of woodland, wetland, pasture, orchard and kitchen garden organically.

For millennia, gardens have been places of quiet and repose, as well as places of industry and food production. For Baha'is they are beautiful spaces in themselves and could exist solely for this purpose. However, they are also opportunities for meditation and self-discovery and places where the relationship between humanity and nature is made tangible. Central to the Baha'i vision is the thought that gardens are also places where relationships between others and ourselves can be enhanced and drawn together. In the Baha'i tradition, gardens are fundamentally spiritual.

CHAPTER 25

Islamic gardens

It is interesting that the last gardening project in which the much-loved *Gardeners'* *World* presenter Geoff Hamilton was involved was his television series on the creation of a 'paradise' garden at Barnsdale. For years *Gardeners' World* had explored plants and planting, garden designs, techniques and materials, but this series heralded a new direction, exploring what gardens are and how people benefit from them.

The Persian word from which our word 'paradise' comes is *pairidaeza*. It means 'walled around' and was the term given to the large gardens, or, perhaps more accurately, parks of the Persian rulers. The first recorded example is that of Cyrus of Persia in the fifth century BCE, whose huge fortress or palace complex comprised buildings with colonnaded porches as well as an inner garden. This was a walled area with a sophisticated irrigation network where water ran along channels that allowed the many trees to survive and therefore to provide more shade and refreshment. The water rills and small reservoirs divided the garden broadly into four parts and the whole design of a quartered garden became a tradition known as *chahar* *bagh*, or 'fourfold' garden. It is thought that Cyrus's garden was itself based on a history of such areas stretching back as far as 3000 BCE. At this time the Sumerians settled and created a whole civilization in the Middle Eastern delta of the Tigris and Euphrates, and included in their culture walled gardens for the cultivation of food and the pursuit of pleasure, especially sport and hunting.

Evidence for these earliest gardens comes through the paintings and stone reliefs in Egypt and throughout Persia. Another source of reference for the later gardens was Persian carpets, which included a whole genre of 'garden carpets'. A garden carpet design was like a bird's-eye view of a typical garden of the time. The material was woven into representations of flowerbeds and divided into squares and rectangles by the portrayal of intersecting water channels. Stylized flowers, plants and trees are depicted on these carpets in geometric arrangements, with a border of animal or plant motifs around the edge. (Similarly, an actual Islamic garden was also planted like a carpet, with certain plants as recurring motifs that produced a general and subtle rhythm of planting. The Prince of Wales's garden at Highgrove has an example of an Islamic *chahar bagh* carpet garden enclosed behind four walls and created with the help of designers and craftsmen from the Visual Islamic and Traditional Arts Programme at the Prince's Foundation in London.) Very often the overall effect of the historic garden carpets was less natural and more flamboyant, as the threads would often be gold and silver, and precious stones and pearls were sewn into the design. However, they have provided a useful record of both the wealth and the lifestyle of the owners and some indication of the importance of gardens to Middle Eastern culture of this period. In that part of the world, surrounded by significant areas of desert, a garden was literally an oasis. It was something to be highly prized and, requiring sophisticated design and care, tended to be the privilege of the wealthy.

By the seventh century CE, the Middle East was controlled by two civilizations: the Byzantine empire stretched across what is now Turkey, Greece, some of Italy, Syria and Egypt, while the Sasanians ruled modern-day Iran and Iraq (effectively Persia, where Cyrus's garden lay – part of the earlier Achaemenian power) and stretched into Afghanistan and Turkmenistan. This was the time when Mohammed's teachings had become the new faith of Islam and his Arab followers moved across and conquered the Sasanians, taking over their cities and their gardens. It was common for the victors to ransack both the land and the cities, but Islam teaches that the natural world, created by God, is sacrosanct and should be treated with respect and care, and therefore the vast orchards, fields, palace gardens and rose beds of Persia were kept intact, and thus the horticultural and agricultural traditions continued to thrive and spread as part of the expansion of the new faith.

In the eighth and ninth centuries, when peace reigned under Harun al-Rashid, Islamic scholars were encouraged to study and Baghdad became a source of knowledge as well as industry. This included studies in botany. Abu Hanifah al-Dinawari drew together the botanic wisdom of the Bedouin oral tradition, as well as that from poetic sources and earlier reference books. In doing so he created an Arab botanic compendium. Latin and Greek horticultural and botanic texts were also translated into Arabic, and other scholars investigated and catalogued the 'new' plants and flowers (including the tulip genus) of Persia for themselves. This knowledge and love of nature, plants and gardens accompanied those who moved into North Africa and Spain before and during the time when Genghis Khan and the Mongols invaded Persia behind them, in the thirteenth century, lacking such a respect for native gardens.

Spain at this time already had a thriving garden culture, which was first brought by the Romans. The Muslim invaders inherited all of this and built upon it. The Islamic gardens of Spain take various forms. Near Cordoba one of the rulers of the Umayyad family, Abd al-Rahman III, built a palace complex (starting in 936) which to all intents and purposes was more like a garden city. He named it the Medina Azahara, after one of his beautiful wives, and spent more than 25 years and vast resources making it the most spectacular garden area for many centuries. It was composed of three terraces: the palace was at the top and gardens on the second terrace stretched out from the palace's main reception rooms. There were cypress-lined avenues, small woods, orchards with pomegranate trees and sunken flowerbeds of roses and lilies. There was also the equivalent of a botanic garden containing a collection of rare plants. Water to irrigate the garden was brought nine miles by aqueduct from hills to the north. The buildings were constructed in pink and blue marble with white limestone, and were decorated with columns, arches and huge stone reservoirs.

Other large gardens, or *bustan* (Persian for 'orchard'), were also often associated with palaces. They contained areas of flowering fruit trees such as lemons, apricots and figs, large man-made pools of still water, and groves of olives or palms. These gardens were largely green and provided shade and water for visitors who would sit and picnic beneath the trees. The Generalife gardens in the Alhambra in Granada are an example of a *bustan* garden. They were created by the Muslim Nasrib sultans in the thirteenth century and were constructed as a country retreat from the Alhambra city palace (which also has wonderful gardens). A great deal of skill was employed in bringing the water from the Sierra Nevada mountains, via aqueducts and reservoirs, to water the gardens and orchards. These gardens grew fruit and vegetables as well as ornamental flowers, and provided food for the population of the Alhambra. They were gardens which brought a small taste of paradise to that part of the earth.

Gulistan were Islamic rose gardens. Rose water, perfume and rose petals were popular across the East and their production had developed into a significant industry. These gardens might be anything from huge areas for commercial production to small parts of a garden with a few rose bushes that either climbed the walls or were grouped together in a bed.

Courtyard gardens at this time were usually designed in a *chahar bagh* style, and might be large or small. They almost always contained a central fountain or pool and were surrounded by the high walls of the house or building. The Cordoba mosque has a courtyard garden where orange trees are planted into a grid of irrigation channels. The garden provides shade, fruit and water: an essence of paradise in this hot place. The Alcazar in Seville has a *chahar bagh* courtyard garden with sunken beds and fountains. It was laid out originally on the instruction of King Peter the Cruel in the 1300s. He admired the Islamic gardens and had Muslim craftsmen and designers employed to do the work authentically.

The Turkish Ottomans became part of Islam from the tenth century onwards. The Turks had a well-established culture that embraced flowers and the countryside, and their travels across Persia brought them experience of the pleasure parks and gardens there, as well as those with a Roman influence in northern Europe. The Ottoman garden tradition therefore became an eclectic mix of East and West in which flowers reigned supreme. The Ottomans wore tulips in their turbans and it was this habit that sparked interest in the flower that would lead to the tulip mania of the 1600s in Holland.

In the sixteenth century Islam extended into India with the Mughal emperors. Emperor Babur, the first of these, didn't just encourage palace gardens to be established as a matter of course and status – he loved plants and gardens and spent much time supervising their construction and enjoying their beauty. He was born in Kabul in modern-day Afghanistan and created *chahar bagh* gardens there. His maternal ancestors included the Mongol ruler Timur, who took power in 1369 and who, with his son Shah Rukh, created stunning palace gardens in Herat and Samarkand. (The glories of gardens at that time were recorded in poetry books by Persian miniaturist artists and these illustrations provide fascinating insight into the gardens of the day.) Babur visited the gardens of Herat and Samarkand and fell in love with the culture of gardening. The gardens at Herat consisted of 99 acres of pools, red tulips and roses: a visit there must have been quite an experience! Babur loved his own gardens so much that he gave them names like the 'Garden of Fidelity', the 'Heart Expanding Garden' and the 'Moonlight Garden'. He was also a plant collector and cultivated new plants such as plantain bananas and sugar cane in the 'Garden of Fidelity'. When he led his troops into northern India he bemoaned the lack of water, but nevertheless created some great gardens with the aid of water wheels or other irrigation technology. He sent back home new discoveries such as mangoes, banyan trees and oleanders, to be planted in the gardens of Afghanistan. Babur also loved to explore the countryside for wild flowers and bulbs and grew many of them on in his gardens; he enjoyed taking cuttings and being involved in hands-on horticulture.

Babur started building a palace and garden at Agra, and it was left to his grandson Akbar to complete the Red Fort, which was based on the Medina Zahara at Cordoba. Akbar then moved into Kashmir and created more beautiful paradise gardens there. His son, Shah Jahan, built Shalimah Bagh as well as the better-known Taj Mahal in Agra, which introduced a new type of Islamic garden, the mausoleum garden, built as it was for his wife Mumtaz Mahal. The Shalimah gardens in Lahore illustrate the perfect harmony between the architecture of the white stone palace buildings, the vast still blue pools of water and the neat grids of fountains, which provide movement, all surrounded by the green trees of the countryside. Shalimah means 'Abode of Bliss or Beauty'.

There are numerous beautiful examples of Islamic gardens, large and small, across the world, although not many in Britain. These gardens are all different, but at the same time adhere to some central principles of design that originate in scripture, in the verses and principles of the Koran. In order to understand what makes a garden 'Islamic', it is necessary to understand something of Islam.

Within Islam there is no discrepancy between the sacred and the secular. There is no reality except God and the spirit of God underlies all things and therefore gives meaning to the material. Thus the first Muslim invaders didn't pour sand into the wells of the conquered people, as those after them did; rather, they respected the creation of agriculture and horticulture as part of a wider care for nature, which is itself a sacred symbol of the grace of God. Furthermore, because the sacred and the secular are one within Islam, gardens are not simply for the silent contemplation of God. Gardens are also places to eat, socialize, laugh, play, have political discussions and enjoy the sound, taste, smell and touch of the plants and flowers around. All these activities are as valid and good as prayer.

In the Koran the many references to heaven or paradise, which is the prize of the believer who acts justly in this life, most often describe paradise as a garden. The words used conjure up the sense of something indescribably beautiful (or blissful) where there is no fear of the experience ending and into which no trouble will intrude. Paradise is like a refuge or a sanctuary from the sort of experiences we have on earth. The most frequently used phrase is 'gardens underneath which rivers flow'.[1]

This accounts for the presence of water in any truly Islamic garden, and preferably running water, which symbolizes the productive richness of the heavenly experience. Paradise is not a place where things run out or stop growing; it has constant resources, an eternal water supply. So the garden is an elevated concept, the ultimate prize for the believer.

Islam means 'peace' or 'submission' and one of the prime purposes of an Islamic garden is to recreate the sense of peace that will be present in paradise, where it is said that the only words to be heard are the murmurs of 'peace, peace'. Moving water in the fountains and irrigation channels cuts out the noise of the everyday and provides a peaceful sound to still the soul. An Islamic garden design should also be restful; the formal layout brings order, simplicity and therefore a sense of calm.

The *chahar bagh* garden is the ultimate example of an Islamic garden, providing the water, the peacefulness, the sensory experience of the plants and flowers and the place to sit alone or to meet others. The fact that it is also in four parts is significant within Islam. Nature is seen to embrace the number four, as there are four elements, four seasons and the four directions of the compass. The heavenly gardens are spoken of as having four rivers running through them. There is also a passage in the Koran which speaks of a heavenly order of four gardens: two for those closest to God and two for the rest of the righteous. Each garden has its own fruit: the olive, the date, the pomegranate and the fig. The number four occurs many times in many ways and represents the way in which ultimate reality is divided up, so a garden divided into four like the *chahar bagh* is the closest expression of truth.

Four elements that are significant in an Islamic garden are water, planting, geometry and architecture. Geometry reflects the over-arching principle of harmony. The Islamic principles of peace and unity are best expressed through harmonious order, and order is very well created through the geometric arrangement of the elements at hand. As Emma Clark puts it in her very helpful book on Islamic gardens:

> An Islamic garden is about the rhythm of nature represented by the plants and trees, with order imposed upon it in the forms of geometry by man in his role of God's representative on earth.[2]

Geometry is not just a way of doing things that is aesthetically pleasing, but it is another symbol pointing to the truth of eternity. Certain shapes echo certain truths, so a circle is symbolic of unity and heaven, while a square represents unity in multiplicity and symbolizes the material earth. A triangle suggests balance and harmony and an octagon is a symbol of renewal and rebirth, representing the eight stages of

1. Koran, LXI:12.
2. Clark. E. (2004), *The Art of the Islamic Garden* (Marlborough: The Crowood Press), p. 63.

heaven through which a person will travel to attain paradise. Muslim master-craftsmen combine the skill of using the tools of their craft alongside their knowledge of sacred symbolism. Their patterns of geometric tiles (Zellij) which line the stone water channels, decorate walls or create flooring are not merely random and pleasing collections of shapes, but interpretations of a higher truth.

It is not considered proper to re-create human shape and forms, nor even the image of any living thing, within Islamic art, architecture or design. Permitted decoration includes calligraphy: letters and words from the Koran or wisdom literature; and the arabesque: curling patterns seen in latticework shutters and screens, ironwork grilles or balconies and on plaster. Calligraphy must be above eye level, as sacred text should never be walked upon; it is more usual in buildings than gardens, but it can occur outside as well as inside. Arabesque, with its swirling forms, is a pleasing contrast to the angles of geometry. Geometric shapes are also used in the forms of the fountains, stone basins and reservoirs and in the stone tile floor plans of Islamic gardens. The overall plan of the garden would also always be a geometric design. The paths and drainage channels always intersect at angles and there is no place for a winding path or a curving labyrinth.

Furthermore, the architecture of a garden in the Islamic tradition is a crucial part of the whole and seeks to present a harmonious balance of the building with the rest of the garden. Within traditional Islamic culture there is a strong distinction between the public and private domain, and the wearing of the hijab or burka is one example of this distinction (they are not worn at home in private). Another example is the way in which houses and palaces were built, with no windows facing out onto the public street; instead they all open onto the inner private courtyard. Islamic gardens are the original 'garden rooms': private spaces where the family eat, talk, pray and sit. In the process of coming in from outside, a sense of mystery is evoked: the inner gardens are never visible from the street because paradise needs to be hidden and not easily discovered. The experience of entering an Islamic courtyard garden is to move from the noise, heat and bustle of the street into the quiet, calm and shade of the garden where water from the fountain is splashing. It is also a metaphorical journey from the outside world to the inner being of one's own soul. The inner garden keeps the wild outside – so a wildflower meadow or wildlife garden such as we know in Britain would not be appropriate as part of an Islamic garden, which must be separated from the wild world outside. Thus the building and the garden are a single indivisible feature; together they express the principle of unity which is central to Islam. Architecture on a smaller scale is also used within the larger gardens to create places of refuge from the sun, or places in which to relax, contemplate or chat, and these structures must fit harmoniously into the whole plan of the garden.

Water, symbol of infinite resources, is another essential element and (like everything else) will be present in a formal way, in fountains, basins, reservoirs and straight irrigation channels, rather than as a 'natural' stream or pond. Ideally there will be areas of still water to bring a sense of tranquillity, as well as moving water to give sound, to moisten and cool the air and to create a sense of vitality and life. According to Emma Clark:

> Hassan Fathy, the great Egyptian reviver of traditional Islamic architecture, suggested that the fountain in a hot country was equivalent in importance to the open fire in a cold country.[3]

The Bedouin have many words to describe water, not because they have a lot of it, but because they don't and it is therefore so special. The appeal of water in a garden, even in a temperate land like the UK, could be an implicit recognition that water has symbolic as well as physical properties. In a desert land, water is a very tangible symbol of God's goodness and mercy and is considered something of ultimate value, even a sacred thing. Water can also be symbolic of the soul and the spiritual life, and washing with water can signify being spiritually cleansed. Water in a pool in the garden will reflect the surroundings and will also be disturbed by the smallest breeze; it thus symbolizes a central concept in Islamic thinking, that this world is merely a reflection of heavenly reality.

A fountain in an Islamic garden would be used for washing and for drinking as well as for aesthetics, and the water would be seen to be spiritually as well as physically uplifting. The water in a *chahar bagh* garden will also have a practical purpose, as irrigation to keep the plants flourishing. It will not be used in a flamboyant way so, although a fountain may be present, it is there to create tranquillity and not to disturb it; an ostentatious display of startling water features is not in line with the spirit of Islam. There are three specific water features found in Islamic gardens: the *chador* is a small and often wide waterfall which creates a 'veil' effect and may be designed so that the water flowing over it is broken into patterns; the *chini-khana* is a small niche behind a mini-waterfall in which a candle or light is placed, thus illuminating the falling water; and a *chabutra* is a small island or platform in the middle of a pool, designed to be a place where one can sit surrounded by water to meditate. Water appeals to all five senses and speaks of the reality of the heavenly paradise garden, the goal of each believer, 'under which waters flow'; without it a garden is not an Islamic garden.

Of course plants are also essential in an Islamic garden. The prophet Mohammed commends the planting of trees as an act of charity, for by them humans and birds can eat and be sustained. Green is the colour of Islam because it is the colour by which the heavenly gardens of paradise are described in the Koran; if a garden lacked flowers, it would still be an Islamic garden if it had plenty of green foliage. In the classic *chahar bagh* garden design the plants would be placed in beds alongside the paths and these beds would be sunk, sometimes metres deep. The thinking behind sunken beds is twofold: first, it allows for more efficient irrigation with less water lost through evaporation, and second, it allows the visitor to walk at the same level as the

---

3. *Ibid.*, p. 88.

flowers and leaves and therefore have a more sensory and soothing experience of them.

As to which plants can be planted in an Islamic garden, there are no hard and fast rules, but there are some principles to bear in mind. Any of the plants mentioned in the Koran can be used, as they will be particular reminders of the earthly journey and the heavenly goal. There are also lists, from the great Arab botanists and horticulturalists of the ninth century onwards, of the plants that were used in historic Islamic gardens. Likewise, Islamic poets and mystics speak of certain plants and flowers that could be used, as their meaning would then also be known – symbolism being as important in the planting as it is with the other aspects of the garden.

Trees are valued not only for their fruit and shade but as symbols of spiritual stability, fruitfulness and growth. The date palm, the fig, the olive and the pomegranate are all given symbolic significance in the Koran, as is the cedar of Lebanon. Other trees frequently planted in Islamic gardens include the mulberry, the plane tree, the cypress, citrus trees, almond, apricot and cherry trees and maples. The interplanting of cypress with spring-flowering trees is not only a visually pleasing combination but symbolizes eternity and transience. Fruit and nut trees, with their obvious bounty, remind visitors of the act of charity that planting a garden embodies, and vines are often included for the same reason.

Shrubs, perennials and annuals all have a place, and choice is limited only by keeping within the principles of providing shade, scent and 'fruit', as well as colour (green being the most important), and remaining in keeping with the orderliness and tranquillity of the design. Climbers can be used to grow against the pavilions or private spaces within the garden. Roses are very welcome. There is a story that the first rose grew from the sweat of Mohammed's brow, and lilies are likewise held in high regard because of their association with the Prophet. Many other flowers have a particular symbolism: the tulip speaks of gracefulness; the violet represents humility; the poppy has an ability to stay dormant for years and is therefore reminiscent of eternal life; and the hibiscus signifies constancy. It is also known that spring-flowering bulbs were much used in historic Islamic gardens.

The way plants are arranged is important. Clashing colours and drift planting are not encouraged, being respectively too loud or too informal, and hybrids are less welcome than the original species of plants. Any plant that is particularly associated with the wild, such as cactus or brambles, should be left 'outside', rather than being brought into a cultivated space. Herbs and vegetables have always been grown in Islamic gardens because, apart from anything else, they can also be eaten. The actual species of plants used are less important than an adherence to the principles of order and harmony, the expression of a link between the physical reality and spiritual truth, and the creation of a sensory experience.

An Islamic garden is to be a sanctuary on earth and a taste of paradise. Redolent with symbolism it uses the physical, natural world to speak of spiritual delights.

CHAPTER 26

Japanese and Buddhist gardens

Japan has a fascinating gardening tradition and culture stretching back at least two millennia and possibly more, although evidence of anything further back into history than the first century CE is minimal. It is a complex task to summarize the essence of Japanese horticulture and some over-simplification is inevitable, but I think it is possible to give an impression of the sort of theory and practice that has operated in Japan over the years.

Like Britain and much of Western Europe, the Japanese gardens of which there are records or archaeological evidence tend to be the large palace or temple gardens. It is clear that the spirituality and thinking of the Buddhist monks and the influence of the Japanese Shinto religion have always been interrelated with horticulture in a deep and perhaps more organic way than, for instance, Christianity and the monastic gardens in Britain.

Gunter Nitschke, in his very informative book *Japanese Gardens*, suggests: 'The history of the Japanese garden is the history of man's search for his place within nature and thereby, ultimately, his search for himself.'[1] He goes on to take a studied stroll through Japanese history to see how spirituality and horticulture have gone hand in hand.

What is immediately obvious from even a cursory look is how different the Japanese horticultural tradition is from ours. In Britain the gardening quest has tended towards flowers, colour and scent, an increasing diversity of plants, and developing new plant varieties for more or better colour, shape, scent, etc. Our garden design has also been constantly evolving and holds within its history huge swings of thinking. We moved, for example, from the formal, controlled Renaissance gardens in the sixteenth and seventeenth centuries to the naturalistic gardens of the eighteenth-century landscape movement, and then on to the colourful, eclectic Victorian borders and glasshouses.

The Japanese tradition has not had such fluctuations of thinking. It has always sought to imitate nature – perhaps to organize it or even abstract it, but it is nature in miniature, arranged as an art form, just as bonsai are trees in miniature, designed as an art form. Broadly speaking, the traditional gardens comprise certain specific

1. Nitschke, G. (2003), *Japanese Gardens* (Köln: Taschen), p. 9.

elements and therefore appear to be relatively simple in design, although the thinking behind them may be complex and there may be many species and varieties planted. They are also generally greener, relying more on leaf form, texture, shape and shade and far less on colour and flowers. One of the early species of plants to come out of Japan was the hosta, a fine example of a foliage plant, found in a variety of forms and textures and leaf sizes and shades of green. Hard-landscaping materials are very much part of Japanese traditional gardens, especially natural rock arrangements and stepping stones, gravel or sand, and bamboo. Structures and ornaments, which are kept to a minimum, include pavilions or teahouses, lanterns and statuary (particularly cranes). Water is another essential part, whether implied or actually present. In many Japanese gardens the over-riding maxim 'less is more' holds sway and plants may be in the minority.

All Japanese gardens are highly crafted. The concept of beauty in a Japanese mind includes both natural and man-made landscapes. Shintoism, the oldest religion in Japan, has within it the idea that something distinctive and unusual within nature – such as a wind-blasted tree sculpted into a certain shape, or a rock formation cut out by water currents, or just a particular rock – is likely to be inhabited by a deity and is therefore given a sanctity and attractiveness. Beauty is thus very much present in pure nature. Equally, though, beauty is revered in something man-made, whether a building, a flower arrangement or a carefully assembled garden. The best Japanese gardens would seek to include both sorts of beauty, the natural and the man-made, and the juxtaposition of the bamboo and paper screen wall of a teahouse and an acer tree outside it is an example of the ultimate in bringing together nature and artifice. John Brookes made his name in modern Britain by insisting that good garden design should bring the house building into the garden plan, but in Japan the practice of designing a space where architecture and horticulture sit harmoniously alongside each other was a 'given' from centuries back.

In the late 1600s and early 1700s, when the new Renaissance garden ideas were dawning on Britain, Alexander Pope decreed that the true man of taste is the one who delights in natural beauty, and it is 'people of the common level of understanding' who like artifice such as topiary.[2] Pope's own garden was carefully 'arranged' with rows of cedars, a grove of lime trees, statuary, a lawn and the like, so his idea of the 'natural' was determined by the Renaissance ideas of the classically perfect, proportioned landscape and had rather less to do with the later Romantic notion of the perfection of wild nature. However, in Britain the debate over 'nature or nurture' with regard to horticulture has historically often held the truly natural and the man-made apart and suggested, unlike the Japanese ideal, that it is best to have one or the other.

That said, Alexander Pope is credited with urging garden designers to 'consult the genius of the place', which is something that Japanese designers fully understand.

---

2. From Alexander Pope's essay in *The Guardian*, September 1713, quoted in Hunt, J. D., and Willis, P. (1988), *The Genius of the Place: The English Landscape Garden, 1620–1820* (Cambridge, MA: MIT Press), p. 204.

The Japanese word is *fuzei*, or 'breeze of feeling', and the *Sakutei-ki*, the classic manual of traditional garden making from the eleventh century, suggests that a designer 'follows the request' of various elements of his design as to where they must be placed. Design is a much more intuitive and spiritual process in Japan than it is in Britain. What has remained important within Japanese garden design over the centuries is the understanding that it is the essence of the Japanese landscape that is being encapsulated, in whatever way, within any truly Japanese garden.

From the 1890s in Britain, in the Victorian age of novelty, display and foreign travel, a surge of interest in and accessibility to Japan resulted in a Japanese garden in Britain becoming the ultimate status symbol of the moment. Josiah Condor published two influential books, one on Japanese flowers and flower arranging, and one on landscape gardening in Japan. Following this, many wealthy ladies and gentlemen of leisure included Japan in the places they would visit on their travels. There was also a Japanese exhibition in London in 1903. However, an amusing anecdote in Charles Quest-Ritson's book, *The English Garden: A Social History*, suggests that perhaps anything that was not obviously Western might be considered 'Japanese':

> The Japanese garden at Gunnersbury was designed from photographs taken by Lionel de Rothschild from Villa Melzi on Lake Como. After it was opened in 1901, the Japanese ambassador said to Lionel's father, Leopold de Rothschild, 'We have nothing like it in Japan.'[3]

Likewise, Lady Alicia Amherst (1865–1941), a botanist and wife of the governor-general of India, said in 1917 that the British Japanese garden 'probably shook the Japanese gardener'. In some cases (of particular wealth or sensitivity) Japanese designers were brought over in order to create something more authentic, raising the question of whether it is actually possible to re-create in another place a garden which relies on distilling the essence of the native country.

So what makes a Japanese garden authentic? In Nitschke's book *Japanese Gardens*, the author takes a close look at the sort of language that is applied to horticulture in Japan and notes initially that the word for 'garden', *shima*, has various connotations. It means 'a bound artefact', 'land which has been taken possession of', 'a section of nature fenced off from the wilderness' and 'a piece of land floating in the untamed ocean'. In Japan a sacred site, either within a temple context or in the wild, will often have an item such as a tree or a rock with a rope around it. This practice of delineating a holy area is known as *shime-nawa* and also draws a spiritual dimension into the idea of gardens. A garden is thus a portion of land that has been taken over and manipulated in some way but, importantly, is still set in the natural context of which it speaks.

Over the course of Japanese history, various types of garden have been in evidence, demonstrating adherence to certain principles of design. It is useful to take an

3. Quest-Ritson, C. (2003), *English Gardens: A Social History* (London: Penguin), p. 203.

overview of some of these types in order to understand the progression of thought within Japanese horticulture.

One of the earliest forms of a garden in Japan is what could be called the naturalistic garden – that is, a specific, marked-out piece of land within a natural context, differing from its context either in a more definite 'arrangement' of the elements that make it up, or simply in being known as a garden area.

For instance, in Japan rice fields have historically had a place under the title of 'gardens'. The ancient shrines of the Imperial Ancestors were set amongst paddy fields known as 'Divine Fields' because daily offerings of rice and *sake* from them were brought to the deities at the shrines. These 'Divine Fields' have become an archetype of sacred gardens. The story is that the deity of the local mountain (since Japan is particularly mountainous, this would be a normal setting) lived in the mountains in the winter, but came down to the paddy fields in the summer. The fields therefore became a meeting place of the gods and humanity, or a 'sacred garden'. Similarly, according to ancient folk beliefs, once a year the sun deity would come down from the sky to a mountain, from where the villagers would take him to the river's edge for a season. A place with pebbles and a tree became symbolic of this sacred meeting place, and a pebbled area in a Japanese garden should be interpreted as having theological significance.

Japanese garden design has been influenced by a variety of different stories, myths (a story carrying a particular resonance) and ideology. Ancient Buddhist thinking saw the universe as a mountain surrounded by concentric circles of other mountain ranges with oceans between them. Earth (or Japan) was represented by four islands floating in one of the oceans. The concept of the mountain at the centre of the universe and the waters of life and death became a powerful one to Japanese minds. Included in this worldview is the idea of an island being the first manifestation of land and therefore a crucial central symbol. Many Japanese gardens have lakes and islands. An ancient Chinese myth, which crossed into Japan with a wave of Chinese culture, speaks of a land of five populated islands. The men and women of the islands flew around on the backs of cranes and the islands themselves floated on the backs of sea turtles. It is an interpretation of a Utopian state and the inclusion of a turtle and a crane island in Japanese garden design recalls both the myth and the ideal.

The gardens of *san-sui* are literally 'mountain-water' landscape gardens, which blend harmoniously with their natural surroundings. They came out of both indigenous Japanese thought and the influence of China from 552 CE and have taken on various forms through the centuries. The Heian era *san-sui* gardens are more like lakes, with small islands or rock features dotted around, to be enjoyed by boat; others have a greater proportion of land to water and can be strolled around. The Heian *san-sui* gardens were to be found in palaces, where huge festivals and banquets were held. Spring and autumn are traditionally the two favourite seasons for Japanese people and spring was particularly full of festivities of celebration and lightness. The southern courtyards of these palaces might be quite empty, but clothed in white sand with perhaps one or two small cherry trees. This provided a pure setting and an empty space for sacred dances designed to invoke the gods, because early emperors were both rulers and priests. Small courtyards within the palace complex might house gardens that contained only one specific plant or one variety. Other gardens were added on to the 'empty space' gardens such as the lake and man-made mountain gardens, with a winding stream and rocks placed along the banks. Small arched bridges sometimes connected islands (which were situated in the main lake) to each other.

The whole landscape of buildings and gardens was laid out according to principles of geomancy – that is, *feng-shui* in Chinese, or *chiso* and *kaso* in Japanese. This recognizes the energy that underlies all material things and asks a designer to intuit where, according to the pattern of the surrounding natural features, all the elements of building and garden should sit comfortably. Generally, south-facing gardens are appropriate and water should flow in from the east, go under the house and come out of the garden at the south-west, but these are only two of the guiding principles and the system is complex.

In Japan there is always an understanding of the links between the outer world of nature and the inner world of humankind, and the *san-sui* gardens were also situated in palaces on city outskirts. In these settings they acted as a kind of mediation between the urban environment and wild nature. The garden of Osawa no Ike still survives and people can still take a boat out onto the lake to admire the moon in early autumn. It is seen as the closest human experience of unity with nature.

The biblical notion of 'paradise' does not seem to have a large place in Japanese thought, except in the early Utopian myths, but it does come into a strand of Buddhism. In Mahayana Buddhism, one of the many world systems of which the cosmic universe is comprised lies under the control of Amida Buddha, an enlightened figure of light who possesses eternal life. The life goal of Mahayana Buddhism is to die and be reborn in Amida's Pureland. Pureland Buddhism is an easier path for the devotee than some other strands, involving chant, prayer and the contemplation of images. It has the largest following within China and Japan and, unsurprisingly, the largest number of temples which have gardens attached to them. The gardens most usually created around Pureland Buddhist temples are *san-sui* mountain-water gardens; these may include a central island for religious ceremonies, conducted while musicians play from boats in the water.

It is impossible to look at more than a few Japanese gardens without realizing that rocks are a central element in their horticulture. Hard landscaping has been part of gardens in Britain through history, and rocks have been used to create features such as the grottoes of Renaissance gardens, the waterfalls of landscape gardens, the giant rock mountain reconstructions of early Victorianism and the rockeries of the nineteenth and twentieth centuries. However, in order to understand the spirit behind the use of rocks in Japanese gardens, it is probably more useful to think of what is left of prehistoric 'rock practice' in Britain: stone circles and standing stones. To the Japanese mind, rocks may well be actually sacred or at least speak of divine qualities such as majesty, permanence, beauty and 'presence'. In Japan, rocks are viewed rather as we might currently see an English rose: they are symbolic, indi-vidual (to the extent of sometimes being given human 'body' parts and described as having a head and a foot, a front and a back), essentially and differently beauti-ful, and appreciated for their form, shape and individual markings.

Rocks are to be found in all types of Japanese garden, but most notably in the rock or dry gardens heavily influenced by Zen Buddhism, in which rocks are the focus and tend to be arranged in groups. A triad of rocks is considered particularly harmonious, especially if it consists of a large, a medium and a small rock; and there may be little else in the garden.

The *kare-sansui* are the classic Zen rock gardens. They are often situated close to a building (often a temple), from which they can be viewed from a number of angles 'framed' by the sliding screen doors. Priests, whose duties in this way made them expert garden designers, originally laid out the *kare-sansui*. Another classic Japanese text on garden design is the *Sansui narabini yakai-zu*, which was written in 1466 in the temple complex of Ninna-ji in north-western Kyoto by these *ishi-tateso* or 'rock-setting priests'. *Kare-sansui* gardens therefore have an overt spiritu-ality. They are icons of meaning, designed to speak of the inner essence of nature rather than its outward lake and mountain forms, and they are often quite abstract. However, *kare-sansui* also occur in other forms, as part of a larger garden design where, for instance, instead of a real stream a dry stream is represented by a wind-ing channel of small pebbles lined by larger rocks on the bank. Sometimes, also, moss replaces water.

In Japan in the time of the shoguns, around the 1400s, Yoshimasa was installed as the eighth Ashikaga shogun. As the arts took more of his attention than military prowess, he handed power to his son and concentrated on building a Villa of the Eastern Hills, which subsequently became the Zen Temple of the Silver Pavilion with a grand garden. The garden had two parts: a lakeside strolling garden and, on the steeper slopes, a dry *kare-sansui* garden. By 1578, this dry garden had taken abstraction to a high degree and as well as the 'water' (or 'sea') being represented with white sand, the mountain rising from its centre was also a sand cone. Often the 'sea' of sand or gravel raked into 'waves' will have a few rocks auspiciously placed to resemble the 'islands', which are found literally in the pond gardens of Japan; they also speak of the mountain of 'inner' Japan. It is thought that the dry gardens have their origins in ancient Shintoism when gods lived in groups of boulders or rocky outcrops, and the form has become more empty and abstract over the centuries.

The gardens created later by Zen monks were designed for meditation. The emptiness is deliberate and is there to show that space is as important as objects (the yin and yang of ancient Chinese thought underlies much thinking related to de-sign and ties in with Zen ideas). Void is at the heart of our experience and 'empti-ness', 'selflessness' or 'objective awareness' is crucial to finding enlightenment. When observing *kare-sansui* gardens, the novitiate sits in front of a view of the space and is enabled to direct a meditative focus towards his own centre of being. In doing so the separate groups of rocks that are usually spaced in the sand merge into a one-ness and cannot be told apart, and so the garden has assisted the meditation. Another technique of Zen Buddhism is to give the one who wishes to meditate a phrase to mull over, known as a *koan*. These phrases are insoluble riddles, but provide an important exercise on the path to enlightenment. The rocks in front of the novitiate may be seen as *koan* and contemplating them may assist in discovering the meaning behind them.

It is not unusual for *kare-sansui* gardens to have one or two trees or shrubs. In the garden of Daisen-in, north of Kyoto, a lone bodhi tree stands in the expanse of white gravel. This is the tree under which Gautama Buddha is thought to have sat when he reached enlightenment. Seeing this symbolic tree in the Daisen-in garden, the visitor would ponder about the significance of the other elements and perhaps realize that the garden is a symbolic representation of the path of life: the river of life springs from the heights where the gods dwell and becomes the stream of youth and, eventually, the winding river of experience, pursuing a path between the rocks that depict the hard lessons of life.

The *Sansui narabini yakai-zu* textbook on garden design written by the early priest-gardeners spends a lot of time explaining geomancy in relation to rocks and therefore where and how to site them. It also includes much detail about naming rocks. The fact that rocks are given names shows that the gardens are encouraged to be symbolic.

Zen Buddhism encourages all sorts of art forms, including garden design, and in all of them certain elements are to be found, including asymmetry, simplicity, starkness, naturalness, depth of thought and tranquillity. Zen gardens are therefore seeking to imitate not the outward forms of nature such as mountains and lakes, but the inner principles on which nature and human existence are built. A Zen garden, for all its dissimilarity to a Western 'paradise garden', nevertheless provides a very peaceful setting in which to enjoy meditative quiet.

In 1603 after a turbulent period of Japanese history since the 1400s, a new Shogun was recognized, having been appointed by the emperor, and Edo (modern-day Tokyo) became the new centre of political power. At this time Christian missionaries from Europe came to Japan and brought European cultural values alongside their faith teaching. The rulers were not comfortable with this disruption to traditional thinking and practice. They persecuted the missionaries and closed Japan to the outside world. Peace was restored within the country for over 250 years and the closed-door policy did much to preserve traditional garden design practices. Thus the *san-sui* pond-island gardens continued, although they became areas to be looked out on from the buildings (many of which were built in multi-storey 'pagoda' style) rather than being gardens to stroll around or be taken through by boat. The pond perimeters became far more convoluted, rock arrangements became bigger and more complex in both *san-sui* and *kare-sansui* gardens, and ostentation in the amount and type of plants overtook previous austerity. Even in the *kare-sansui* gardens, trees and shrubs were in evidence and they were exhibited in a new style.

O-karikomi was the 'new' art of topiary, clipping shrubs or trees into shapes. It had always been a small part of Japanese horticultural practice, but now emerged as a main focus. Kobori-Enshu was the main practitioner of this extreme form of *o-karikomi* and he sculpted the waves of the ocean in a temple garden of Raikyu-ji, as well as being the inspiration behind a topiary treasure ship created in the Daich-ji Temple of the Great Pond garden.

At the end of the sixteenth and beginning of the seventeenth centuries the increasingly grand palaces which were signs of a nobleman's wealth and status became also centres for the arts, including *wabi-cha*, or the tea ceremony. Tea drinking in a social and quasi-religious setting was common in China from 206 BCE and came to Japan in the first wave of Chinese influence, but it wasn't until this later stage that it was formalized into a specific ceremony. The lords wanted to demonstrate both their warrior past and their power as well as the fact that they were men of learning; they therefore wanted to be seen as people who understood and encouraged the tea ritual, often combining it with lavish festivals and parties. The Zen monks, who also saw the value of the tea ceremony as part of the process to enlightenment, had a much more ascetic approach and it was they who influenced and shaped the *Roji* or 'tea gardens'. Many masters of the tea ceremony were also garden designers and the new style of secluded garden was introduced at this time into larger gardens. The tea garden had a few simple elements. A path and a rustic hut were the main components, and various gateways, washing houses and waiting rooms developed over the years as the process of walking to the tea house became part of the ritual. The path is always winding or zigzag (the Japanese word is *ganko*, 'the pattern wild geese fly') and is designed to slow down the participants as they approach the ceremony, stilling their bodies and their minds. Stepping stones became the norm for these paths and this allowed moss to be grown on the ground around the stones, as well as further concentrating the walkers' focus on their way to the tea house. The Buddha's methods of meditation include both sitting and walking, so the spiritual aspects of the garden were maintained in the tea gardens. Tea ceremonies took place during the day or at night and lanterns were used to light the path. The stone lanterns traditionally found in the temples have been iconic elements of Japanese gardens ever since.

From the mid-1600s, various social laws brought changes to the traditional hierarchies. The warrior nobles were obliged to spend half the year in Edo, the capital city, and half in their home area, and great cost was involved in this constant migration. The urban merchants became rich instead of the warriors, but the arts were still encouraged and sponsored. New artistic methods and forms, as well as an increasing awareness of Western technology, brought new developments of thought and practice. There were still *san-sui* and *kare-sansui* gardens, but a new style evolved which developed the ancient practice of borrowing features of the natural landscape outside the garden and highlighting them as a feature of the garden itself, a technique known as *shakkei*. Thus a mountain in the background would be framed through the trunks of two trees, for example.

Gradually from this a garden style emerged called 'the strolling garden', in which owners or visitors could walk around and enjoy a number of 'sights' either borrowed from the landscape behind or re-created in the garden in miniature. For example, these gardens would display miniature versions of various well-known and revered actual or mythological Japanese sites (say, by re-creating Mount Fuji as a grass-covered mound in Suizen-ji Park in Kumamoto), or they might depict an aspect of Japanese life or culture such as 'rural life' being represented by a copse of cherry trees. These gardens would usually include the basic elements of pond, waterfall, stream, rock, tea houses, hills, bridges, footpaths and stepping stones, as well as the newer features such as *shakkei*. Apart from the specific 'sights' that one of these gardens might feature, they were on the whole more naturalistic and realistic than ever before.

It is thought that the strolling gardens came about because the *daimyo* warrior lords were obliged to stay in one place for months at a time. Their palace gardens thus literally became the outside world to them and provided a substitute for travel. They were secular gardens and offered no spiritual meaning or symbol, although a similar phenomenon also began in spiritual circles. Pilgrimage circuits, whereby devotees hiked around a number of temples in order to earn merit and therefore secure a place in paradise, had been around since the twelfth century and they re-emerged in the 1600s. At this time numbers acquired magical properties, and certain numbers were particularly favoured. The number of temples one visited on the pilgrimage needed to be one of these magical numbers. This system became gradually abstracted, so that the pilgrim need go no further than his own garden, where he could ring a bell a certain number of times – a bell that had been cast with the images of the temples on it. Alternatively, a strolling garden could represent the temples in some way within the confines of the garden, and the pilgrim would still have 'visited' each one.

Hermitage gardens evolved out of the tea garden tradition. Two examples survive: Shisen-do in Kyoto and Jiko-in in Yamato Koiyama. Like the tea gardens, the goal is to reach a building in which the visitor can experience stillness and meditation, but the path to it is particularly tortuous and often confined to quite a small piece of land. Various techniques are employed along the path to give visitors an impression that they are covering a much greater distance and to slow them down to prepare them for meditation. Katagiri Sekisho (who succeeded Kobori Enshu, the ultimate master of tea) created the garden of Jiko-in. The visitor to the garden starts in an environment of open fields and enters through a very small gate. Although the space inside is small, it appears large after the diminutive entrance. The next feature is a path which has been cut below the level of the surrounding land and planted with thick undergrowth on either side. It therefore has the appearance of a tunnel, and two zigzags in the path mean the end of the 'tunnel' is not visible at the beginning so that the path appears to be longer than it is. The visitor is slowed down after the 'tunnel' by having to pass through another gate, then by having to choose between three paths to the destination, and by ending up in a dark space just before the entrance to the building. Once in the building, a view of the *kare-sansui* garden can be seen through the window. The building itself imparts a sense of vast space, although visitors speak of it as an awareness of inner space rather than of what is physically around them. Thus it is the process of visiting a hermitage garden, rather than the planting or landscaping itself, that brings the spiritual experience.

At this point in history, social change was once again having an impact on gardens and garden design. From the eighteenth century, Japan was a more urban than rural country, and gardens were in demand from the ordinary townspeople rather than just the *daimyo* warriors. This new market required the services of a newly formed profession of *niwa-shi*, or 'garden masters', who still had the secret knowledge of the Japanese tradition of horticulture. Inevitably but sadly, these master gardeners were superseded by garden manuals. In 1735 Enkin Kitamura wrote *Transmission of Making Mountains and Creating Gardens* and in 1828 a second volume of this was published. Although they were beautifully illustrated, they tended to simplify the creative spirit of gardening into formulae and possible combinations of options to produce something that had the appearance, but not the depth, of the traditional gardens.

Meanwhile, in a law of 1871 the larger gardens of the former warrior-lords were declared to be public parks. Many of them were not in the best state of repair and in order to bring them up to a suitable level, gardeners were sent to Europe to study park design. On their return, they created quite a different style of garden which incorporated both Japanese and Western features. This style was accepted as part of the new enlightenment and openness to the West, and pure Japanese garden design was relegated to history until the early 1900s, when an interest in naturalism and native garden tradition was rekindled. In 1895 a new shrine was commissioned to be built in Kyoto. It was to be a replica of Heian-age architecture with a garden around it, but spirituality was not foremost in the garden design. The shrine fulfils a religious purpose, but the garden around it is seen more as a public park where worshippers take a stroll after visiting the shrine, rather than in itself being an expression of spirituality.

Japanese horticulture and garden design evolved further in the twentieth century. In the late 1930s one of the well-known garden designers was Shigemori Mirei, who studied the old garden tradition and practices and produced 26 volumes of research. He felt that the most important principle from the great textbook the *Sakutei-ki* was that designers should be influenced by the past, but should also be concerned to create something new in every piece of work they took on.

Today gardens have been assimilated into the increasingly urban Japanese culture and are to be found in office building courtyards, or at the entrance of public or government buildings. Sculptors and artists have joined garden designers, all of whom now study at degree level, and the resultant gardens are very carefully thought-out renditions which refer back to previous tradition but are not limited by or slavish to it. Rock is used extensively, but it is carved rock, rather than being left in its natural state. The rocks are given form and shape according to the imagination or thought of the artist. They have become 'mindscapes' rather than landscapes. Likewise, geometric shapes representing paths and streams are also widely used. In 1989 the winner of the competition to design a garden for the Shonandai Culture Centre in Fujisawa was an architect. Her creation is all about making a 'second nature', so the design comprises a winding stream edged with trees and crossed by bridges. She looks back to traditional Japanese garden design elements, but this garden is made out of metal and concrete. The trees are stylized metal sculptures and the garden is in effect synthetic.

At the end of his book *Japanese Gardens*, Nitschko concludes that what has happened in modern Japan is that the garden designer no longer wants to display nature in all its glory and to be hidden himself; rather he wants to display his own ideas alongside or implanted onto nature. He wants to be seen as a separate force alongside nature, rather than someone who is at one with it. A dualism has emerged but it is a philosophy which, when taken to the final degree, is behind environmental and climatic damage, and Nitschke calls for a return to an understanding of the spiritual relationship and oneness of humankind and nature. He feels certain that a garden can be that bridge between the two.

I am struck by both the unity and diversity of Japanese gardens. There are certain specific elements, in addition to plants, without which a Japanese garden could not be called Japanese, such as water, rocks and a pathway. There are also very specific styles of garden such as the tea garden or the *kare-sansui* dry garden. What is evident from an overview of Japanese horticulture is the incredibly strong tie between the spiritual and the material, which is an over-arching principle of every garden. Although this has been diluted in recent times because of the assimilation of many aspects of Western culture and thought, today there are calls for its return, because a fundamental understanding of the unity of the spiritual and the physical has so many implications (not least ecological) for every aspect of our lives.

CHAPTER 27

The Pureland
Buddhist garden

Clearly the place to go to really experience the Japanese approach to gardens and garden design is Japan itself. The poor opinions expressed at the attempts of the English to create a Japanese garden did not encourage me to visit examples of Japanese gardens in Britain today. However, curiosity got the better of me and I went to see the Japanese garden at the RHS Garden at Tatton Park. This has many traditional elements and is a good example of a strolling garden. One follows the winding path around and over bridges that cross the small lakes, catching the view of the tiny tea house and the larger temple-like structure across the water. The garden has moss and cloud-pruned shrubs, sculpted cranes, buildings, lakes, water lilies and azaleas, although I don't recall too many rocks. The smaller and more secret tea garden within it is hidden in the larger pond garden landscape, and the only absent feature is a *kare-sansui* dry garden. Overall it is a pleasant stroll in slightly unfamiliar territory with definite English-park overtones, and is perhaps in this way more typical of the more modern Japanese gardens, which assimilated East and West. Spirituality is somewhat lacking, but it is a fine introduction to many elements of Japanese gardening.

Shortly after my visit to Tatton Park, however, I was introduced to the 'Pureland' Japanese garden in the East Midlands, which is an authentic Japanese garden that has been both created and lived in by Buddha Maitreya.

Maitreya was born and raised near Nagoya in Japan. He has studied Buddhist theology and for a time lived the life of a Zen Buddhist monk, but he came to the conclusion that monastic life was too harsh and inflexible for true spiritual growth. At this point he left Japan and travelled to Thailand, India and Nepal before coming to England at the invitation of a friend. He taught in Cambridge, Reading and Lancaster and on a visit to Nottingham learned about a property and land for sale outside Newark. The 1.5-acre field and buildings have become the Pureland Japanese Garden and Meditation Centre. It is open to visitors who wish to see the garden or who come for meditation teaching. Buddha Maitreya also makes delicious scones accompanied by either 'heavenly' or 'earthly' tea, which tickled me, especially when a distinctively British visitor was offered the option while I was there and politely but firmly chose the 'earthly' option. Buddha Maitreya made it with as much care as the 'heavenly' tea, and with perhaps just the slightest twinkle in his eye.

Initially the site was used just as a meditation centre, but in 1980 Maitreya started work on the garden. He has no previous horticultural experience of any sort. He is the sole designer and gardener, and the garden is a credit to his devotion, hard work and instinctive approach.

The garden entrance is through an old brick barn, which feels very English. Once through the other side, however, the visitor is obliged to walk on three stepping stones and cross a tiny stone bridge, which serve both to slow the pace and to help the visitor realize that things might be very different from here on. The café that adjoins the house is now immediately in view ahead, across a small lawn, and to the right stands a line of ceramic pots containing acers, cloud-pruned shrubs and rock arrangements, as well as a small Buddha statue and a pagoda. To the left of the café is a rectangular area outlined with small polished granite cylinders. Inside the rectangle are two arrangements of curiously shaped rocks sitting amongst pale gravel – a small *kare-sansui* garden of islands and dry 'sea'. There are various other compositions like this throughout the rest of the garden: different shapes are marked out with the cylindrical rocks and in the centre there are either just rock arrangements or also perhaps plants: an acer, an acer and a bamboo, and so on. Interestingly, the highly polished surfaces of the cylinders mimic water, in reflecting the light and the objects around them. This is a curious twist on the more conventional symbol of rock as earth and the infill gravel or sand as 'sea'.

The garden proper starts to the left of the more English café and tea lawn. It is a stunning combination of small paths, bridges, pavilions, water and plants. I was surprised to find that, although my impression was that these plants were all Japanese, on closer inspection they are mostly naturalized British plants, but tended in a Japanese way through pruning or by association with other artefacts. (I was struck initially by a small clump of leylandii soaring out of surrounding shrubs –their vertical trunks have been pruned of any side branches so they are bare to 15 feet or more and just a top ball of green has been kept.) The harmonious balance of vertical accents with round forms, tightly clipped balls next to free-form bamboo, stone adjacent to water, open space and busy planting, is particularly impressive, and perhaps it is this perfect balance that contributes to the extraordinary tranquillity of the place.

At the entrance there are choices as to which path to follow first. One leads into the larger *kare-sansui* Zen garden of white marble chips and round concrete stepping stones. This was my first choice. Within this dry garden there are two 'islands', although with a twist on the traditional rendering they are sunken spaces rather than raised mounds, filled with diminutive shamrock and thyme, the green mingling with tiny pink and yellow flowers. These are very restful to the eyes amidst the sometimes dazzling white of the marble chips. A single small birch tree to one side of the white 'sea' has a wisteria twining its trunk and over-arching its umbrella-clipped canopy with weeping leaves and lilac blooms. At the back of the Zen garden is an example of one of the many hidden spaces within the garden. This is a small pavilion created largely with bamboo canes, bamboo fencing walls, a bamboo screen roof and a hanging bamboo curtain suspended halfway down from the roof to the floor at the entrance, which moves in the breeze with a wooden clinking sound. Inside it is a completely private, intimate space with a bamboo cane seat for reflection. I can testify that it is possible to sit there for a long time, quite at peace with the natural world, hearing the birds sing and the wind rustling the leaves of the bamboo that grows next to the pavilion.

A path from the Zen garden is sunk into what feels like a carved rock channel path that winds past hillocks covered in moss-like shamrock. A large weeping acacia tree drips its white blooms from high above, and other small weeping evergreen trees that are grown as 'standards' line the path by the hillocks. I look around and see there are camellias, irises, thrift, berberis, Solomon's seal, wild strawberries, a blue spruce and stonecrop, as well as ferns, bergenia, holly and asparagus fern. Yet it all looks very Japanese. The path winds back to the perimeter of the two 'lakes', which are cut in two visually by a bridge. Candelabra primula stand tall at one side, fish swim lazily across and back again and a Japanese lantern projects over the water, in order that its light can be reflected at night. There is a central tea house with sliding screens, and the only thing that disturbs the mood is my own frustration that someone else is sitting in the other 'hidden' pavilion with a view over the water, and they are clearly not going to move quickly!

The garden is not huge, but that is not obvious and is also well compensated for by the amount of detail at every turn. I found myself stopping sometimes at every step, and sometimes for many minutes, just drinking in the sights, sounds and smells, and appreciating the feel of the leaves as they brushed against me in the breeze. The wide path in and out of the main garden is lined with alliums and ferns and the sound of the water moving fast along narrow channels to feed the smaller ponds is alluring and calls the visitor back into the paradise behind. It is quite difficult to leave.

Buddha Maitreya balances his day between what he calls 'being-ness' and 'doing-ness' and sees both action and passivity as equally important. He meditates morning and night and in between does the work of three men, tending the garden, teaching, baking and housekeeping. He has summed this up in a poem he wrote:

I am nearly sixty-eight
But I do not retire
Retiring is retreat
From the harsh reality
Of life as well as from
The joy of one's creativity
As long as I live I deal
With the pain of the world
Also harvest the joy
Of creative life.[1]

---

1. A copy of this poem was given to me by Buddha Maitreya when I visited. He wrote it on 8 May 2008.

In the Pureland Japanese garden, Buddha Maitreya has followed the traditional Japanese practice of reflecting nature and creating a miniature Japanese landscape which is balanced and harmonious. The Zen garden is a stark garden of rock and sand. It symbolizes earth and heaven, island and ocean. It is a meditation garden. Rock is the elemental symbol of the earth and stands for solidity, steadiness, immobility and stillness. It is one of four elements in the garden along with water, both moving and still, the sun (as fire) filtering through the leaves of a tree and the trees that concentrate sunlight into them through photosynthesis. The air all around, moving through the leaves and coaxing the water into ripples, is the fourth element in balance here. Maitreya's understanding is that we all belong to nature, but have lost our connection with it in the stressful world we inhabit. This garden is a coming home and, as he says, 'that is spirituality' – to come home to understanding our connection with the natural world. 'Sit,' he says. 'It is important at Pureland to find peace and relax, to forget about the world and melt into the atmosphere.'

> People walk around the garden and sit and replenish their own spirit.
> They are revitalizing their soul and they really appreciate it. The garden
> is nature; God, creation, paradise, Eden and we should belong to nature.
> The truth is not far away but close to you.
> Everyone has the divine life force so sit and be and appreciate what you are.[2]

It is clear that the Pureland Japanese garden, as well as being beautiful and a fascinating example of a Japanese garden, is also a very spiritual place. It is impossible not to be stilled by it and, having experienced the tranquillity it offers, one leaves reluctantly.

*A Buddha statue in the Pureland Japanese garden in
North Clifton, near Newark in Nottinghamshire*

---

2. Buddha Maitreya in conversation, 10 June 2008.

CHAPTER 28

Christianity and horticulture
– theology and practice

I come to Christianity with a number of questions. Historically the great 'Christian' gardens of the past are monastic gardens, but how much were these just what the monks did in order to be self-sufficient, and how much were they expressions of their faith? Were nature and gardens as well embedded in Christian faith as they are in Islam, for example? Furthermore, is this happening within Christianity today?

In Britain people commonly divide Christians into 'non-practising' and 'practising', i.e. those who hold to a Christian background but don't actively pursue a personal faith, and those who do. The practice of the Christian faith is an attempt to live out the principles of Christianity, as expressed in the Bible. I therefore want to look at what the Bible has to say about the natural world, and therefore by extension how and where gardens can come into the thinking and practice of the Christian faith today.

Moving through the Bible from start to finish (and this is not the only way to approach what is essentially a collection of different books), the first principle that relates to nature is found at the very beginning in the book of Genesis, and is that of 'creation': 'God created the heavens and the earth.'[1]

From a Christian standpoint, the material world is an instinctive expression of the divine: since it is, and will always be, something that comes from God, it enjoys, if you like, the divine seal of approval. It was intentionally conceived, desired and brought into being; and then God sat back and took delight in His creation, much as we are gratified by taking time to walk and enjoy a forest or a coastal path. God has therefore sanctioned 'nature': it is a good thing. However, there is another reference in the Bible that explains God's *ongoing* relationship with nature, through Jesus: 'He holds all creation together.'[3] God has not set the universe spinning and then backed away. He remains, mystically through Christ, at the centre of it, keeping it going.

For horticultural purposes, it is interesting to note that in the whole cosmic creation process God is described as taking time specifically to make a garden: 'Then the Lord God planted a garden in Eden in the east …'[4] He seems to bring it about as part

---

1. Genesis 1:1.
2. The three biblical references Psalm 102:27, John 1:1 and Hebrews 13:8 need to be taken together.
3. Colossians 1:17.
4. Genesis 2:8a.

of a whole energy-burst of generation, but when he has a human figure to place somewhere, the purpose for this particular site is clear: '… and there he placed the man he had made.'[5]

A view from beneath the Liriodendron (Tulip Tree) at
The Elms Quiet Garden, Draycott in Derbyshire

A garden is chosen as the right context for the man and woman. In the perfect climate balance of the time, a building was perhaps not necessary and wild nature was perhaps too alien for them, but a garden – which has both things to eat and things to delight the senses – was a perfect situation in which human beings might flourish and work. The context in which humanity was designed to be most at home was a garden.

The creation process itself is also interesting. I think it is worth noting that God created man from the dust of the ground. Moreover, nature also grew from the dust or soil of the ground. We have a close relationship to nature in that we are of the same stuff, quite literally, and science has since demonstrated that the same elements or chemical constituents that make up our human bodies are also to be found throughout the world of nature.

So in the beginning there was the spiritual world, which God and the angels inhabited, but the divine intention was that the spiritual world was not the be-all and end-all. The material world was created as a manifestation of divine qualities, particularly creativity, variety and unity, but also of God's care, and he pronounced it 'very good'. The spiritual and physical worlds were not separate entities. There is a

---

5. Genesis 2:8b.

delightful image in Genesis of God 'walking' in the Garden of Eden in the cool of the day – something to which we can all relate, if we have ever wandered out into a garden at dusk when the air is cooler and rich with sound and scent.

The spiritual force of evil also comes slithering in, taking the form of a serpent. The third chapter of Genesis gives an account of what is known as the Fall, or the doctrine of original sin. God said that the fruit of the tree of the knowledge of good and evil was not to be touched, but the man and woman decide not to follow these instructions and ate it anyway. This process of deliberately rejecting God's directions is given the term 'sin' and serious consequences stem from it, which also affect the material world. God curses the ground, thorns and thistles come into being and the activity of tending the garden becomes a struggle rather than simply a joy – something to which gardeners ever since will attest! The material world is no longer perfect, but blighted.

In the light of this, Christians could shun the material in favour of the spiritual, a path taken by many over the years, following Greek Platonic thought which separated out the higher spiritual forms from the baser, material reality perceived through the senses. Ascetic monasticism and fervent Puritanism are historical examples of this rejection of the material in favour of the spiritual. If the doctrine of original sin were the only teaching, I think that a rejection of the material world might be justified, but there are other Christian doctrines to take into consideration.

A major part of the Bible relevant to an understanding of the Christian stance on the natural world is the beginning of the New Testament, in the Gospels of Matthew, Mark, Luke and John. The first three simply give accounts of the birth and life of Jesus of Nazareth, and they give Jesus two distinct titles: the Son of Man and the Son of God. We are therefore given to understand that Jesus holds within himself both humanity and divinity. The Gospel of John is more of a theological treatise and explains the concepts in more detail. Originally, in the pre-creation state of being, without matter, God the Father and God the Son, or the Word, were together in glorious isolation: 'In the beginning was the Word, and the Word was with God, and the Word was God.'[6]

This one God, who is revealed elsewhere as being of three parts (in Genesis 1:1 the 'Spirit' of God hovered over the waters), created everything that has been made, i.e. all the material world. After the infiltration of everything that was good by the darkness of evil, the 'Word' had another task to do: 'The Word became flesh and made his dwelling among us.'[7]

God became man, and was called Jesus. The theological term for this process is 'incarnation', or the embodiment of the material by the spiritual. To anyone walking the streets in the region of Galilee at the time, Jesus appeared to be a human being just like everyone else. However, his teachings and his actions of healing, as well as other miraculous happenings, are highlighted as evidence of innate divinity. What is important for the development of a philosophy of nature, however, is the initial

---

6. John 1:1.
7. John 1:14.

act of incarnation. By taking on human form, God is sanctifying the physical world. Incarnation strengthens the initial recognition, in the act of creation, that the material is good and makes even more of it: the material world is not only good, but so good that it is a suitable medium for the containment of the divine.

In his life on earth, Jesus spent his time telling people about God and explaining his qualities and his purposes through stories and examples of everyday happenings, and then demonstrated those qualities of patience, compassion and service in his own life. He lived in a rural area and used stories of the natural world to illustrate his points, bringing a holistic understanding of who we are into his spiritual teaching. At one point he suggested that we should make nature our study: 'See how the lilies of the field grow.'[8]

The one example of Jesus' own understanding of incarnation comes at the Last Supper, when he sits down to eat a meal with his disciples on the evening before his arrest and trial. As would be usual at a Jewish meal, Jesus blesses the bread and the wine, but then he adds something that was not at all usual: 'Take and eat, this is my body,' he says, and, 'Drink from it, all of you. This is my blood of the covenant, which is poured out for many for the forgiveness of sins.'[9]

This ceremony, which Jesus is here instituting, has become known as 'Holy Communion' or 'the Eucharist' and is central to both the theology and the practice of Christians today, as it has been now for two millennia. It is not known exactly what Jesus originally said, as 'this is my body' is not a possible combination of words in Aramaic ('This is what I am like: I am to be torn apart and poured out' is possible). However, the gist is clear: 'These material elements of bread and wine illustrate what is going to happen to me, and what I am for you.' In other words, Jesus is depicting a profound theological lesson and in doing so reminds the disciples that he has allied himself with the material world in the deepest way. In the Gospel accounts of Jesus' crucifixion, it is said that (perhaps because of this relationship) the physical world reacted to Jesus' death: at the moment he died there was an earthquake and darkness fell. Jesus had taken on a material body and established an intimate connection with the natural world, and he is to be perpetually remembered and celebrated through bread and wine. For Roman Catholics, who hold to the doctrine of transubstantiation, the elements physically become the body and blood of Christ; while for Protestant Christians the bread and wine are rich symbols of Jesus' atoning sacrifice. Jesus' act of dying and rising from the dead was done in order to bring humanity – alienated from God through disobeying him in the Garden of Eden – back into the possibility of relationship with God.

At the same time, this act of redemption was for more than just human beings:

> Through him [Jesus] God reconciled everything to himself. He made peace with everything in heaven and on earth by means of Christ's blood on the cross.[10]

---

8. Matthew 6:28.
9. Matthew 26:26–27.
10. Colossians 1:20.

Against its will all creation was subjected to God's curse. But with eager hope, the creation looks forward to the day when it will join God's children in glorious freedom from death and decay.[11]

The natural world was put under a curse on the day that Adam and Eve ate the fruit of the tree of the knowledge of good and evil, and Jesus' sacrifice on behalf of humanity lifted that curse from the earth, so that it too will have a future in the time to come.

Eschatology is the study of the end times and this is the final theological point that the Bible makes about the factors that inform the Christian relationship with nature. The book of Revelation, the last book of the Bible, gives a picture in its final chapter of what the future holds for the believer. Contrary to popular theology, it seems that humanity is not going to be floating around on clouds holding harps and fraternizing with angels. Rather, we are going to enter an entirely new heaven and earth, depicted as a physical city, decorated with jewels and precious stones, and with trees and water to enjoy. Back in the Gospel accounts (Matthew, Mark, Luke and John), when Jesus explains something of what is to come to his disciples, he talks in terms of a great feast with eating and drinking, laughter and socializing. Through this we can understand not only that the present material world is a good thing, a place God himself inhabited and enjoyed and 'made holy', but also that at the end of this material age there is a new universe prepared for us which is also physical and to be enjoyed.

There seems to be plenty of encouragement within the Bible's teaching to inspire Christians to maintain a healthy relationship with nature. The teaching or doctrines of creation, original sin, incarnation, redemption and eschatology all have a direct bearing on the Christian attitude to the natural world, most of them overwhelmingly positive, and over the centuries there have been different attitudes within Christianity to nature and to gardens.

The first Christian communities to have a strong relationship with the natural world were those of the Desert Fathers in Egypt. St Anthony (251–356 CE) was an anchorite, or isolated holy man, who lived in the desert alongside others who had turned away from the evils of urban life. They felt that true spirituality could only be found in the quiet and hardship of the desert environment. These hermits and holy men and women were the forerunners of monasticism and from the beginning had an equivocal relationship with the material world. They lived in extremely close association with nature and enjoyed a relationship with creatures, used plants to their benefit and appreciated the beauty of the landscape around them, while at the same time they eschewed the materialistic and hedonistic world of the cities of their day.

The earliest Christians in the British Isles were the Celtic saints and early missionaries (St Patrick, St Non, St David and the like). They saw God in all of nature and

---

11. Romans 8:20–21.

themselves as a part of the whole cosmos, and therefore conceived of no separation between themselves and the natural world they inhabited. Celtic Christianity came out of a pagan, nature-centric culture, and took to heart the Old Testament emphasis on creation and the example of the Jewish Patriarchs who lived amongst nature and understood, for example, that to mark a place as holy you put a stone there.

It is important to remember that, to the inhabitants of third- and fourth-century Britain, the world of nature was the world they inhabited: the sun, rain, winds and tides were as intrusive and immediate to them as sirens, traffic noise and pollution are to us, and could have even more direct or disastrous impact on their lives. Their relationship to nature was a working one. From the plants around them they gained food as well as materials to build shelter, make clothing and prepare medicines. They also had a mystical or spiritual bond with the natural world, which was a source of beauty and wonder to them. Celtic prayers are full of natural images and references to the cycle of the seasons, and they speak of nature herself as a life force living alongside them to a degree that can sound almost idolatrous today.

> I am wind on sea
> I am ocean wave
> I am roar of sea
> I am bull of seven fights
> I am vulture on cliff
> I am dewdrop
> I am fairest of flowers
> I am boar for boldness
> I am salmon in pool
> I am lake on plain
> I am mountain in a man
> I am word of skill
> I am the point of a weapon
> I am God who fashions fire for a head.[12]

Celtic Christians had an embedded and instinctive understanding, love of and feeling for nature. They worshipped the Creator God who can be seen in all aspects of the created material world. One of the great Celtic writers and theologians was John Scotus Erigena, who was Irish and lived in the ninth century. His work *De Divisione Natural* was a meditation on the first chapter of Genesis and celebrated God as Creator. Such Celtic natural theology taught that the existence of God could be verified through contemplating the natural world, both through the beauty of nature and through its science – the way it is ordered and comprised. Celtic Christians were most at home in the 'wild' places of Britain, the coasts, cliffs, islands and

---

12. From the Celtic poem 'Amairgen', in O'Malley, B. (2002), *A Celtic Primer* (Norwich: Canterbury Press), p. 147.

forests, not seeking to move anywhere else that might have been more hospitable. Being a hermit was a popular career path. It was seen as the ultimate in spirituality – a position where one could be thoroughly immersed in nature and alone with God – and many of the early saints such as St Patrick lived almost entirely outdoors.

For the Celts, God was quintessentially a presence just as, in the biblical story of Moses leading the Israelites out of Egypt, God was present in the pillar of cloud by day and the pillar of fire by night. God was really *in* things. Esther de Waal, in her book *A World Made Whole: Rediscovering the Celtic Tradition*, points out that the ordinary daily prayers and graces of Celtic peasants were woven into their everyday life so that every activity they did, such as damping down the fire or churning the butter, had an associated blessing that was said or sung while the activity was performed. They lived in a truly religious world. Herbs with healing properties were associated with Jesus' time on earth and any plants that were heard to have had anything to do with his crucifixion were never used. As the essence of all things, God was seen to be there alongside them in daily life and in the natural world all around them. Creation was therefore an expression of the presence of God, as well as a sacrament, a material means by which God's spiritual grace can be experienced. Water was reverenced for its healing and life-giving properties and sacred springs became a big part of Celtic life and tradition.

Moreover, in Celtic thinking God is always there in creation. He didn't create it and disappear: he is present and always will be, conducting an ongoing relationship with the natural created world.

> Our God is the God of all things,
> The God of heaven and earth,
> The God of the sea and the streams,
> The God of the sun, moon and stars,
> The God of the great high mountains and the deep glens,
> The God above heaven, in heaven and under heaven.
> And he has a household – heaven and earth,
> And the sea and all that they contain.[13]

As we saw earlier, Jesus came to redeem (through his death and resurrection) the created world that had suffered the consequences of the Fall along with humanity. The Gospel accounts of Jesus' death talk about darkness falling over the whole land and an earthquake shaking the ground – and the Celtic Christians took on board this idea that all of the natural world took part in the Passion of Christ. Perhaps *the* summative symbol of Celtic Christianity is the Celtic cross, in which the created world, represented by the circle, is cut through with the symbol of the cross, signifying that Jesus has broken through into the world and incorporated it into his redemption venture.

---

13. Ancient Irish poem, in *ibid.*, p. 195.

Celtic Christians understood that they were one with nature, not separate. There are many stories of Celtic saints who developed special links with animals. St Kentigern (or Mungo) adopted a hound and was guided by birds; St Brynach of Pembrokeshire lived with wild stags, a cow and a wolf, which used to perform daily tasks for him, as did St Ciaran's wild boar, badger, deer and a fox; St Colomba instructed his monks to take care of an injured crane as they would a sick monk; St Cuthbert was cared for by otters and St Kevin is said to have stayed still in one place, waiting for the eggs laid in his hand by a blackbird to hatch (he was known for extremely long prayer vigils). The elements were both friend and foe, to be treated with the greatest respect for the good and the harm they could do; and the rest of creation such as the animals were to be looked after, respected and loved. It was a symbiotic, ecological and thoroughly theological union.

Whilst the significant influence of Celtic Christianity was confined to a relatively small area on the edges of the British Isles vast expanses of northern Europe were suffering from the over-enthusiastic and large-scale agriculture of the Roman period, which was leaving land and labourers exhausted.

Into this milieu came institutional monasticism, beginning in 515 with the Rule of St Benedict. Many monks and nuns viewed their relationship with nature in the same way as did the Celts in Britain. A delight and appreciation of creation would have been part of their religious experience, although a theology of nature was less pronounced. The monasteries nevertheless cultivated farms, gardens and woodland with restorative and healthy techniques in the use of fertilizers, drainage and woodland and pond management. Their influence went far beyond gardens, including agriculture, viniculture, arboriculture and fishing. Within the confines of the monastery gardens, however, they developed much knowledge and skill. Their experience with medicinal herbs brought basic hospitals into being, often part of the monastery complex and supplied by the physic garden. There would have been a separate herb garden, which was the model for the future kitchen gardens of the great estates, where they grew culinary herbs and vegetables.

Although there was a strong element of simplicity to their lifestyle, and many monastic orders took a vow of poverty, the flip side of the coin was a concern to celebrate properly all that God has given, and feast days were very important. Much care was taken to make food flavoursome and good to eat. In the heyday of the monastic period, when abbots and priors were significant political as well as religious figures, they enjoyed the same sort of provision as noblemen and even kings. The 'obedientary garden' was a private garden for the abbot/abbess and was constructed like any other nobleman's garden of the time with a trellised courtyard, turf seat and beautiful scented roses and honeysuckle. Flowers and plants were given religious significance and became symbolic of saints, angels, the Virgin Mary or healing. These private gardens in the monastery are likely to have had lilies, which the Venerable Bede describes as the Virgin Mary's emblem; the three-leaved clover, which St Patrick associated with the Trinity; and roses, whose thorns spoke of the suffering of Christ and whose red petals symbolized his blood. The white rose was another symbol of Mary, as were irises, which represented faith, wisdom and courage in their three petals, whereas daisies celebrated innocence.

Places for contemplation were clearly important to a monastic community. The most obvious is the cloister. Sometimes the area in the centre of the cloister court-yard would be developed as a garden with plants, but often it was a quieter area with simple symbols. It would be divided into four parts and covered in turf. The green of the grass represented rebirth and eternal life and the four parts were the four corners of the earth. There was often a fountain or some sort of water feature at the centre. As the monks walked round the cloister they could see the grass, hear and see the water and be reminded of the Trinity, because water comes in three forms (water, ice and mist), and because they were surrounded by the three elements of earth, air and water.

Another area for contemplation would be the orchard, which often doubled as a cemetery. In medieval times there was less fastidiousness about death, and to meditate upon one's own mortality in a place where people were buried was con-sidered a healthy practice.

The monks also grew flowers for the decoration of the church and for the glory and worship of God. The sacristan was the monk in charge of all the objects associated with worship and he arranged flowers to adorn the altar. Even more importantly for the future of horticulture than the creation of the various types of monastic garden was the fact that the monks kept records, hence their skills and knowledge could be passed on and further developed.

Outside the monastery boundaries, the medieval period (from the retreat of the Romans to the dawn of the Renaissance) was clearly no stranger to gardens and gardening, although most of the evidence comes from paintings which were likely to be idealized and may only suggest the reality. The 'pleasure' gardens of the nobility were very similar to the abbot's private garden. They were always enclosed by walls or fences to keep out the uncivilized and often lawless world, and were places to meet friends, family and lovers, where ladies read and sewed and gentlemen played music and wooed. There was water and there were fruit trees, as well as individual flower specimens, a 'flowery mead', turf seating and a trellis with scented climbers.

These secular gardens were remarkably similar to what became known as the *hortus conclusus*, or 'enclosed garden', which took on a religious purpose and sig-nificance and was associated with the monastery. A painting from 1410–1420 by an unknown Rhenish artist shows the Virgin Mary surrounded by saints in a beautiful walled garden full of flowers symbolic of her virtuous qualities, including the iris, lily, lily of the valley, wild strawberry and many more. The *hortus conclusus* was a living, growing example of theology and religious symbol. Gardens may originally have been enclosed as a protection against the ancient belief that pagan gods and evil spirits inhabited forests, lying in wait for the innocent and to corrupt believers, but the locked garden also alluded to the words of the Song of Solomon in the Bible, where the bride is described as being like an enclosed garden. The bride was also the Church, the fountain in the garden was a symbol of baptism and the flowers represented the Virgin, the saints and Christian virtues.

The medieval period saw a flowering of Christianity in that strong monastic culture, in which gardens clearly played a significant part. However, when the effects of the Renaissance reached Britain and permeated all thinking, including that concerned with landscape and gardens, it was seen to be appropriate to exert humankind's control and domination over nature, rather than to praise the Creator. Renaissance gardens are typically highly organized and geometric, extending out into the forests and bringing them under the sphere of human influence.

Later still, the English landscape gardens of Repton, 'Capability' Brown and Kent were a pendulum swing away from this formality, and brought nature right up to the large houses once again, although this was now more about appreciation of the pastoral landscape and romantic wildness than an attempt to bring God back into the picture. The nineteenth century in Britain was the age of Enlightenment, when science was far more interesting and relevant than the Church and there were no links between gardens and faith.

Probably the only strong connection between Christianity and horticulture in British history after the medieval period came in Victorian times. Death was not then a taboo subject and Victorian cemeteries were developed as a cross between gardens and public parks. They were tended by teams of gardeners, visited much more frequently than our cemeteries today, and enjoyed as places of natural beauty.

Within Christianity in Britain in recent times, the Quiet Garden Movement has been the main organizational representation of a theology of gardens. More generally, the subject of gardens comes up every Easter when many churches make Easter gardens, either literally in their grounds, or in sand trays within the church porch or building. The Easter story features both the Garden of Gethsemane, where Jesus went with his disciples after the Last Supper to pray and where he was arrested, and the burial garden where his disciples placed Jesus' body in a tomb borrowed from Joseph of Arimathea. Gethsemane seems to have been more of a typical Eastern 'garden' consisting mainly of olive trees, while the burial garden is not described in detail but does apparently have a gardener tending it, because Mary Magdalene mistakes the risen Christ for the gardener. Church Easter gardens re-create the burial garden where the resurrection took place and are full of flowers (often bulbs) symbolizing new life.

In the Roman Catholic Church there is a history of 'Mary' or 'Marian' gardens. These are often small, fenced-in patches of ground with plants and flowers grown around a statue of the Virgin Mary. I found one on a slope on Eriskay in the Outer

Hebrides, surrounded by a white picket fence and filled with flowers growing round the statue. Similarly, the Quiet Garden at Limbo Farm in Sussex has a variation on a Mary garden. Both these bear a relationship to the Marian shrines on the highways and byways of Europe with their statues and floral offerings.

Today, as ecological and sustainability issues come to the fore, Nature and gardens are once more creeping back into the edges of Christian thought and practice. Churches can become eco-congregations, and this includes consideration of church grounds (*www.ecocongregation.org*). The Christian organization A Rocha is a conservation movement that was started in Portugal in 1983. It is now an international organization, undertaking research and conservation and offering ecological education programmes for all ages. In Britain it has been recently involved in a project called 'Living Waterways' in Southall and Hayes in west London. There, volunteers are working with the local councils to turn a 90-acre wasteland site into a recreational space and conservation area, with a brief to open people's eyes to the beauty of God's creation around them.

Furthermore, Christian aid agencies such as Tearfund are increasingly concerned with climate and landscape issues because they recognize the implications for the world's poor of bad land management. They offer advice and practical suggestions for ways in which Christians can become active conservationists and environmentalists.

Christianity has a deep theological underpinning for a doctrine of nature to exist within the faith, and a rich heritage of traditions such as the Desert Fathers, the Celts and the Orthodox from which to draw inspiration. However, there is little evidence today of a strong contemporary relationship between Christians and their natural surroundings, and the earlier tradition of faith which planted nature and spirituality in the same bed has been seriously neglected. Although most Christian theology underlines the importance of our relationship with Nature, this seems to have been outweighed by our reading of the Creation story, which emphasizes our role as subduers of the land, rather than co-workers with it, and perhaps an over-emphasis on sin being embedded in physicality. I am slightly shocked that my own faith tradition is so weak in this area by comparison with, for example, Islam, Buddhism and the Baha'i faith.

CHAPTER 29

Growing together in faith – an interfaith garden at Chelsea

It was clear to Chris and me, through our own knowledge and experience of the world faiths, that gardens have a part to play in most faiths and in some they are particularly prominent. Historically, the Abrahamic faiths of Judaism, Christianity and Islam have gardens rooted within their sacred texts and, to a certain extent, their theology. The temple spaces of Buddhism, Hinduism, Sikhism and the Baha'is tend to be cultivated as gardens, with spiritual principles incorporated into the garden design, as well as in the flowers actually used in worship. As faith producers within the BBC, we also had a good working knowledge of interfaith projects and were convinced that the process of building a garden together could be a very good focus for interfaith dialogue.

Chris was the chaplain at Capel Manor Horticultural College in Enfield, which has extensive, beautiful and much-visited gardens within its grounds. Furthermore, Capel Manor is a college of further education within Greater London, with campuses in Castle Green in east London, Crystal Palace in south London, Edmonton Green in north London, Gunnersbury Park in west London and Regents Park in central London. The college is therefore committed to an inclusive and diverse student body and we felt sure there would be students of all faiths currently studying there. The college also holds an annual Federation of City Farms and Gardens Harvest Festival service: a day when people of all faiths and none are welcomed. Having had a long relationship with the college both as a student and as chaplain, Chris felt it would be appropriate to approach the director, Dr Steve Dowbiggin, to see if it would be possible to establish a multifaith garden within the grounds.

We came away from our initial meeting with Steve both delighted and a little surprised. Not only would it be possible to create a multifaith garden at Capel Manor, Steve suggested, but also why not first take it to the Chelsea Flower Show? We needed little persuading – few enthusiastic horticulturalists would turn down such an opportunity – and the 'Growing Together in Faith' garden for the Lifelong Learning marquee at the 2007 Chelsea Flower Show was conceived.

We began a busy year. The RHS demands nothing short of absolute perfection for a Chelsea gold medal and we had just eight months to produce it. Steve assigned Capel staff member Julie Phipps as the designer and co-ordinator and we were also extremely grateful to be under the watchful eye of Roger Sygrave, the gardens manager at Capel, who has a lot of experience of exhibiting at Chelsea.

Our proposal was that every world faith has an appreciation of the created natural world. In many religions this has meant associating people of faith with particular plants and flowers, and developing faith stories and even theology with horticultural elements. Plants are also often used in rituals and traditions. The 'Growing Together in Faith' garden would demonstrate how the rose has become entwined in four faith traditions.

The rose is a rich and universal symbol. It represents perfection, being ideal in its beauty, colour and shape – but with thorns! It speaks of hiddenness and depth, a flower whose secrets can only be revealed to those who seek.

It seemed reasonable to base the design of this rose garden on the *chahar bagh* four-quartered garden. It has been a traditional design in the East for several millennia and, as most faiths originated in the East, it felt appropriate. We had then to choose four faiths and settled on the three Abrahamic faiths and Hinduism, if for no other reason than that the rose in particular features strongly within each of these faiths.

Hinduism is the religion of India, the oldest of the world faiths. The rose is present in Hindu myth: the goddess Lakshmi was born of a rose comprised of 108 large petals and 1,008 small petals. The god Krishna associated himself with roses ('I am the flowery spring season', *Gita X*). Secondly, the rose is rooted in Hindu theological concepts: 'Kali' is the beginning of faith or a new prophet – a beautiful bud or a fragrant rose; and 'Darshan' is spiritual insight – like a rose opening from a bud. Finally, in Hindu religious ritual the act of worship, *puja*, can be translated as 'the flower act', and rose petals and rosewater are routinely used as offerings in worship at temples or home shrines. Rosewater is used for washing in temples.

Judaism is the earliest of the Abrahamic faiths. The rose features first in Jewish legend, which records that the colour of dawn is made by the sun being reflected from the roses blooming in heaven; that a righteous man will have a tent in heaven with 800 roses in it; and that roses will bloom in the desert when the Messiah comes. Roses occur within the Tanach, the Hebrew Bible. The Rose of Sharon is mentioned in the book of Isaiah and the Song of Songs. The burning bush that Moses saw was thought to be a rose bush and St Catherine's monastery in the Sinai, on the site of the burning bush, has a rose growing in the grounds. The book of Maccabees also features roses. Roses played a part in Jewish history: in 1941–1943 a student movement to expose the Nazi Holocaust was called The White Rose. The Golden Rose is the name of the first Russian synagogue, built in 1852, which was closed by the Bolsheviks in 1922. It was given back to the Jews in 1996 and rededicated in 1999. It is a symbol of the Jews' turbulent history.

Within Christianity the rose is associated with the Virgin Mary, who is 'La Rosa Mystica'. She is represented by the white rose, symbolizing purity, and by the thornless rose, symbolizing perfection. The rose was soon also linked to Christ, whose crown of thorns (as myth has it) changed from thorns to a red rose briar. The red rose became associated with his blood. Various Christian saints were also symbolized by roses, for example St Rose of Lima, whose symbol is a rose garland (pink roses), and St Mark of Venice, where a St Mark's rose is supposed to flower on 25

April each year. In a more general way the red rose symbolizes martyrdom and the white rose symbolizes celibacy. A yellow rose is a symbol of papal benediction. It is not surprising, therefore, to find roses built into Christian architecture, and rose windows feature prominently in cathedrals such as Durham and York. Although the rosary was not necessarily a product of roses, nuns at the St Teresa of Avila convent still make rosary beads with rosebuds. American Carmelite nuns in Colorado Springs make rosary beads with roses painted on them. Roses were so closely associated with holy people in Christianity that in medieval Britain ordinary people were forbidden to grow roses because they were so potent a symbol.

Islam also has rose stories. One tells of a time when Mohammed was away fighting. When he returned he asked that, if his wife had been faithful, anything she was carrying when he saw her would stay the same colour when she dropped it in water. She was carrying red roses, which turned yellow when dropped into water, but she remained nevertheless his favourite wife! Turkish legend says that roses grew from drops of sweat from Mohammed's brow. Since Islam flourished in Persia, the home of mass rose-growing, it is not surprising to find many references to roses. Omar Khayyam, a famous poet who was a Muslim, wrote *The Rubaiyyat*, an epic poem all about roses. Mahmud Shabistari, who was a Sufi, wrote a poem called 'The Secret Rose Garden'. I also found on the internet a modern poem, written in July 2006 by Ibnabuashher, entitled 'Islam is a Rose'. Islamic ritual includes the rosary, as well as traditionally using rosewater for the washing before prayer five times a day (*wudu*). Attar of roses was widely used as perfume in Persia, and therefore by many historical Muslim leaders.

Having established the thinking behind the 'Growing Together in Faith' garden, we started to translate that onto the information boards which explain the gardens at Chelsea, onto the Capel website pages and onto the leaflet which would be handed out to visitors during the show. At the same time we were all researching the actual species and varieties of rose that were available and appropriate for each section of the garden. These needed to be not just chosen, but then ordered and nurtured to perfection in the greenhouses and polytunnels at the college under Roger's watchful eye.

Other plants would be used alongside the roses in the final garden and we felt that all of these should be appropriate to each faith section. This meant more research into plants associated with each faith. For Hinduism this proved particularly challenging, as one of the central plants is the lotus. Julie spent many an hour of nail-biting, patience and kindness trying to trace the right sort of lotus that was available at not too disproportionate a cost and didn't have to be shipped from India. It was then equally tricky trying to find the right sort of basil, as holy basil is not the same as the normal culinary basil. Holy basil, or *tulsi*, is purple-leaved and smells rather unexpectedly of aniseed. There were moments when nothing seemed straightforward. Judaism was slightly easier, as many vegetables and fruits play a part in festivals and are also mentioned in scripture. We managed to find an olive tree, a pomegranate and a fig, as well as 'bitter' herbs, lily of the valley and cistus, hibiscus and hypericum, the latter two being alternatives for the biblical 'Rose of Sharon'. In Christianity, lilies, either calla or Lilium candidum, are another symbol of the Virgin Mary, as is the iris and the foxglove, or Alchemilla mollis, which is known as Our Lady's mantle. Yew, hawthorn and rosemary were also possibilities, and we needed plenty of options as only the plants that would be at their peak during the second week of May were going to be used in any of the sections. The Islamic garden needed to be altogether less colourful, as green is the colour for Islam and tranquillity and harmony needed to be the ultimate impression conveyed by this section of the garden. Lilies and narcissus were acceptable, as was Alchemilla mollis, the name of which comes from the Arab word for 'alchemy'. Aloe vera – *Aloe barbadensis* – was a favourite of Muslim traders, and Arabian botanist Ibnal Baithar used tarragon to dull the taste of nasty medicine.

It was a constant challenge to find plants that fulfilled the thinking behind the garden and were related to each faith, as well as providing a harmonious whole – a greater undertaking when the Hindu garden needed to reflect the bright, clashing colours of the Indian markets, while the Islamic garden required something much more subdued. Each garden section also required an artefact to bring the faith element alive, and further fun and games ensued as we tried to find a fitting Hindu Sarawati goddess statue and a Jewish Menorah candlestick. The London markets and the Board of Deputies of British Jews came up trumps respectively and we breathed easily once again.

Disasters happened frequently. March and the beginning of April were freezing cold, so roses were moved to greenhouses where they promptly flowered and had to be put into cold storage. The jasmine came on too early and the irises too late (or was it the other way round?). The first rose window cracked, the fountain setting leaked, the lotus refused to open its bud and the *tulsi* (holy basil) only arrived at literally the last moment.

One of the great successes of the whole project was the involvement of the Capel students. Having bet our back teeth that faith students galore would volunteer, Chris and I put an advertisement up in college with just a fluttering of nerves. Our hunch was proved right, however, and we were delighted to find and talk to students who were Muslim, Hindu, Jewish and Christian of various denominations, all of whom took the project to heart and spent happy hours tending the plants beforehand, some tedious hours tying prickly roses onto the trellis of the stand, and one or two proud moments dressed in their religious finery at the service of affirmation on the literal day of judgement.

Whatever you know in your head about Chelsea being *the* show to end all shows, it is more spectacular still when you're there, not just on the day of judging, but through the last weeks beforehand – watching the rain, the mud and the wind, the hard landscaping not quite behaving, then the furious last 48 hours of shift work, sometimes day and night, placing each perfect specimen in the perfect place. I was not expecting, on the day, to trace the now-familiar path through neighbouring stands and turn the corner and almost literally have my breath taken away. The garden did look beautiful. We were awarded a silver gilt medal, and for a first attempt we were well satisfied to be just one down from gold; even Steve beamed from ear to ear. One of the several Royal parties asked to take a turn past our garden and, better still, we heard many a rumour about how long the judges had debated whether it was worth a gold. They didn't quite come down on our side, but we did at least cause a stir: no one had done 'faith' in the Lifelong Learning tent before and many judges thought it a fine example of horticultural collaboration and education.

The 'Growing Together in Faith' garden can now be viewed at Capel Manor Horticultural College gardens, where it was re-established after Chelsea. A memorial plaque was placed there in memory of Chris in 2008. He and I both knew not just that it had been not just a medal-winning garden and a fine example of the professionalism of Capel Manor, but that the process of putting it together was also a practical example of the garden as a meeting place for faiths.

CHAPTER 30

Journey's end

The genesis of this book was founded on nothing more scientific than a hunch. All my life I have had an inbuilt susceptibility to and connection with the natural world. Family and friends will verify that if leisure time can take in either a seascape or a hill, even if only for the tiniest glimpse, then I am a happy rabbit. I am drawn to stand at the water's edge, or to climb a slope, and if I haven't been able to do this for a while it becomes an almost physical longing. I'm fortunate in having some friends who share this yearning, and others who are tolerant of it, and for that I am grateful! Unsurprisingly, given the nature of the 'meaning through horticulture' project ('mYth') in which we were involved, Chris Bard and I also shared the same awareness of landscape, and we do confess to just one diversion on one research trip when, in driving from Warwickshire to London past the Malverns, it was necessary to take a small detour in order to stand on Sugarloaf Hill.

For many years this relationship with nature was something I took for granted as part of the human condition, but marriage brought with it the recognition that not everyone shares this affinity – in fact, many people (including most of my own family) consider it a mild form of insanity. Even I was surprised one summer when, at the end of our family holiday, the drive slowly and inexorably away from a quiet beach in mid-Wales was accompanied by an almost physical ache of separation at the prospect of returning to a landscape devoid of sea or hills. Probably from that point to this I have kept a small part of the back of my cerebral cortex busy in mulling over the possible alternatives to suffering from a minor form of madness. It is therefore with special interest that I have pursued the idea of the relationship between humanity and nature, and this book has been a formal drawing together of other people's thoughts on the subject, as well as my own.

As I reach the end of this particular journey of exploration, I am aware of everything else that I haven't been able to include that is nevertheless relevant. In particular I would have liked to have explored paganism, with its very strong Nature culture. I wanted to have time to visit some of the Maggie's Centre hospital gardens around the country. It was striking, in the course of the 'mYth' project, to find few Jews who had a feel for gardens or thought they were a means to spirituality, and it would be interesting to explore the whole historical and theological relationship between Judaism and nature. I would like to have visited some contemporary monastic gardens. I am also aware of the many Quiet Gardens internationally that I would have loved to visit in order to discover their stories and gain further perspectives. Jack Goody has written a fascinating and comprehensive account of the use and place of flowers in societies across the world,[1] and it was very tempting to talk about this – but inevitably, as with anything creative, there have to be boundary lines laid out and roads 'less travelled'.[2]

There were many paths we weren't able to take. However, like a ball of string in a labyrinth, the question I wanted to keep present through all the conversations, meetings and garden visits was: 'What is a garden all about – what does it do, or what is it for?' I think there is a danger that 'makeover gardening', as illustrated in many popular horticultural magazines and on television, might give the impression that creating a garden is simply a matter of aesthetics and design – that a garden is just a collection of material things that can be assembled in a certain way once a plan has been conceived in someone's head. My intuition, confirmed through conversations with all sorts of people, is that gardening offers much more than simply the aesthetic and material. It connects with parts of us beyond the physical and the cerebral, and therefore allows us to develop, so that we are more fully human and more fulfilled when this relationship is active than when it is not.

The dynamism, relationship, or, as Tim Richardson terms it, 'psychotopia' that occurs when we as human beings encounter nature (or specifically a garden) has physical, mental, emotional and social dimensions to it. Spirituality in its broadest definition is all about qualities that are intuited, felt and sensed: qualities which may originate from sensory experience, but which go beyond the purely physical. Experiencing nature through a garden is therefore not just a physical but also a spiritual experience, and my premise is that horticulture and spirituality are therefore unquestionably intertwined.

Chris and I planned four dimensions to the 'mYth' project. first, we wanted to find out how some of the most influential gardeners and garden thinkers of our time reacted to the idea of spirituality and horticulture, and how they understood their own gardens. Secondly, we looked in some detail at the Christian Quiet Garden Movement to investigate an example of the outworking of spirituality within horticulture. Thirdly, we researched other faiths to explore their attitudes to gardens and the role that gardens play within those faiths. And, fourthly, we wanted to establish the practice of creating interfaith gardens within communities in Britain, which started with the creation of an interfaith garden for the 2007 Chelsea Flower Show.

This book has described the results of this exploration, which from the start was not an academic exercise but a journey. We literally travelled across Britain to meet people in their gardens and, in the process of assimilating what they said and what they demonstrated in their own environments, we also travelled into new ways of thinking and perceived new experiences within those gardens. In this way, the

1. Goody, J. (1993), *The Culture of Flowers* (Cambridge: Cambridge University Press).
2. This refers to the concept and last line in 'The Road Not Taken', a poem by Robert Frost.

project has been that particular type of journey which is known as a pilgrimage. At its end, certain conclusions can be drawn but, perhaps more importantly, the process of the journey itself has allowed me to develop in my thinking and in my approach to other people and to nature.

As far as the conclusions go, we asked the question: 'What is a garden for?' Charles Jencks, Beth Chatto and Sir Roy Strong all told us that gardens are places of meaning and identity, of relationship and story. Gardens can become profound and sacred places. They are created out of, and become redolent of, all the experiences of being human. Moreover, the act of creating these places is as important as the final product (if there ever is such a thing with a garden).

Joe Sempik has spent a good part of his academic life researching the benefits of horticulture. He concludes that horticulture is therapeutic and the therapeutic nature of horticulture is internationally recognized and scientifically proven. It has been investigated and found to be of value to human beings in many ways and often includes a spiritual dimension, whether or not this is theistic.

The Chelsea Flower Show is probably the primary opportunity in which to demonstrate current horticultural philosophy, as well as to offer design ideas and gardening expertise. The leading assessor spoke about the elusive quality that judges are looking for in a really successful garden, which is a sense of 'uplifting-ness' – something close to the spiritual. At the shows in 2007 and 2008, the idea behind many of the gardens was to provide places of significance, sanctuary and even sometimes spirituality for busy people on their life journey.

The Reverend Philip Roderick founded the Quiet Garden Movement. In his own life and studies he has recognized the significance of natural spaces as catalysts to spiritual development. He feels that the importance of providing silence and space for people in a natural setting cannot be overstated. To this end, the openness, the meeting and the hospitality which the Quiet Gardens offer provide the atmosphere in which humans can grow and develop spiritually.

All the Quiet Gardens offer the opportunity for people to take time out in a natural space and to enjoy a particular combination of plants, flowers and trees. They all also have a particular 'atmosphere' or 'influence'. Arley has presence: it brings the profound experience of encountering the 'other' in really grand trees. At Rydal in the Lake District the overwhelming impression is of power, energy and vitality. Epworth brought quietness – not aural quiet, because there were plenty of tractors turning onto the street beyond, but an inner quiet that had steeped the house and garden for centuries. Priors Mead at Clehonger in Herefordshire, with its expanse of lawn and wonderful views all around, imparted a sense of space, freedom and time out. The small but dramatically placed Quiet Garden at Musgrave in Westmoreland breathed community, particularly the value of the rural farming community. Waltham Place was a community of nature and offered the chance to be in a place where humanity was less significant than nature. The wonderful hidden garden at Charlcombe near Bath oozes ancient history and calmness. In the Quiet View garden in Kingston near Canterbury, I felt the importance of other people, of strangers, friends and the sanctity and permanence of relationships. Bridlington was a place that spoke powerfully of the journey of life. With its statue of the hug, it has become a place where you sense you are being cared for, a place of acceptance. Stainforth offered robustness: this was clearly a garden of sanctuary, but also of renewal and hope. The tiny garden at Witham was a paradise of abundance and fruitfulness. Glastonbury brought a sense of refreshment and the delight of discovering something so secret and hidden. And Burrswood Christian hospital offered serenity and support. Each of the Quiet Gardens, through the stories behind them and through their own specific setting and design, contains a wealth of experiences that the visitor may tap into or discover there.

Metropolitan Kallistos Ware feels it is literally vital that networks like this exist where people can recover their own vitality and experience something of the fullness of life that comes from having one's roots in the soil. To him, all nature is a means of experiencing the presence of God and contemplation in a natural setting brings us closer to God. For any Orthodox Christian, there is no question that heaven and earth are one, and any separation, in thought or practice, between the material and spiritual worlds is to our detriment as fully human beings.

Of course there are critics of the idea that a garden can have 'meaning'. In 2005 Jane Gillett wrote a paper for the American *Landscape Journal* called 'Can Gardens Mean?' She maintains that it is impossible for real gardens to mean anything. This is because the physical features of which they are made are so much more limited than the vocabulary of words on a page. It is only possible to fill a garden with a relatively few physical features and therefore at best a garden can only be a 'one-liner' (her words). Conversely, though, she explains that gardens can also be so subject to the limitless subjectivity of their visitors that almost anything can be read into the elements and their arrangement in any garden.

> It is only to the degree that a designer can control the initial code that the meaning of the artefact is saved from the illimitable associations of the reader.[3]

Gillett is sceptical that gardens can 'tell a story' because stories are ubiquitous. They are the default mode of the human being and therefore anything can claim to have a story behind it. Likewise, symbols are open to all sorts of different meanings and therefore cannot be useful within a garden setting. One of Gillett's premises is that, as human beings, we are fundamentally separate from the rest of nature. This creates an anxiety in us and we will therefore make all sorts of associations in order to prove that this dualism does not exist, including attributing meaning, story and significance to gardens and landscapes. In her thinking, we have a strong emotional desire to be at one with the material world, but in truth most gardens simply provide 'one pleasant distraction after another'.[4]

---

3. Gillett, J. (2005), 'Can Gardens Mean?', *Landscape Journal* 24, p. 97.
4. *Ibid.*

I agree with Jane Gillett that meaning is not simply about cognitive information. I also agree that we as human beings have become separated from the rest of the physical universe – this book is a plea that we recognize that separation. Unlike Gillett, though, I would maintain that gardens are exactly the medium in which an experience of relationship with the rest of the physical world can begin, and that this is a necessarily subjective and intuitive process. I come to this conclusion having listened to everyone associated with the 'mYth' project, and having read about the 60,000 people currently benefiting from what the charity Thrive offers through gardens.

Buddha Maitreya has great sympathy with the dualism dilemma that Jane Gillett describes. He teaches, however, that this dualism is an illusion and those who become enlightened will discover that humanity and nature are one. His Pureland Buddhist garden is one environment in which the tranquillity necessary for meditation and contemplation of the nature of reality can be found. It was fascinating to find that spirituality has always been a part of traditional Japanese horticulture, and that some contemporary Japanese garden thinkers are calling for a return to the understanding of an organic relationship between horticulture and spirituality in twenty-first-century Japanese garden design.

The Baha'i faith sees gardens as the perfect context in which human beings can intuit the spiritual dimension, and in so doing draw closer to the ideal of unity with each other and with God. For Baha'is, spiritual values are inherent within the natural landscape as well as in the teachings of spiritual leaders, and God is present in nature. These are Islamic beliefs too. Muslims hold that the only reality is God and God is in everything, including underlying the natural material world. Islamic garden design is based on principles that demonstrate or symbolize spiritual truths. Moreover, gardens and nature are not just to be enjoyed and cherished in this life, but they will form a fundamental part of the world to come.

Christianity subscribes to the central concepts of creation, incarnation and redemption, each of which describes a relationship between the material and the spiritual. The physical world has been created by God and is currently held together by him. The material world was deemed fit to contain the divine in the person of Jesus, and through Jesus' death and resurrection the physical world is redeemed from the curse put upon it at the Fall, and will be made new in the new heavens and the new earth.

There is no doubt that many of the major world faiths celebrate nature and call for a recognition of the relationship between humanity and the wider physical and material world. Many also feel that gardens can be a means to this relationship, and to an understanding of what is spiritual. Secular society also recognizes that horticulture is therapeutic in a spiritual sense, in that it connects people to what is outside them and imparts qualities such as tranquillity, satisfaction and fulfilment. Moreover, the many gardeners and garden designers, well known and otherwise, who have been consulted in the writing of this book testify similarly. Thus the answer to one of the original questions – 'Do gardens provide a medium in which to explore our own spiritual side, whether we are "religious" or not?' – is in the affirmative.

The question that now remains could be couched in the immortal words of comedienne Catherine Tate: 'Are you bovvered?' Why does it matter that horticulture can develop spirituality? I think it matters very much. If we get back in touch with our rooted identity in the earth, we get back in touch with our souls. If we recognize and give room to our souls, we once again give room to intuition, relationship and reflection. It is well recognized that we live in a technologically rich, sound-soaked, fast-moving world. But, if that is all our lives are composed of, we will develop as stunted and impoverished specimens of humanity. Appreciating gardens and, even better, becoming involved in the process of gardening (whether it be planting a windowbox or a few herbs in pots by the kitchen sink, designing for a garden show, or tending an allotment) is a means to reflection, to hands-off thinking and stillness time, and therefore to regeneration. These are vital tools to counteract the many stresses and demands of the world in which we must live, and to enable us to become fully and maturely human.

In ideological terms I may be preaching to at least some of the converted; but, as many of the world faiths would attest, faith without actions is dead. I would therefore ask that we might not simply recognize in our thinking that gardens are a medium to discovering and enriching our spirituality and possibly our faith, but that we might do something about it. I would love to see more community gardens in city centres, created and maintained by the local community of business people, faith groups, retail workers and the like. This could be through 'Britain in Bloom' schemes, local councils or independently. I would love to see more faith woodlands planted, such as that established in Peterborough in 2007 through the BBC's *Breathing Spaces* campaign, or through the Tree Council, the Forestry Commission – or any other way. I long to see gardens and horticulture on the National Curriculum, and Britain taking a lead in that from the many American schools' initiatives. The Quiet Garden Movement is starting to investigate the possibility of Quiet Gardens in prisons, and this seems an avenue full of potential. I want churches, mosques, temples and any other religious building to plant and maintain a Quiet Garden in their grounds, such as the Bible garden outside the Jewish synagogue in Maidenhead. I would like to see more bodies established like the Alliance of Religions and Conservation or the Quiet Garden Movement, which are actively drawing together people and nature in innovative ways. Above all, I would love to see Christianity really grasping the nettle again and owning its relationship with nature in its theology and its practice, especially through garden spaces.

There are so many reasons to get into the garden. Apart from being good physical exercise, a means of creating beauty, producing healthy food and creating more sustainable urban environments, gardening is, I would argue, most significantly also good for the soul.

Bibliography

Books

Brookes, J. (1991), *John Brookes' Garden Design Book* (London: Dorling Kindersley).

Causley, C. (ed.) (1999), *Poetry Please: 100 Popular Poems from the BBC Radio 4 Programme* (London: Phoenix).

Clark, E. (2004), *The Art of the Islamic Garden* (Marlborough: The Crowood Press).

De Waal, E. (1991), *A World Made Whole: Rediscovering the Celtic Tradition* (Michigan: Fount).

Dixon Hunt, J. D., and Willis, P. (1988), *The Genius of the Place: The English Landscape Garden, 1620–1820* (Cambridge, MA: MIT Press).

Ferris, J., Morris, M., Norman, C., and Sempik, J. (eds) (2001), *People, Land and Sustainability: A Global View of Community Gardening* (Nottingham: PLS).

Frewer, R., and Machin, D. (2008), *Charlcombe Parish Church of the Blessed Virgin Mary* (Charlcombe: Charlcombe Parochial Church Council).

Frost, R. (1916), *Mountain Interval* (New York: H. Holt and Company).

Gallis, C. (2007), *Green Care in Agriculture: Health Effects, Economics and Policies* (Vienna: University Studio Press).

Goody, J. (1993), *The Culture of Flowers* (Cambridge: Cambridge University Press).

Hobhouse, P. (2002), *The Story of Gardening* (London: Dorling Kindersley).

Hughes-Hallett, P. (ed.) (1990), *My Dear Cassandra: Jane Austen, the Illustrated Letters* (London: Collins and Brown).

Jencks, C. (2003), *The Garden of Cosmic Speculation* (London: Frances Lincoln).

Jencks, C. (2005), *The Iconic Building: The Power of Enigma* (London: Frances Lincoln).

Kingsbury, N. (2005), *Vista: The Culture and Politics of Gardens* (London: Frances Lincoln).

Merton, T. (1972), *New Seeds of Contemplation* (New York: New Directions).

Nitschke, G. (2003), *Japanese Gardens* (Köln: Taschen).

Norfolk, D. (2000), *The Therapeutic Garden* (London: Bantam).

O'Malley, B. (2002), *A Celtic Primer* (Norwich: Canterbury Press).

Palmer, M., and Manning, D. (2000), *Sacred Gardens* (London: Piatkus).

Pavord, A. (1999), *The Tulip* (London: Bloomsbury).

Quest-Ritson, C. (2003), *English Gardens: A Social History* (London: Penguin).

Sempik, J., Aldridge, J., and Becker, S. (2003), *Social and Therapeutic Horticulture: Evidence and Messages from Research* (Reading: Thrive).

Sempik, J., Aldridge, J., and Becker, S. (2005), *Health, Well-Being and Social Inclusion: Therapeutic Horticulture in the UK* (Bristol: The Policy Press).

Sempik, J. (2007), *Researching Social and Therapeutic Horticulture for People with Mental Ill Health: A Study of Methodology* (Reading: Thrive).

Shelton, R. (2007), *Allotted Time: Two Blokes, One Shed, No Idea* (London: Pan Books).

Strong, R. (2000), *Gardens through the Ages* (London: Conran Octopus).

Voltaire (1947), *Candide* (London: Penguin Classics).

Ware, K. (1979), *The Orthodox Way* (New York: St Vladimirs Seminary Press).

Wilson, E. O. (1984), *Biophilia: The Human Bond with Other Species* (Cambridge, MA: Harvard University Press).

Journals
Gillett, J. (2005), 'Can Gardens Mean?', *Landscape Journal* 24, pp. 85–97.

Acknowledgements

The writing of this book has been a thoroughly enjoyable experience, excepting only when my computer had frequent mid-life crises (and thank you to Ben – technical back-up – for rescuing me on more than one occasion!). I am grateful for it's reluctant efficiency, but I do not love it! However, the rest of the process I *have* loved, and I freely admit I am forever in the debt of my family – Philip, Ben, Charlotte, Byron and Joel (who undoubtedly will elicit payback). They have allowed me to interrupt their comfortable lifestyle by disappearing regularly to hole up and write. You know this is one of those things I wanted to 'do before I die' and I love you all deeply and forever for bearing with it! I want to apologise to all the friends who have been horribly neglected in the last month especially, when I have had to put the book before pleasure and your company. I am really grateful to Chris, one of my oldest and perhaps most tolerant friends who figured that if you can't beat it you can join it and spent happy hours assisting me with photographs. I will also love forever Tony, Domini, Sarah, Michael, Rosie and Tom who opened their home to allow me to periodically scuttle into a corner, borrow laptops and drink liberal amounts of carbonated water (to say nothing of homemade wine!). The Quiet Garden at Draycott is Domini's domain, it is utterly beautiful and there is no more hospitable and delightful place this side of heaven.

I want to say a big thank you to Charles Jencks, Beth Chatto and Sir Roy Strong for their generous time, welcome and insights. It was a privilege to understand these great gardens with the direct help of their creators.

I am very grateful for the creativity and vision of Philip Roderick in starting the Quiet Garden Movement in the first place. Chris and I have been overwhelmed by the welcome and willingness to share of all the Quiet Gardeners we met. In particular I'd like to mention Penelope in Bridlington who suffered two early morning visits, Joy in Westmoreland for the best porridge I have ever tasted, Philip and Sue at Clehonger for calmness in the face of ever-changing time schedules, Tom at Rydal for not worrying how wet he got, Burrswood for socialising with chickens, Nigel at Arley for whom we were regrettably always late, Eddie and Father Mark in Huyton for buying us cream cakes, Lizzie and John for not minding it was practically dark when we finished, and Vinnie for being so real – and allowing me to see the Berkshire pigs! I'd also like to thank Maureen Douglas who has written an insert into Chapter

16 from her much more copious study and understanding of labyrinths than I could hope to bring. Metropolitan Kallistos Ware, I thank you for your example, your time and your simple words. They will stay with me.

Being invited into other cultures is always a treat and not something I take lightly. May Buddha Maitreya's heavenly tea and scones never run out and neither Garry's creativity and enthusiasm, and the welcome of the community at Burnlaw.

I am deeply grateful to all my Faith Producer colleagues at the BBC who have taken an interest in gardens to heart and put up with the enthusiasm of Chris and I over the years, especially Ashley and Naomi who have been such a support – you are a lovely bunch! Chris, this was the best of projects, I am gutted you have not seen the outcome of it, but we thoroughly enjoyed the doing of it, your irrepressible optimism has paid off! And finally thank you to Steve Dowbiggin and the team at Capel Manor Horticultural College. If Chris could have burst with happiness on the day the medals were distributed at Chelsea, he would have done. We were both thrilled at the opportunity of working alongside such professionals as yourself and of the chance of being the other side of the garden gate at Chelsea.

SUSAN BOWDEN-PICKSTOCK